D. Donovan, Senior Reviewer, Midwest Book Review

"A difference between her story and others is her focus on not just coming of age and leaving her country, but living in it through regime changes. Her warm observations of her country, its people, and its culture offer simple reflections on daily life challenges and objectives: "I realized people in cities all over Iran longed for freedoms as simple as running a business without bribes."

My Persian Paradox is an outstanding synthesis of personal experience, social change, and political insights both in Iran and in the U.S. Its revelations about the emotional growth required to immigrate and reconcile two countries' cultures makes for an inviting, educational, and thoroughly engrossing account which is especially recommended for any library strong in immigrant experiences and the psychology of integration."

My Persian Paradox

Memories of an Iranian Girl

Shabnam Curtis

Editing: Mathina Calliope

Cover Painting: Saya Behnam

Cover Design: Parnian Emami

Author/Publishing Name
Shabnam Curtis
www.mypersianparadox.com

Editing: Mathina Calliope
Cover painting: Saya Behnam
Cover Design: Parnian Emami

Publisher's Note: This is a work of non-fiction.

Book Layout © 2017 BookDesignTemplates.com

My Persian Paradox – Shabnam Curtis – 2nd ed.
ISBN 9781733598811
Library of Congress Control Number: 2019900654

To Parnian, who is my motivation to continue growing, and to Arash, whose existence inspired my passion for writing this book.

"[T]he paradox is one of our most valuable spiritual possessions ... only the paradox comes anywhere near to comprehending the fullness of life."
~CARL JUNG, CW 12, PARA 18

Acknowledgments

Along my journey to create a book, many supporters have poured love into the project, creating heart-to-heart connections as they did. More people than I can name here supported me directly and indirectly; I appreciate their help so much.

Heartfelt thanks to my immediate family, Mike, Parnian, and Jennifer; my parents, who helped me with the daunting process of retrieving difficult memories; editor Mathina Calliope; cover-page artist Saya Behnam; Cover-design, website designer, and public-relations specialist Parnian Emami; beta readers Edward Curtis, Meredith Burton, and Nance LaRussa; friends Sahar, Faranak, Suri, Mahnaz, Sara, Shiva, Mona, Mojgan, Saya, Ghazal, Marjan, Holly, Ayeh, and; the Arlington Creative Nonfiction writing group; and my friend Captain, who asked me to write this book.

Author's Note

To protect their privacy, I have changed some characters' names and distinguishing features. The facts in this story are true as far as my human memory allows, especially given the challenging circumstances described.

CONTENTS

Foreword

One September afternoon at work, I was trying to force myself to finish a tedious financial report. When I heard Mary's voice, I got up, stretching and complaining about my boring report. Her eyes were shining.

In a happy, mysterious tone, she said, "Do you want to hear my latest news?"

Beth, my close friend sitting in the cube next to me, joined us too.

Bubbly Beth said, "Go on, girl. What's the news?"

Mary said, "I'm becoming a grandma!"

Beth and I both said loudly, "Whaaaat? Your daughter-in-law is pregnant?"

Closing her eyes, she sighed. "Noooooo, it's my daughter."

It was her son who had gotten married last year. Her daughter was not in a relationship as far as we knew. We were now on edge and wanted to hear the whole story.

Mary said her daughter, Sandy had just announced she was three months pregnant. "Poor girl!" Mary said. Not knowing who the father was, Sandy had been too embarrassed to talk about it, but she also didn't have the heart to go through with an abortion. She was keeping the baby.

Mary hesitated for a moment, then with a firm, kind voice said, "We want to support her. She is excited. I'm so excited and a little nervous. I'm becoming a grandma!"

We hugged her and congratulated her.

Giggling, we went back to our cubes, but as I sat down I felt tears coming down my cheeks.

I typed a message to Beth: "Is it time for a coffee break? I need to talk."

She immediately typed back: "Let's do it, girly."

I had started working at a defense contractor General Dynamics in December of 2014. Beth and I immediately became close friends. She was going through a challenging divorce and I had been dealing with a life dissatisfaction for the past few years.

In 2011, at age 39, seven years after immigrating to the United States, after years of riding an emotional roller-coaster, I had finally settled down, with my 16-year-old daughter, a wonderful partner, and a well-paying job. The future looked bright too, but I was lost. I still felt unfulfilled. I had everything I had wished for and yet felt a deep personal dissatisfaction. I felt crazy and ungrateful.

Though I didn't like the past, I constantly went back to it. The more I tried to escape from it, the more it came back to me. The desire to go back and read my journals from the time I lived in Tehran was irresistible. I dug down through memories, major milestones, and important people in my life. So many bittersweet memories surfaced.

I found interest in Persian poetry again, and it reminded me of the power of writing. Something began to blossom in me. Reading my favorite poem, "Life is Beautiful," by Siavash Kasrayee made me emotional. When I mentioned it to my father over the phone, he started reciting it. I wiped my tears as he said,

"Yea, Yea, Life is beautiful

Life is an everlasting fire-temple

If you brighten it, you'll see the flames dancing in every direction

And if not, it will be quiet, and that will be our fault..."

Mastering English had been my focus since 2004, but in 2011 I craved the sound and sight of Farsi; I wanted to read books in my own language again, my favorite old books I grew up with.

The Little Black Fish, by my beloved Samad Behrangi, reminded me life is not limited and offers many opportunities for new adventures. I remembered the horror I felt watching my father take his books to burn to avoid arrest by the Islamic regime. He left only a few, including this one.

The Unbearable Lightness of Being by Milan Kundera made me realize dictatorships like the regime in Iran could repress but not kill people's desires to live. As I reread it in Farsi, I listened to the audio book in English and noticed that censorship in the Farsi version that changed the story considerably.

At the same time, to honor my heritage, at non-Persian events I offered to cook Persian food, making it as authentic as I could. It felt important to introduce Persian cuisine to others. I presented everything perfectly. I felt accepted when there was not a grain of rice left in the dish and people came to say, "That was delicious. What are the special seasonings you used in that dish?" My proud answer was, "Persian seasonings, like cinnamon, turmeric, and saffron." I made sure to say saffron with a little louder voice to make people excited to want to know more about it. I needed so badly to share my culture.

I wanted to stay away from Persian gatherings to avoid refreshing painful memories, but when invited I politely accepted and joined. I even enjoyed mingling and dancing–at least for a few hours. Yet I disliked our personal interactions–full of male-dominant behavior–and I was not shy about expressing my resentment of it.

If I asked why women were in the kitchen while men talked or played cards, ladies answered, "You've become so Western. It's the women's job. We know how to do it better."

When my friend's husband commented, "My wife didn't have to become a dentist. Taking care of the kids is the priority. I make enough money for all of us," I expressed frustration, but she just rolled her eyes and motioned me to shut up. I wanted to shout, it is not about money! And oh, by the way, why did he use her income to the last penny towards family life then? What about her talents, her years of education, her dreams of building a career? I felt out of place.

It made no sense: Among my American friends, I wanted to emphasize my Persian side. Among my Persian friends, the Western side of me wanted to scream.

Confused by these mixed feelings, I was not sure what I was looking for. What did I need to change?

Was it my lack of fulfillment in my career? The status-oriented Persian culture that forced me towards an education path that clashed with my personality? Did I need to do something other than analyzing financial data just because the pay was good?

If I stopped thinking about the past and got a job where I could see tangible changes in people's lives, would I feel fulfilled and overcome the confusion? What about teaching? I loved to nurture and help others. Could I do it? Not if I wanted to keep my lifestyle and help my daughter with college. A friend suggested volunteer teaching. She assured me it would be rewarding. So, I started to teach English as a Second Language (ESL). It was rewarding, but the good feeling was short-lived, and as soon as the class was over, the confusion monster was waiting for me outside class to remind me about the big hole in my heart.

I felt helpless. Why couldn't I enjoy my life? Whenever this thought was at its peak, releasing excess cortisol in my brain, I messaged Beth. "Nice day out. Coffee break?"

Beth would answer, "Let's go."

As we circled the pond in front of our office building, we moved deeper and deeper into the mysteries of our lives, walking round and round, making spirals.

She said of her marriage, "I felt no more intimacy after our 10th anniversary. I had a strange feeling about him, but I blamed myself for being negative. Why didn't I realize he wasn't into the marriage?"

I said I never felt any emotional intimacy with my second husband but hoped he would change, hoped he would love my daughter (from my first marriage), hoped he would accept me as a mother.

A rush of relief flooded me every time I told her a story of my past. The connections between our life stories showed me bitter events are natural parts of life.

At the same time, circling the same pond and repeating the unpleasantness of the past through different stories felt like chasing our tails. Beth's 20 years of marriage, her constantly changing mind about divorce. Sweet and bitter emotions from the past, plus fear of the future, confused her. I suggested she take some time without forcing herself to make a final decision.

I realized Beth was a mirror for me. I was as confused as she was. We both needed time. The difference was she had only two choices, divorce or not divorce. Marriage wasn't my problem; twice divorced, I lived with a man I loved devotedly. But I still wasn't happy, and I had no idea whether I had any choices, or if I did, how many.

I shared with her a quotation from The Art of War by Sun Tzu:

"In the midst of chaos, there is also opportunity."

We decided to accept and welcome the confusion and be patient with it. We were confused. Voila!

There was no more fight or resistance. We still walked around the pond, but now we listened to each other with compassion, trying to understand the day-to-day emotional change each one experienced. We didn't offer solutions. There was only empathetic listening and support. One day I shared a sweet story from the past, feeling good about life, and Beth shared a good memory and decided to stay with her husband. The next day, I shared a bitter memory of the hated culture I grew up in, and felt empty inside. She remembered some of her husband's abusive behavior and felt she could not tolerate him.

Accepting the confusion with compassion allowed me to slowly discover my need to overcome my resentment and hate for my bitter past. Resentment created by the male-dominant, rigid culture that made me feel scared and trapped all the time. But how? It was tough since I was exposed to so much freedom in America. The comparison was like day and night.

America, where I had lived since 2004, this "work-in-progress" democracy that is no-where near perfect yet, felt perfect to me.

In America I could freely say to a young missionary boy who knocked on our door: "No, thank you. I am not religious," and have him respectfully say goodbye. If I said that in Iran, the least reaction was an eye roll, and the greatest the death penalty.

In America I didn't have to find an underground market to buy books. I ordered any book I wanted online or borrowed it from a library.

In America I talked about my political views without fear of arrest.

In America I wore any clothes I liked without risk of government punishment or being harassed by men in the street for a visible strand of hair or (God-forbid!) nail polish.

In America I lived unmarried with someone I loved.

In America I freely listened to any music in the street without fear of arrest.

In America I felt a lot more equality of rights as a woman, while in Iran I had no right to divorce an abusive husband unless he agreed.

In America people empathized with my pain at leaving my only child in Iran while trying to build a future for her, rather than judging me for leaving her behind. To my

American friends I was not a selfish woman and careless mother.

And last but not least, in America I could, if I wanted to, have—and legally raise—a child out of wedlock.

How could I not hate the male-dominant culture heavily influenced by Islamic dictatorship that had stolen those opportunities from me during the first thirty-one years of my life, filling my heart with guilt and shame?

And yet, I counted days that I had no one to speak Farsi to. And yet, I cried when I heard the Iranian national anthem. And yet, I screamed happily when Iran's soccer team made its way to the World Cup.

I thought this confusion must be related to all the pain buried in my heart.

Beth, a capable, professional woman who could live independently and did not want to accept humiliating treatment anymore, still showed fear of being alone. I could not forget the shame and guilt created by the culture I grew up with and believed I was not worthy of enjoying life.

Listening to Beth's analysis of her past and its negative impact on her marriage, learning about the Midwest Michigan environment she grew up in, I realized the culture we grow up with came as a package with all its sweet and bitter impacts on people.

Culture, this one word with a world behind it. Countless cultures all around the world, different and yet similar.

My learning and searching taught me that a male-dominant culture, especially one empowered by dictatorship, is a social hierarchical structure that causes power struggle. This power struggle shows itself in all different ways in people's lives, but one common and devastating thing it does is erode emotional intimacy from personal relationships and trust and empathy in all human relationships. Failing to fulfill these very fundamental needs–emotional intimacy, empathy, and trust–results in dissatisfaction, resentment, and a void in the heart. It forms an invisible confusion.

People still try. They still build life around the limitations, with what possibilities are available, but no matter what they do, they remain unfulfilled.

However, under dictatorship, the resentment created within society raises the curiosity of some (but not many) people who think more deeply and see things differently. Those are people who don't go with the flow. Those are the creators, the keepers. Poets, writers, translators, artists, singers, musicians, and journalists become depressed but don't stop creating. When they are banned from their work by Islamic law or stopped because they are women, they go underground but do not quit. The desire to connect through fine arts is a natural instinct in humans. In a lot of cases, their creations speak the language of the dark current circumstances of life, mainly the missing closeness, honesty, and empathy.

If the Islamic regime's ultimate goal has been to kill fine arts, the limitations created more artists. If many women have suffered from lack of equality of rights under the regime and under their fathers, brothers, and husbands, the suffering has caused women to strive for independence by going for higher education and professional careers. If society has been anguished because of lack of trust and empathy and excess of corruption, people still keep the rituals, ceremonies, and traditions. Persian language, Persian new year, Persian dance, Persian hospitality, Persian cuisine, and Persian poems have stayed strong and survived the harshness of the regime and the negative side of the culture, and that keeps us going.

A person, a culture, a life: nothing is perfect. A human gains inner peace once he or she accepts his or her imperfection and dark side without hatred or feeling shame. I am no exception. I would gain my inner peace once I accepted the imperfection in myself, my life, and my culture. That's when I would recognize those cultural aspects that I still wholeheartedly loved and those aspects that I resented. There would be next steps to shed light on the dark parts for healing the pain in my heart. That realization gave me hope, but I didn't know how to move forward.

Through the years, sharing my concerns with Beth and others and receiving their care and empathy as well as learning about their concerns and feeling empathy for them, I learned how fulfilling it could be for a human to build trustworthy connection with others.

A big personal change was revealing itself as a result of the deep confusion; I just didn't know what.

****

That sunny September day after hearing Mary's news, when I stepped out of the cube with my coffee cup in hand and tears on my face, Beth looked at me with her lively green eyes and, as always with her bright tone of voice said, "Uh-oh. My friend Shabnam needs some girl talk."

The patio outside the building faced the pond with geese floating on it. We picked two chairs under the shade of the tall trees. With my tears still running down, we had a few moments of silence.

Then: "Tell me what happened," Beth said.

"I'm happy for Mary and her daughter, happy Sandy can keep the baby. I hope they appreciate this opportunity. But hearing their story brought a bitter memory of my own experience."

Beth listened attentively. "Shabnam, what are you telling me?"

"Beth, you remember I told you my love story with Captain?" After my divorce in 1998, the married "Captain" and I had had a secret romance for almost two years. We had both tried hard to break it but couldn't until he finally left Iran, perhaps to avoid any damage to his wife and children.

"That's one juicy story you have. I'll never forget that one. Then what? You are killing me."

"About three weeks after he left Iran in the fall of 2000, I found out I was pregnant."

I told her how I had been thinking about emigrating, too. I wanted to build a better life in the West for myself and my little daughter from my first marriage. I also dreamt that outside Iran, in a land with more freedom, I could have a baby from Captain. He didn't belong in my life, but his baby could. I explained how under Islamic law you could not get a birth certificate for a baby out of wedlock. If you had no legal relationship with the father, you literally could not legalize the baby. That meant you could not send him to school and in the future, he would be unemployable. He would have no identity. Not only that, it would be a big shame that under no circumstances I could reveal to my family or people around me. It was intolerable in that culture.

I had no choice but to have an illegal, risky, and expensive abortion.

"I was already depressed by losing Captain. When I found out I was pregnant, I didn't think about any other possibilities."

Beth's eyes were doleful.

Tears coming down again, I continued. "I didn't have time to think differently, so I didn't tell Captain back then. Just like that, I lost the dream baby I wanted so badly."

Beth sighed. "I am sorry, Shabnam."

She put her hand on my cold hand. We were silent for a few seconds, then she asked, "Did you ever tell him?"

"We never lost touch. I told him, but not until 11 years later."

"What did he say?"

"He had an emotional response, and then he asked me to write a book, the story of my life." My tears were now uncontrollable.

"Girl, you have told me a lot of stories before, but this is something else. Captain is right. You should write the story of your life. I know your story will show me, and probably others, I am not the only one who deals with tough life challenges. It will be inspiring. You should write it, Shabnam!"

If sharing the story of my Persian paradox with Beth was helping us understand the past better, sharing it with more people could certainly bring more understanding and connection between me and others. That is what stories are about, right? To understand the natural growth of life and to create empathy and trust, we need to learn about each other's differences through our common feelings. I saw a new light coming through my heart.

I wiped my tears and began to glimpse a possibility of a passion for something new. The coffee break was over, but my work had just begun.

CHAPTER ONE

Fall of 1978 - 1984

We were sitting in the corner bedroom, a little candle our only light, when the shooting started. I jumped into my mother's lap and asked her whether they were coming to kill us. I had only seen shooting in movies. Nervously, she held me tightly and reassured me, "No, they are not killing us. They won't be able to come in. The doors are locked."

My mother, Manzar, blew out the candle to darken the room. She closed the door behind us and carried me to the family room in the middle of the apartment, away from all windows. In the dark we held each other tight. The apartment was one level above the garage. The fall wind blowing through the door hinges sounded like steps on the staircase right outside the apartment door.

The shooting didn't last long. After a long few minutes waiting and listening, we went back to the bedroom to try to fall asleep. That was impossible; the two of us lay in bed in silence.

At age seven, I was old enough to understand circumstances were unusual but young enough to be confused about what to do.

Not able to fall sleep, I remembered conversations my mother and her brother Mohsen had had a couple weeks before.

For a couple of months, we had been staying at Uncle Mohsen's house while my parents' divorce went through. He was my mother's biggest supporter, encouraging her to leave my alcoholic father and go to America with him and his family.

This plan was moving forward until one day Uncle Mohsen came home in a rush and ordered his American wife, Judy, and their two daughters to pack as quickly as they could; they had to fly back to the States that night. Uncle Mohsen was giving orders to his family in English and telling my confused mother in Farsi that he had received threatening phone calls. Islamic fundamentalists who were protesting the Western policies of the Iranian shah, Mohammad Reza Pahlavi—and his friendship with the States—had threatened to kill Judy and burn their house. I understood the Farsi part of the conversation and internalized the fear, if not the political complexity, without speaking a word.

Judy and my two cousins left Iran immediately with tears in their eyes. Judy hugged my mother and me and said she had a great time during her past five years in Iran with all the fun parties and trips they had, especially to the Caspian Sea. She asked my mother to ensure she got our plane tickets as soon as her divorce was final to fly to the States, and with an emotional but reassuring voice she said, "See you soon, but in America. *Khodahafez*, goodbye."

A week later, Uncle Mohsen decided to follow his wife to the States when the political upheaval worsened. My mother and I remained in his house with his family's helper, Belinda, but she was from the Philippines and planned to leave soon, too.

To control the roads, the Shah's government enforced a sunset curfew, and a power outage became a nightly occurrence in Tehran, where we lived, and in most other big cities in Iran.

After Uncle Mohsen's departure, my mom's sister, Aunt Sara, and her husband checked on us every evening before the curfew started. Unlike Uncle Mohsen, Aunt Sara and her husband were not encouraging the divorce. Aunt Sara told my mom, "You need to go back to your husband. Only Moshen was in favor of your divorce, but he's gone now. You will have a hard time in this society being a divorcee. How will you handle money matters? How will you handle people's judgments? And now that the situation in the country is so dangerous, how will you handle you and your daughter's security?"

My mother kept saying she could not go back to her husband. My father's alcoholism and violent behavior were too frightening.

I loved my father. I had a hard time understanding what was going on and cried when I missed him. During my stay in my uncle's house, I looked forward to every visit we had. He took me to my favorite restaurant, to his office, to the park; he bought me ice cream. But I hated their fights. I always tried to avoid doing anything that might cause a fight between them, but it didn't matter. They fought about everything Aunt Sara or Uncle Mohsen said to my mother, they fought if my mother had forgotten to bring something to a trip to Caspian Sea with her, they fought all those nights my father came home drunk. I think my father hated my mother's family. He always complained that his in-laws insulted him.

After he left for the States, my uncle called every night, asking whether my mother had finalized her divorce and gotten her ticket. My 28-year-old mother, emotionally paralyzed by the political unrest and by being alone in her brother's house, came up with excuses every night and put it off.

She was a teacher. Every morning we pretended life was normal: We got up, got ready, and went to school. She dropped me off at my school and went to hers. School was a good distraction, but my anxiety would grow as we got closer to 2:00 pm. I was a first grader, and my cousin Marjan, Aunt Sara's daughter, was a fifth grader at the same school. She would come and hug me before we went home. Our evening routine was my mother yelling at me to rush to get my homework done before the power outage, and then us sitting in the dark being scared, waiting for another crisis like the shooting the other night.

Sometimes Aunt Sara picked up Marjan and me from school, and my mother got me from their house later. When I was at their house, I hated to hear all the bad things they said about my father. If they didn't like him, why did they want my mother to go back to him? I was confused, and I missed my dad.

I wanted him to take me to the park and play hide and seek with me. Once, in Shahrara Park close to our condo, I couldn't find where he'd hidden, so I panicked and started crying. When he came to me from his hiding place, I yelled at him, asking why he had left me. He gently said he would never leave me. I wanted my parents take me to the Caspian Sea to the villas by the beach. The labor department, where my father worked, provided the houses free to its employees for one week per year. Everything was included: clean beaches, food, and dance parties at night. I loved the yummy food at the buffet and the dancing nights. My maxi dress with white-and-blue small creases on the top, flowed down to my ankle that was a hand-me-down from my American cousin was perfect for dancing. I wanted to go back.

Uncle Mohsen's house was a 10-minute drive from Aunt Sara's house. Aunt Sara was nervous that we were alone at Uncle Mohsen's house, especially after the shooting. One night, about a week after my uncle left Iran, Aunt Sara came to check on us as usual. That night, though, she was furious. My mother's face grew tense waiting for her older sister to start her advice. Aunt Sara said, "We don't know what to do with your husband. He comes to our house drunk and starts yelling and shouting at us in front of the neighbors. He thinks we encouraged you to get a divorce. Remember Shabnam's birthday in our house. You need to decide, Manzar."

My mother started crying. I went to the bedroom while still trying to listen to them. At my birthday party a couple of months ago, my father had come to Aunt Sara's house to pick me up, discovering the party in the process. My mom's whole family was there. He started yelling at Uncle Mohsen that he was stealing his wife and his daughter. Someone from the crowd grabbed a silver candle stick and hit my father in the head. Blood covered his face. My father turned back to me with a miserable expression and said, "You see what they do to me?" and he walked out leaving me there as I cried hysterically.

I was thinking about that night when my mother answered her sister: "He is violent. I am scared of him. I am scared here too. The shooting the other night was terrifying."

Aunt Sara had to leave before the sunset and the power outage. As she left she said, "Isn't living with him probably safer than living here alone?"

Half an hour later the doorbell rang again. My mother hesitated to answer and tried to see who was there from the front window, but my father started banging his fists on the door to the building.

Probably embarrassed in front of the neighbors, my mother buzzed the intercom and opened the door to calm my father down. He came in shouting. He had found out that my uncle had left us alone in Tehran. Belinda was home that night. I ran to the bedroom while my mother and Belinda got my father out of the house. The power outage happened. My father still shouted for a while outside, threatening my mother with violent consequences if anything happened to his daughter due to her stubbornness staying in that dangerous house. He said, "You have no legal right to take my daughter out of the country!" But eventually, he left. I am sure neighbors were listening to all of this but didn't show up. My mother cried for the rest of the night. Thirty years later she found out that she actually could have taken me to the States because my father had given up legal custody. My father, with his law background, knew this but took advantage of my mother's ignorance. Uncle Mohsen was not there to tell my mother, "Manzar, he is bluffing. Don't believe it."

Over the next days they spoke on the phone. I could hear my mom's voice, soft. To avoid further conflict, she decided to disconnect from her relatives and focus on her marriage. My father came over another afternoon. I was happy to see him and happier he was kind to my mom. He lifted me and put his arm around my mom's shoulder saying how sorry he was, "Manzar *bebakhshid* ! I was angry but I will make it up to you. I love my family." I could see the tears shining in his eyes. Putting her head on my father's shoulder, my mother started crying silently too. In a few days, we lived with my father again.

****

Dr. Abbas Milani explains the situation in Iran thoroughly in his book "The Shah". During the 37 years of the shah's power, he had modernized the country but kept an authoritarian power. Major opposition groups including radical Islamic, secular nationalist, religious pro-democratic, Marxist communist had formed against him, each with different visions for Iran's future but all agreeing that Western countries interfered excessively in our military and economy. Especially after the 1953 coup lead by British and American forces to overthrow the democratically elected Prime Minister Mosadegh, who nationalized oil in Iran, most of the political parties felt a big distrust against Britain and the States.

My father, with his Marxist communist beliefs, felt positive about the protests. Years later I would learn he had a long history of fighting against the shah's dictatorship. He had been arrested by SAVAK (the shah's secret police - Organization of National Intelligence and Security). When he graduated from Tehran University with a law degree, he was prevented from taking the board exam because of his political background.

In December, the protests grew stronger. My father took me to street protests. Tall and handsome, he carried me on his shoulders, so I was taller than anyone else. I usually carried a banner that said, "shah must leave." From up there, I could see a huge gathering filling all the wide street close to our house. Everyone shouted, "Down with shah!" It was fun and even heroic. I felt like a protagonist in one of the stories I had read.

My father and I loved stories by our favorite author, Samad Behrangi. My heroes were the sweet little Oldooz, whose talking doll helped her stand up against her mean stepmother; the little black fish, who wanted to leave her family and her boring life in the stream to find out what was beyond her little world, to see the big ocean; and Yashar, the young boy who lived in poverty and despite his difficult life always tried to help others. Those books shaped my ideas. I began to despise poverty and believe everyone deserved a happy life. My father believed rich people like the shah and the queen created poverty, and he taught me if everyone lived modestly, it would help people in poverty to live better. I believed my father.

When the protests became more serious and violent, schools were closed. My mother probably felt better that way. My teacher had asked my father to come to school one day. She told him that when she had brought the shah and queen's picture to class, I had said those were bad people and should leave the country. She was afraid of spies in the class, even among little kids, and said she thought I must be parroting what I had heard at home. But I loved my books and their stories. It felt as the characters lived with me in real life. I was not simply a parrot; I had those ideas seeded in my mind as well.

Like most people back then, my parents had an arranged marriage. My paternal (Aunt Zari) and maternal (Aunt Soghi) aunts were next-door neighbors to each other. As my mother says, when Aunt Zari started looking for a wife for her younger brother, Hossein 30 years old, my father, she chose her neighbor's younger sister Manzar, my mother, 19. She asked Aunt Soghi for my mother's hand. Aunt Zari said she and her sisters were tired of being worried about my father. At college at University of Tehran fighting along with other like-minded protesters, he had been arrested many times by the shah's regime and he continued that way after college too. Hossein needed to get married and settle down.

My maternal grandmother had passed away when my mother was 16. She was dealing with her father's old-school discipline under her stepmother's authority. Marriage sounded to her like a good way out; my father was an educated young man and held a respectable job in the department of labor. So, she said yes.

My father was from a low-income suburban family and believed in human equality following Marxist ideas. My mother came from an upper-middle-class, conservative, traditionally religious family more privileged than my father's. Her family looked down on poor people, trying to help them with sympathy and not empathy. Coming from a privileged family, my mother's ideal house had chic and valuable objects and furniture while my father with his upbringing and socialist ideology was anti-materialistic and anti-luxury.

My father was a government employee and my mother was a middle-school teacher. We were middle class. My mother and her siblings thought my father could do better with his degree. I heard this from my father, who said it with hatred and disgust. Uncle Mohsen came to our house, cleaning his shoes on the rug in the living room. "Can't you afford a more valuable rug? We are Persian. We should own expensive rugs." To my mother's family, it was stupid to have a law degree without making a lot of money. My father loved his job because he was in charge of defending laborers' rights, but he didn't make enough money for a life of luxury.

After we moved back in with my father, for a little while things were calm because he was busy with protests and my mother was disconnected from her siblings.

By wintertime, the political chaos had gotten worse. All the conversations at home revolved around what was going on in the streets. People were being shot by military police. Because of the curfew, my father and other protesters were active only during the day. People were asking for a democratic government and wanted the shah to leave power.

****

As the political situation deteriorated, the Shah got to his weakest point. When he left Iran on January 16, 1979, people celebrated in the streets. Everyone hoped for a bright future for their beloved Iran.

I had seen and heard about one cleric, a religious leader who had become popular recently. I had seen people carrying his pictures in the protests and his words were respected. Even my father said Ayatollah Khomeini was an honest man and wanted the best for people in Iran.

Khomeini had been exiled for an inflammatory anti-shah speech in 1964 and now lived in France. Since the early 60s, while the shah promoted secularism and created more connection to the West, Khomeini spoke against the shah's policies in cooperation with America and Israel. His lectures were recorded and smuggled into the country. Many listened to them. He spoke about freeing the people from the West's grip on Iran, giving the poor power, and making a fair system, ensuring the oil industry invested in everyone's favor—no attachment or dependence on the West.

Ayatollah Khomeini said he would return to Iran to settle things, then would move to Qom (the Vatican of Iran) to focus on religious leadership. On February 1, 1979, with the shah deposed, he flew to Tehran from Paris.

I watched it on our black-and-white TV. The streets were packed by people all the way to Mehrabad airport, in southern Tehran. People welcomed him and celebrated his arrival. At Tehran's main cemetery he delivered a speech. Everyone was so eager to hear his words. After he expressed his condolences to people who had lost loved ones during the revolution, he said, "We need to contemplate why this nation has experienced such disasters ... such bloodshed, looting, and oppression ever since they raised their voices? What have our people said to deserve such doom?"

He added that the government of the shah was raised unlawfully, and that everyone in that government should be considered criminal and should stand trial. "I will appoint the administration and I will punch the current government in the mouth. I will appoint the administration with the help and support of the nation since the people have accepted me."

That same month, Khomeini appointed the interim government of Mehdi Bazargan. Bazargan was the head of the engineering department of Tehran University, and his Islamic but liberal-democratic school of thought inspired hope for open-minded, non-Islamic people.

Bazargan assigned my father's close friend, Daryoush Forouhar, who was the leader of the National Party of Iran, as the minister of labor. Forouhar and my father had known each other since college.

My father had not been able to get management positions during the shah's era because of his communist beliefs and activities. He felt positive and hopeful when Forouhar selected him to lead one of the most sensitive industrial areas in the country in Ghazvin, ninety-three miles northwest of Tehran.

My father always wanted to give poor people more power. Ghazvin's industrial area contained big factories with valuable goods and was the site of labor strikes and protests asking for improvement in factory workers' benefits and wages. My father left Tehran for Ghazvin immediately.

In a couple of months, late spring of 1980, my mother and I joined him there. My mother started working at an all-boy's middle school, and I attended the elementary school next to that.

By spring, the new government held a referendum on whether people wanted to have an Islamic Republic. Ninety-eight percent of eligible voters in Iran voted yes. Or at least that is what the new administration announced. My parents voted no. They asked for a democratic, secular government. My father was an atheist and my mother believed religious practice was a personal matter.

As Dr. Milani has said in his book The Shah, something Ayatollah Khomeini never mentioned in his speeches during the revolution and in his early days following his return to Iran was his strong belief for the Guardianship of the Islamic Jurist—*Velayat Faghih*. He and his supporters did not openly present themselves as radical fundamentalists. Especially since he had temporarily appointed a pro-democrat Islamic prime minister, no one thought Iranians would live under *Velayat Faghih*. People trusted him to free Iran from the West and create a strong economy with less social and economic inequality.

Dr. Milani explains some people believe the shah's fear of the Soviet Union, along with his personal religious beliefs, created an unintentional undercurrent of power for the Islamic fundamentalists. The shah's modernization policies during the 60s and 70s had caused mass immigrations from the villages to the cities. People who immigrated to the cities hoping to find some of the money brought to the country by the high price of oil found mainly blue collar jobs instead and remained uneducated. They also kept their traditional and religious beliefs and remained separate from the educated class. They supported Ayatollah Khomeini mainly because of their religious beliefs and dissatisfaction in the shah's unfulfilled promises for a modern life for all Iranians. They respected Khomeini and believed what he said. Their population was a good percentage of the society.

Dr. Milani reveals in The Shah, there are recently unclassified documents showing the American ambassador William H. Sullivan had secret meetings with Khomeini. After the shah was gone, Sullivan believed Khomeini was the only leader who could stand against the Soviet Union at the time. He stoked the fire of the revolution in favor of Khomeini taking the power.

In Ghazvin, my father came home late every night. His face was grim and dark. He was not talking to us much, only smoking until late. He was busy talking to labor unions and trying to get more rights for laborers. He was encouraged by the victory of the revolution, but it was not such an easy job.

He soon realized he was under pressure by Islamic forces who were speedily taking everything over. They were urging him to calm the protests organized by labor unions by using fear and that was not my father's way.

Soon, the regime's guardians occupying all the security jobs told him he needed to attend morning and noon group prayers. He was criticized for eating lunch and drinking tea during Ramadan. My father's atheist beliefs did not fit that environment.

Although many people of different opinions, including Islamic pro-democracy, Marxists, and secular nationalists still hoped to build a free Iran released from the monarch as influenced by American and Western imperialism, the Islamic regime's new constitution followed Islamic rules *Velayat Faghih*.

While many people dreamed of a strong economy to free the country from importing high-value goods and instead using oil profits on infrastructure, an Islamic constitution put faith in the power of God and God's representative, the supreme leader of the country. Ayatollah Khomeini became this leader. Under the new constitution, banking systems needed to follow sharia law-compliant finance rules. Interest payments on investments and loans were defined as *riba* (unjust gains made in trade or business). The punishments also became more severe; a convicted thief was sentenced to, at the very least, amputation of the full length of four fingers. Punishment for adultery for women became stoning. Women lost all the rights they had fought for and gained under the previous regime: divorce, training and education for such jobs as pilots, sailors, judges, the president, military ranks, and many others.

I was too young to understand, but in November 1979 when I heard the American embassy had closed and people who worked there had been arrested by the regime, I knew it was serious.

It was one of the longest hostage crises in history. Muslim Student Followers of the Imam's Line were the group who attacked the U.S embassy in Tehran on November 4th. Their complaint was that the States was the biggest ally of the Pahlavi regime and was undermining the Islamic revolution in Iran. Fifty-two American diplomats and citizens were held hostage for 444 days.

As a result, the U.S. government applied economic and diplomatic pressure. It ended the oil imports from Iran on November 12, 1979, and two days later an executive order from the U.S. Office of Foreign Assets Control froze nearly $8 billion (USD) in Iranian assets in the United States.

Also in November, Prime Minister Bazargan resigned, acknowledging his government had failed to prevent the U.S embassy takeover. Forouhar, the labor minister, and other ministers stepped down as well.

My father felt out of place among Islamic fundamentalists. He did not see the point of working in Ghazvin anymore and requested a transfer back to Tehran. Waiting for the transfer a couple of months later, watching all other people being fired for connections to non-Islamic groups, my 41-year-old father requested early retirement (using one of the constitutional amendments with minimum pension) to avoid accepting Islamic rules in his career. We moved back to Tehran. His decision created financial difficulties in our family.

Until then, all I knew about Islam came from watching my mother doing her daily prayers or her older aunt voluntarily wearing a scarf to cover her hair from men's eyes. Religious practices were inside the house for those who wanted to practice them. No one was forced into it. Religious people who were serious did not mingle much with secular people, but no one disrespected each other in public. Now, Islamic rules had become the law of the country and everyone had to follow them regardless of their beliefs.

Not even a year after what was now called the Islamic Revolution I could see how my parents were shocked every day by new surprises from the regime. Adults around me said this was not what they had expected. Open-minded people who started the revolution hoping for a modern and democratic Iran with different political groups free to be active hadn't realized Ayatollah Khomeini, as an Islamic leader, opposed democracy and in fact any modernity.

My parents talked about my mother's co-workers and neighbors who changed their lifestyle, practicing Islam in public to keep their jobs and earn promotions.

The only change that sounded good to my mother and me was the regime's alcohol ban. We were happy my father could not come home drunk every night. But he soon found an underground market and drank even more, at home, sadly watching the unexpected changes his country.

Starting in September 1979, schools were gender separated, and female teachers were only allowed to teach in girls' schools. As a result, many female teachers, including my mother, were left without a job. My mother had to check in at the education office every day. At first, she followed the same business dress code as before the revolution. Then, she started noticing women wearing long, loose dresses and loose head scarves. These women received new assignments. My mother tailored a long, loose dress with a floral pattern and wore it to the office. Soon after that she was assigned to a school, but far away from our house. Because she was among the last to change her dress code, she lost a lot of benefits. The benefits started being affected by non-documented, arbitrary evaluations based on teachers' Islamic behavior; first and foremost was an Islamic dress code.

****

Over the course of winter of 1979 and spring of 1980, many leaders who had served in the shah's government were executed after summary Islamic trials. Many fled the country and left everything behind to save their lives. One word against the regime could put people in trouble; even normal acts of life that could be interpreted as protest were not overlooked.

My paternal grandfather died in July of 1980. The tradition in Iran asks for close relatives, especially women, to mourn for 40 days by wearing black clothes. My younger aunt, Soraya, who was an office employee working for the Navy in the southern part of Tehran, followed the tradition. In an unfortunate coincidence, the shah had just died of lymphoma, and some people wore black to mourn him and protest the regime.

Despite all the documentation she provided to the contrary, along with those grieving the shah, after more than 20 years of work, Aunt Soraya was fired. Because of her "non-Islamic behavior" she didn't qualify for severance. Her husband, a Navy employee as well, was lucky to keep his job, but removing one income from the family hurt their budget. Soraya grew depressed, and her husband moonlighted as a taxi driver to make up the gap.

****

For the next school year in 1980, beginning on the first day of fall, women and girls 9 years old and older were required to wear head scarves and cover their bodies from head to toe. I was 9. My mother, who never missed her daily prayers, said angrily, "If a man is aroused by my hair, he should go to hell. Why do I have to protect him?" Islam taught that even a strand of women's hair or inch of naked skin could force a man to sin.

My ugly uniform: dark-gray, loose, long dress with no front buttons, loose long pants, and gray head scarf. Every morning, security officers trained by the Islamic staff at school checked our drab clothing to make sure it met the standard. I wasn't allowed to wear my red jacket or white shoes. We had to buy black jackets and black boots.

Open-minded people were shocked, trying to digest the new tyranny. They had naively believed Khomeini's words. Islamic fundamentalists had stolen the revolution, repressing anyone who believed anything different. That was not how the revolution was supposed to go.

Then, as if those shocks were not enough, in September of 1980 Iraq attacked Iran and started a war.

In summer of 1980, we had moved to a different neighborhood in Tehran, far from my mother's relatives and closer to where my father had grown up.

The sheer fear I experienced on the first night of war has never left my heart. On September 22, 1980, the national TV channel announced its beginning. Shortly after the announcement, the TV provided a training on different sirens; red with short frequencies was the sign of an actual air attack, yellow with shorter frequency intervals was the sign of a likely air attack, and white with monotonous sound was the sign that an air attack was over and everything was safe. They told us to go to the basement or somewhere with no windows in an air attack.

My mother and I sat paralyzed in front of the TV. My father was out somewhere with a friend. His friend's house, a top-floor apartment, was a block away, and my mother and I walked there to be with the friend's wife and children. When we arrived, their TV was on. Within a few minutes the red siren sounded on the TV. We children clung to our mothers. We all ran downstairs, joining neighbors in the first-floor unit. The loud siren was disturbing. Then, in about 10 minutes the TV announced a white alert. Confused and shocked, we headed back upstairs. A few minutes later the TV announced the red siren had been a drill. By then, my father's friend arrived and said that my father had gone to our house. On the way home, I could not control my fear and wet my pants. That was the first time I experienced such fear.

The Islamic regime's takeover jeopardized Iran's diplomatic relationship with the West, and our economy weakened. Before the revolution, the U.S. dollar was worth seven Iranian currency, *touman* but that quickly jumped to 110 *touman* and was getting worse. Importing necessary goods from the West was reduced, banned, and expensive. The government's budget, all from oil, went mainly to the war.

Staples such as meat, eggs, milk, bread, and rice became scarce. Grocery stores had long lines. The government started distributing food stamps. That winter it was cold. One night, after a few hours standing in line, my mother came home with a few bags of rice, sugar, cooking oil, and loose tea. Her hands were purple. She hadn't thought she would have to wait so long and had not taken her gloves. She walked in, dropped the bags on the kitchen table, and started crying. Then there was a fight because my dad had stayed home and had not helped. There was always a good reason to scream at each other.

Our building's heating system, like most others in Tehran, used oil, which was also scarce. That winter, my father and three neighbors paid triple the normal amount on the black market. Even the driver who brought the oil was scared of being caught. Even so, the delivery gave us only warm water, not proper heat. We all slept in the living room with one small electric heater.

In November of 1980, Iraq captured Khoramshahr, a strategically important city in southwest Iran. Khoramshahr was next to Abadan, with one of the biggest refineries in the Middle East and many oil products that brought money to the country. We were all afraid Iraq could win the war. Our love for our country was separate from its dictatorship.

My mother cried as remembered her memories, "Khoramshahr and Abadan used to be the modern cities of Iran, a vacation place having the best concerts with the most popular singers before the revolution. I never forget our trip there when you were one year old. We have many pictures from that trip."

The pictures of these two cities in my 9-year-old head were like post cards with palm trees and the beautiful Karun River joining Arvand River (Shat-ol-Arab) on the border of Iran and Iraq. I wanted to go there myself to get the city back from Iraqis. I felt so patriotic. At school, we gathered in groups discussing the news feeling like adults. One said, "My uncle is at the front line. He said Iraqis capture Iranian solders and torture them. They stole everything from vacant houses in Abadan." The other one said "I hate Iraqis."

We had no idea hate couldn't return our beloved Khoramshahr to us. Soon that news became old, as the war was progressing and we all got distracted by other news either about the war or the new Islamic rules we needed to understand.

****

During 1980 and 1981, when I was 8 and 9 years old, my father met with his comrades, sometimes in our house and other times at theirs. My parents told me not to talk about those visits with anyone. If they met in our house, I went to my room after saying hello. The meetings were long and I made myself busy behind the closed door.

I liked those secretive meetings at our house. People who came to our house were well dressed and spoke politely and kind to me. Even as a child, I was visible to them. Getting that attention made me feel special. One of them, a handsome fellow in his early 30s whom I called Uncle Behrooz, was always kind to me. On one of his visits to our house, I told him my parents had gotten me a small microscope, and I was trying to learn to work with it. I was proud of it. Because of the war between Iran and Iraq, our family struggled financially, so the microscope was precious.

Uncle Behrooz asked my father to bring me to his house so I could see his telescope to compare what I see between too far and too close in those two devices. I was so thrilled.

A few days later, one afternoon, my father asked me to get ready to go to Uncle Behrooz's house. I put on my best clothes and combed my hair. In the mirror of my white vanity, I tried to make sure I looked good. My always impatient father called me. "I am leaving, Shabnam. Hurry, if you are joining me."

Uncle Behrooz's apartment was close, so we got there quickly. It was in an upper-class neighborhood in Tehran, in a five-story building. It felt so romantic to take the smooth elevator with the modern design on the floor and a few small lights lighting the painting on the wall.

When we walked into his apartment, I felt I was walking in my dream land. All the bookshelves were full of Farsi and English books. With his big smile, he welcomed us and asked me to feel free to look at anything. The bedroom door was open, and I immediately spotted the telescope. He said we had to wait a little until it was darker, then he could show me the stars. He fixed a drink for my father and they started talking. I was wandering and playing with books imagining myself living in that apartment. I even dreamed of being his wife. I wanted that lifestyle. A small, chic apartment in a nice neighborhood in Tehran full of Farsi and English books.

While I daydreamed, I heard their conversation. Uncle Behrooz said, "I'm worried about completing my education. I left everything incomplete in California to join the revolution. What is this now? We are still hiding ourselves. I heard the regime has arrested so many of our comrades already."

I pretended I was busy with Uncle Behrooz's books but listened carefully, a wave of fear rushing to my heart. I loved my father even if he drank every night and shouted and yelled at us. He was the one who brought me books; he was the one who brought classy people to our house and took us to their houses. He was the one who wiped my tears if I was scared or awoke from a nightmare. He was my father. Would they arrest him too?

When it got darker, while adjusting his telescope with a naughty smile Uncle Behrooz asked if I wanted to see the neighbor's house through their window? My father objected, "No Behrooz. Don't teach her to be nosy."

When he put me behind the lens, I was fascinated. Although the stars didn't look as big as I expected with the telescope, his explanations of the location of the stars made sense. He showed me Orion. The world was much bigger than Iran. I wanted to see other places.

On the way home, we were silent, my father was deep in his thoughts. I asked him, "Baba, will they arrest you and Uncle Behrooz?"

He mumbled, "I am not going anywhere. You don't have to worry about that." But he was depressed. Every word coming out of his mouth used up so much energy and he could barely talk.

From that night, I developed a habit to go to my parents' room in the middle of the night to check if he was still there. I started crying, and when my mother asked what I was worried about I said, "What if Baba has to go to the front line to fight with Iraqis?" I was trying to be a secret keeper and not tell my mother what I heard from Baba and Uncle Behrooz. She hugged me, reassuring me that my father had finished his mandatory military service when he was young and at his age now he was past the mandatory calling for the front line. That didn't calm me down since that was not the real reason for my fear, but I said nothing.

One day, my father came home in a rush asking my mother to help him to gather all his books. He said, "They arrested a few of my friends." He walked towards his bookcase in the corner of the living room and continued, "Hassan, my childhood neighbor who joined the Islamic guard, just told me his boss ordered them to search houses of the suspects for books and documents."

If he signed a paper stating that he would not continue his political activities, he explained, they would leave him alone. "But I still need to get rid of the books, all of them. Not just the ones about Marx or Lenin or Kianouri" His face was white. There seemed no life left in him. His ideology was his dignity, and now the regime was taking even this.

"What will you do with them?" My mother asked, her eyes looped with concern.

Baba stared at the book in his hand and reprimanded, "My brother agreed to burn them in his shop outside of Tehran. I have to go there now."

Puzzled and angry, I watched them collecting the books. None of those unpleasant characters I had learned about in my books did such a thing. This was like filching our books, forcing the owners to do the dirty job of gathering them. I held my tears to avoid making the situation worse. I had planned to read all those books as I grew up. I was so proud of having them. My father always reminded me, 'People who read books understand more and are better people.' It felt like they would burn a part of me. If I felt like that, I imagine my father's entire existence was going up in flames.

In a couple of hours, more than 1000 books from the bookcase in the living room and their bedroom closet were gathered in two big suitcases and a few bags. My parents each grabbed one of the suitcases, holding their breath, quietly carrying the heaviness of it physically and mentally down to the garage. They placed everything in the trunk of the car in the garage, hoping not to attract the neighbors' attention. We had three neighbors living in the same building using the same garage.

I was sitting on the counter-top behind the kitchen window and watching outside. In a few minutes, my pale-faced father came out of the garage and drove away to destroy his beloved books. I went back to my room to look at what remained. Luckily, The Little Black Fish, Oldouz and Her Talking Doll, and all other series written by my favorite author Samad Behrangi were still there.

My father had encouraged me to take special care of our books. We wrapped them with newspapers when reading them to maintain them in good shape. He had told me that under the current regime, there would be few translations of foreign books, and those would be censored. Whole, intact books like the ones he had were not permitted anymore. The few books left were my treasure.

My father signed the paperwork that indicated he would step down from his political activities. However, a piece of paper at the local police station did not guaranty the ever-changing arbitrary laws of the regime. Those sophisticated people I liked very much never came to our house again. Uncle Behrooz returned to America. Many people I had met in their elegant parties, including the great Iranian poet Fereidon Moshiri, had to step down from their political activities. Whoever did not sign the paperwork or leave the country was arrested. They had unthinking, few minutes trials only to hear their punishment. They were forbidden to hire lawyers. Under the Islamic trial cases, they were mostly convicted of being the Soviet Union's spies. The majority were executed right away.

Only more alcohol could help my father.

****

Our building was at the end of a dead-end alley next to a big and beautiful orchard. Almost everyone in that alley knew each other. After the revolution, all the streets' and roads' names had changed and ours was named after a neighbor, Nejat, who was shot and killed by the shah's soldiers in one of the protests at the time of revolution. His wife and two children still lived in their house on the alley. Their house was unique with modern architecture. It looked new and had a cream-colored exterior and many small, unaligned windows. A medium-size window at my height next to the entrance let me peek inside and see a little, but I was curious to see more.

As soon as my mother met Mrs. Nejat, they became friends, and her daughter, Sanam, a year younger than me, became my best friend. During the summer, we spent almost every day together in their house. As I had suspected, the inside was beautiful.

When Mr. Nejat was killed in one of the protests, Sanam was six and Seena, her brother, was 8 months old.

Mrs. Nejat kept her job as an architect, and her mother lived with them to help her with raising the children.

Mrs. Nejat was about 35 years old, but wrinkles in her face and gray hair framed her beautiful eyes. She told my mother she preferred to keep her look old to avoid men's disgusting offers at work.

After the war started, the government allocated pensions for martyrs' wives, but receiving them required filling in mountains of paperwork. Many widows were housewives with no income. Under Islamic law, men could have four legal wives and unlimited part-time wives through *sigheh*. Men in power in the offices working on those processes would take advantage of women's despair and ask them to be their part-time wives. If they accepted, this would result in higher priority for their paperwork, expediting the pensions. It seems this did bring some money to the family in need.

Mrs. Nejat (along with her late husband) was an architect who had graduated from the National University of Tehran. The couple had built their house based on their own design. It was their dream house and they had so many dreams to realize in that house. Although he was not there to help her realize them, she was still an architect at a good company with a reasonable income and said she was lucky she didn't need government—or other men's—financial help.

I loved to spend time at their house. Sanam was a happy girl, and her grandparents were almost always there and very kind. We had so many opportunities to play in their big house, to use their swimming pool. After swimming, we went to the top deck and collected blackberries fresh from their old tree in the backyard. Seena, now a three-year-old, sometimes joined us and sometimes played on his own, telling us we were too girly for him. We loved him. Usually around eight at night, either my father or my mother came to take me home. I always had such a good time that I didn't want to leave. Going home meant being alone in my room, waiting for my parents to start another fight, especially after my father drank. That was the biggest fear I grew up with; sitting in my room with the door closed and waiting with fear for them to start fighting.

However, that was not how Seena saw my life. To him, I had a kind father who took me home for dinner each night. He had asked his mother where his father was so many times. Mrs. Nejat always said "in heaven," but heaven was not tangible for little Seena.

One day, Sanam and I planned to swim in the pool in the morning. It was still cold and Seena didn't like cold water. He asked why we didn't wait till the afternoon. We giggled and told him this was our plan and he could follow us if he liked.

As we were playing in the pool and I was in the deep section, something hit my head hard. Before I knew it, Sanam started yelling at Seena and he ran away. I got myself to the corner of the pool, and Sanam jumped out and ran to help me to get out of the pool. Her grandmother rushed to the yard hearing Sanam yelling at Seena. I looked at my hand in my head and saw blood. I started crying. Sanam told me Seena had thrown a big stone at me. Her grandmother went to our house and called my mother. They took me to the emergency room.

It was not anything bad and didn't need stitches. The bleeding stopped soon. I stayed home for the rest of the day.

After Mrs. Nejat got home from work that day, she heard the story and came to our house immediately, worried about me. Sanam and Seena were with her. She asked Seena to say he was sorry. He had a hard time saying that. She said he had no bad intention, and he had a big heart loving others, like his father had. She was sad, and we all knew Seena missed his father dearly. He had asked his mother a couple of days before why Shabnam's father was not in heaven but his was.

That incident made a deeper place in my heart for little Seena. We played for the rest of the summer and tried to engage Seena in our activities. Grandmother was watching Seena's behavior carefully, but he did not show resentment anymore.

Once I heard Sanam and Seena's grandmother talking to my mother while wiping her tears: "I am bitten by both regimes." She had lost her son-in-law during the protests by shah's guard and then after the revolution, they executed her son, a high-ranking military general. "What can I say? My heart wants to explode every minute but I keep going watching over my grandchildren."

We all loved when Sanam's grandma told us stories about her life, especially stories of Tehran before the revolution, during our afternoon snack.

Mrs. Nejat told us stories about Mr. Nejat's kindness and sense of humor. How he had made Mrs. Nejat and her sister dance in the hospital room, when they were worried sick not knowing why Mr. Nejat had so much pain in his digestive system for several days. We laughed and could see in her eyes and her voice the love and affection she still had for her husband. With a confident voice coming from her heart, she ended each story with: "I want him to be your role model. He was such a great person."

She taught us a tough life does not have to damage our dignity.

****

Every year we went back to school, the rules were more severe.

Schools traditionally had tall cement walls around the yard with the building at one end. A large metal entrance door surrounded by the tall walls made the doorway. Our school – a girls only school, added an extra layer of security. Once we passed the door, before entering the yard, there was a small space of almost 10 by 6 feet, shielded by a thick curtain. That's where the security officers— students in higher grades trained to be guardians of Islamic law—inspected our uniforms and searched our bags.

There was no official list of banned items. Although we generally knew what was prohibited, it was arbitrary and subjective based on the security officers' interpretation. If we had music cassettes or non-textbooks, we hid them in our underpants; otherwise the item would be confiscated and we would have to deal directly with the principal.

In winter, the year I turned nine, one day I carried a small sticky, black plastic spider to school. It looked pretty realistic and was fun to scare other girls with. I hid it in the bottom of my backpack below my pencil box. I was one of the first students to arrive and the security officer was fresh and had all the energy to do a thorough search. I didn't think about that part. When she started searching my bag to the bottom of it and touched the sticky spider, she screamed and asked me to take it out. When I did, she screamed louder. Scared and disgusted, she immediately took me to the principal's office.

It was still early. The security girl asked one of the secretaries to watch me until the principal showed up. I stared at the floor, embarrassed and scared. The principal's deputy, a young pregnant woman, showed up in few minutes. She addressed me (by last name, routine back then): "Shahmohammad, you look embarrassed. What have you done? You don't usually make trouble."

"She has a nasty plastic spider in her bag," the secretary said.

The deputy's face turned mad, and as she frowned ever more deeply she said, "You are a big girl. You still have toys? You should be learning about more serious things in life. What was your score in your Koran course? Show me what you have in your bag."

I slowly brought the spider out. It was not completely out when she screamed and sat on one of the chairs on the side of the room far from me. Then the principal came in. Her deputy, ready to cry, said, "Look what she has brought!"

The principal looked at it with disgust and asked for my home phone number. While the phone was ringing, she said, "You are usually an obedient girl. Who influenced you to make such an embarrassing mistake? Is that what we have taught you to do at school?" My father answered the phone, and she asked him to come to school at once.

My father arrived in less than half an hour, which felt like hours while I was waiting for him in the pantry behind the principal's office. At least I was alone there. When I heard his voice, I started crying and walked back to the principal's office.

My father, looking at the black spider, said, "You asked me to come here for this?"

"Mr. Shahmohammad, your daughter scared my pregnant deputy. What if, God forbid, she lost the baby? You need to watch your daughter's behavior more carefully. Isn't your wife a teacher? We didn't have the Islamic revolution to raise rebellious girls like this. We need to raise good, obedient girls who follow the rules to become faithful Moslems in the future."

"How could a plastic toy misdirect them from their faith?" He said. "The school should teach girls to become fearless and independent."

Our principal, not looking at him, pretended she was writing something. In Islam, women are not allowed to look at men's eyes directly. It seemed like she was being a good Moslem woman, but in fact she was twisting the rule, dismissing my father.

Finally, my father grabbed the black spider from my hands and without looking at me said, "Don't bring such things to school anymore. Go to your class. You are late." And he left.

The secretary quickly wrote a letter to explain why I was late and walked to the class with me to hand it to my teacher. I don't know what the letter said, but my teacher hid a smile when she read it. I felt a little better, but guilt and embarrassment still overwhelmed my heart.

At least my father was the one to come to school. It would have been much worse, with follow-up punishment, if my mother had been home to answer that call.

At the break after that class, with hate and rage I told the whole story to my close friends, being careful not to let girls who might have been the principal's spies hear us. I hated them all.

That semester, for the first time, I lost 2 points out of 20 on my discipline grade, which was part of my GPA. I earned 20 out of 20 in all other courses.

A few weeks later, our religion teacher said she wanted us to watch a movie during her class. We were all excited since watching a movie was a luxury. After the revolution, not only had all the textbooks changed to include Islamic rules, all pictures of women had scarves on their head. Even the hens. In fact, the entire curriculum changed. Courses such as religion and Koran were now mandatory, while art and essay-writing hours were reduced. Overall it didn't matter because except for math, all classes sounded like religion class anyway. History, sociology, literature—they were all designed to focus only on the Islamic part of the culture and history. The history textbooks in Iran are largely fiction.

That day we got so excited to watch a movie. Our teacher said it was called "*Tobe Nasooh*" (becoming clean of all sins). The name didn't sound appealing but we were still hoping for a good movie. Our school was fortunate and owned a VHS and a TV. It was set up in the prayer room.

The first scene was at the cemetery, then moved to a morgue. A man woke up, found himself among the dead bodies, and ran away, realizing he was almost dead. When he escaped being buried alive, he decided to become a good person and make up for all the sins he had committed, but he constantly had nightmares finding himself in that cold room again.

That night, I woke up from a nightmare, calling my parents. The next night, I refused to stay in my room alone and instead slept on the floor next to my parents' bed. The third night, my mother stayed with me in my room until I fell asleep, but I woke up with that nightmare again. My father came to my room and stayed with me until I fell asleep again.

After a week of this, my father was fed up and came to school. I was scared of him starting a fight with the principal and went to my class worried sick. When, by the end of the day, I had not been called to the principal office, I felt better, and when the bell rang to release us to go home, I bolted out, avoiding all the staff in the yard. At home, my father was calm, so I kept my worries to myself. At night, he told my mother: "That sick woman who is sitting there teaching our daughters is a whore herself. She is an idiot and there is no point to talk to her but at least I hope she knows by now she shouldn't show those type of idiotic movies to small girls."

My mother gently said, "Well, we need to make sure we communicate our complaints without making them mad at Shabnam."

"Ah! You are so scared of everyone. You can never stand up for your rights. You are a weak woman." I was waiting for a fight after that, but my mother's answer was silence.

She indeed didn't know how to stand up for her rights, especially to my father. Predicting her reaction—silence or screaming—was hard. Back then, her behavior never made sense to me. Every time there was a fight and screaming, she rattled off everything that made her angry during her marriage from day one. The list only got longer with no resolution.

****

The war was not calming down. Although Tehran was far from the frontline, we could see the impact everywhere. There were on-and-off air strikes on Tehran and other major cities, but the frontline was mainly in the southwest along the border with Iraq. The main provinces affected by the war directly were Khuzestan, Ilam, Kurdistan, and Kermanshah. In those provinces, people fled their homes, taking minimum belongings, escaping in a rush to safer cities. Everyone who had a teenage son worried it would soon be his turn. Compulsory military service was 24 months for boys 18 or older. A few of my cousins fled Iran with the hope of finding refuge in a Western country. As far as we knew, they stayed in Turkey since it was between Iran and Europe and did not require a visa from Iranians. They stayed alone under harsh financial circumstances and fear of an unclear future until they could find an asylum opportunity in a Western country that was accepted refugees at the time.

Meanwhile the regime was trying to become stronger. The state-controlled news suggested Iran was ahead in the war, but we did not trust it. Every night at 8 o'clock, my father demanded silence as he tried to tune in the BBC Persian news on our old radio. Any noise my mother or I made, including washing the dishes or my record player, made him shout at us to shut up. BBC Persian usually had more truth than the regime-controlled national news, but the regime sent higher frequencies to create background noise on the BBC Persian channel.

One afternoon in May of 1982, my mother and I were at my mom's sister Aunt Soghi's house. By then my father had allowed my mother to link back to her siblings; this caused more fights.

They fought because my father believed everything my mother said was influenced by her family. My mother did have closer emotional connections to her siblings and not much with my father, especially since my father kept telling her: "Your ideas and thoughts are not yours. You have a weak personality and allow others to decide for your life. You are like a mold shaped by your sisters' and brothers' opinion." My mother in return cried and screamed that he was wrong, stopped talking to him for a while, and then resumed her relationship with him, repeating the same process.

That day in May, my mother and I were at Aunt Soghi's house for afternoon tea with my cousin Shahrzad and her friend Zohreh, who was from Khoramshahr, in the south near the frontline and invaded by Iraq. She and her family had had to escape, leaving everything behind, to save their lives. They were lucky not to have lost anyone in the war. So many families lost loved ones in bomb attacks, and entire populations of many western and southern cities lost their houses.

We were sitting in the living room talking and sipping on tea with windows left open to let in the spring. Suddenly we heard loud marching music outside. It sounded like the music came from a mosque close to the house. Aunt Soghi switched on the radio in a flash. An announcer said the Iranian army had bravely won our beloved Khormashahr back through a long and heavy battle. Hearing about the large number of the casualties on both sides was unbearable, but Khoramshahr had been released.

Zohreh started screaming and fell on the floor on her knees. She threw her head on the ground, sobbing and screaming and saying "Thank you, God!" We all cried, feeling proud of Iran's army and sad for all those who lost their lives in that battle. Everyone, even me as a child, hoped that victory would bring an end to the war. Sadly, it didn't.

When I look back at those years, I remember a Tehran with always overcast weather. Tehran is a beautiful city surrounded by mountains and is usually sunny but that is not how I remember it from those days.

****

My mother made some friendships with other likeminded teachers at school. They held gatherings she liked and took me to—without my father.

While I was instructed by my mother to focus on my homework, my focus was on what they were taking about.

They talked about nostalgia for the lifestyle they had before the revolution. My mother referred to the time before her marriage and the parties with music and dancing she would attend with Uncle Mohsen and Judy. She didn't have much happiness after her marriage except when she talked fondly about the London trip she and I made in summer 1977 right before the revolution. She always longed for the pre-revolution lifestyle. Others also talked about their parties, European vacations, and Caspian Sea trips with fun beaches. Now European vacations were a dream. Obtaining or renewing a passport was not easy; it required many government approvals. Such a trip was not financially possible for most people. Europe and America became unreachable dreamlands.

Since I was so young, I didn't have a clear picture of what they were missing. These conversations, though tedious since I would rather be with my own friends, at least gave me a glimpse of pre-revolution Iran.

In those gatherings, the women tried to cook and garnish the same dishes they had eaten in luxury restaurants before the revolution. We were eating one such meal when my mother's friend Giti said, "Yum! Do you remember this at Chattanooga?" She recalled and described the restaurant. "They had such a great environment with great music. You could listen to Chattanooga Choo Choo every time you went there. I loved that place. Its food presentation was beautiful and the deserts were always top notch. Do you know after the revolution the owner was beaten almost to death because of his Western-style hospitality and for serving alcohol? He escaped the country."

Her reminiscing about Chattanooga called to mind the kind of clothing they could no longer wear out of the house. "I want to show you the clothes I brought from Italy when I went there in summer of 1978. I don't know what to do with those clothes anymore. When I bought them, I planned to wear them at work. I love them and want to keep them. They remind me of the glorious time." She brought out a V-neck, sleeveless navy dress; a pair of bright-green pants with bell bottoms; and a white shirt with short sleeves and small white flowers embroidered around the round neck that would go with the green pants perfectly. Her clothes were chic indeed.

Soon the conversation turned to their crazy principal at school. A woman in her early 20s who showed up overly conservative with chador—a black scarf to cover herself from head to toe, she carried a Kalashnikov to show she was ready to join her brothers on the frontline if only they would allow women to fight. This was supposed to inspire girls at school to be pro-war. Every morning, rain or shine, at prayer time before school started she read a verse from the Koran and said students should follow Islamic rules to become faithful Moslems and obedient wives, fighting for Islam at their future husbands' feet.

Then my mother and her friends described how rude the principal was to teachers, who were all older than her with a lot of experience, while the teachers had to be silent and swallow their pride to keep their jobs. The principal had full power to fire a teacher if she didn't follow Islamic rules there.

My mother taught a course called Technique and Vocation. After the revolution, since there were no more co-ed schools, separate textbooks came out: one version for girls and one for boys. Girls learned how to become housewives, learning sewing, cooking, and house cleaning. Boys learned about careers so they could choose one that fit their talents.

The books were carefully reviewed and published by the department of education under strict Islamic supervision. Still, the principal warned my mother to be careful when she talked about the small section in the book about pregnancy. It didn't explain anything about girls' cycles or how girls become pregnant. It talked only about taking care of their health during the pregnancy. Yet, my mother told her friends, the principal had said, "Mrs. Askari (women don't change their last name after marriage in Iran) be careful! You women who think you are open-minded, who came to work with improper dress code before the revolution, may transfer too much information to girls. Focus on what is in the book. Make sure you don't answer any questions girls may ask out of curiosity. Watch your behavior." My mother added, "She talks illiterately, so cheap and rude."

Pretending to be busy with a book, I listened and was surprised hearing that. With me, my mother was traditional and never talked about anything related to my body or sex. Those days, parents believed if they talked about sex, they awoke the desire in their girls ahead of the right time. To them, the right time was when the girl got married. I was eleven and had secretly learned some in books with pictures at my uncle's house a few years before, but it was not much. Despite my strong curiosity about sex, I didn't dare asking my mother about such private matters. I could imagine her serious, angry voice saying: "You will learn about it when you are an adult. Focus on your school homework." So we never talked about it.

CHAPTER TWO

1985 – 1989

On the first day of eighth grade in the fall of 1985, I noticed a new girl in class, tall and skinny. Her oval face was pretty with long eyelashes, but a lot of pimples made her dark skin bumpy. She looked shy, and it was obvious she didn't know anyone. She sat in the back of the room. Our school was large, with about 40 students in each class. We had two rows of benches. Each row had probably ten benches, and two or three of us sat on each bench. I walked between the rows toward the new girl and she looked up. I introduced myself and asked her name. "Arezoo," she said. She said she was originally from Abadan, near Khorramshahr in the south, but when the war started, she and her family had left everything behind and escaped. Her father was killed in the first year of the war, and her mother took her four children to Isfahan, a big city in central Iran that accommodated many refugees.

Her mother remarried in Isfahan, and the family had just relocated to Tehran.

As she saw my sad look while she was telling her story, with dignity in her voice, she immediately said, "We like our apartment now and we are happy." I liked her. We shared our snack on the first break and started a friendship. I knew a lot of people at school since it was my third and last year in the middle-school, so I introduced her to other kids. In no time her open personality helped her to be part of the class.

I invited Arezoo to our house. She said her mother and her stepfather were strict and wouldn't let her visit a stranger's house, so my mother called her mother to get permission, and she came home with me from school one day. We went to my room to change out of our uniforms before heading to the kitchen for lunch (we ate lunch late, after school). Arezoo looked around my room curiously for a few seconds. Then she said sadly, "I shared my bedroom with my sister in Abadan when we had our big house there. We had a big yard where I played after school until my father came home. He lifted me up and took me inside for dinner. We had our own beds. Now, my siblings and I all sleep in one room. Our apartment has only one bedroom. My mother and her husband sleep in the living room." I felt she must crave privacy, and I felt empathetic, but I was too young to show this or comfort her in any way. I blankly looked at her and suggested we go and eat lunch.

A couple of weeks later, she invited me to her apartment. I was surprised to see two little girls in their house—her newest sisters. "My stepfather likes to have a lot of kids," she said. Her pregnant mother came out of the kitchen just then. She hadn't brushed her hair, and she wore a smelly, stain-splashed dress. She said hello to me in a hurry and in a nagging voice told Arezoo, "Hurry up, the kids are hungry. I have been busy all day. Change their diapers too!" Arezoo took care of the kids skillfully as I watched in disbelief, and then it was our turn to eat. I was starving, but lunch was a simple stew without much meat. We sat on the floor in the corner of the kitchen and ate quietly. I was so uncomfortable. Her sisters came home and went into the one bedroom. I eyed the living room, hopeful we could do our homework there, but her brother came home and turned on the TV. I enjoyed houses with a lot of kids around, like my uncle's house, but in this cramped place, I was lost. When I said I could do my homework at home, relief flooded her eyes. I left confused and sad for her to have so many responsibilities and no solitude. My room at home was my sanctuary.

My schoolmate Negar did not have as much sympathy for Arezoo. Negar and I had started out enemies, fighting about whether her class was better than mine and which kids were cool and who knew everything better than everyone else. Then one day in 7th grade my father was driving me to school and saw Negar and her aunt waiting for a cab on the side of the road. He remembered Negar's aunt from a school meeting, and her uniform made it clear we went to the same school. He stopped and asked them to join us. Negar and her aunt sat in the back seat. Negar and I didn't want to talk to each other, but my father and her aunt started chatting and got us engaged, asking questions about school. After the car ride, we waited together in line for our bags to be searched. We smiled at each other.

Our friendship had grown, and I respected her ideas, believing she knew more than I did. But her reaction when I told her what I had seen at Azeroo's surprised me. Annoyed, she said, "I feel for her but never liked her behavior." She said Arezoo kept her emotions hidden and had an agenda.

"But she is nice to me, and we have to understand her situation."

Negar insisted. "I don't know but I can't trust her."

If she had read Samad Behrangi's books, and if her parents had taught her how to feel for poor people like my father had taught me, she wouldn't judge Arezoo like this, I thought. I ended the conversation.

Arezoo's description of her big house in Abadan stayed on my mind. What has war done to our people? How would her father feel if he saw his daughter's life today? When I arrived home that day, I hugged my mother and started crying. I hated war.

****

Arezoo and I shared the same path walking home from school. We had become close friends and shared our secrets. So, one day we were walking home and I pointed out the boy I liked, Reza. "I am so happy when I see him, and I think he looks at me too." I didn't dare talk to him or look at him directly. The thought of talking to him, as sweet as it was, created a wave of fear in my heart. I would be in big trouble if I spoke to him in public. People would tell my parents, and I would be punished or be arrested by Islamic guardians, *Basij* who acted as moral police. . Instead I kept it in my diary and in my heart.

But Arezoo just said, "Why don't you talk to him?"

"Are you crazy? My parents will find out."

She laughed. "Oh, my stepfather beat the crap out of my sister when he found out she was talking to a boy over the phone. But that didn't stop her. Now she uses the public phone to call him. You shouldn't be scared. We'll find quiet roads. Let's change our path and pick alleys that are quieter. You should tell him to come to those alleys."

To my horror she motioned to him, and he started following us. We walked to a quiet, empty alley. The houses were hidden behind big yards surrounded by tall walls. It looked safe, but my heart was pounding, so I let her talk to him. Just his presence felt good. They chatted a bit; she told him what school we went to and asked about his school. Then she said we had to go. "See you tomorrow at the same time," she added. Both of us giggling, we started walking fast to get back to the main road. She said, "You see? That was easy. Tomorrow you talk to him."

But I didn't talk to him, neither tomorrow nor the day after; I was too scared and shy. I started feeling bad about our detour, watching Arezoo and Reza talking and entertaining each other. Within a week Arezoo said she didn't want to go home with me. I had a bad feeling and sure enough saw them together, talking and laughing and walking toward that quiet alley. I wiped my tears going home. My mother asked what was wrong with me when I got home grumpy. I said I didn't get the best grade at school, went to my room, closed the door, and hoped she wouldn't insist I tell her more. She didn't.

I didn't complain to Arezoo for her betrayal. It was my fault I hadn't talked to Reza and that Arezoo was more fun than me. However, it affected our friendship, and I talked to her a lot less, which seemed fine with her. All I could think about was my broken heart, and the first trimester report card showed my GPA had dropped, placing me the third in my class. I had always been first or second. My mother didn't like that. "You need to work harder. That girl Arezoo is distracting you with her family drama, and you are letting others get ahead of you. Focus on your homework."

No one taught us about our changing hormones or what a sex drive was. Not recognizing such strong changes in my body, I thought I was in love with Reza. My first experience of sexual desire was a disaster. I was confused but couldn't talk about it to anyone, not even

Negar. I was embarrassed to have such silly thoughts—strong desire I didn't understand and felt bad about. Of course it was hard to study. I wanted to stay in bed and think of a boy who would wrap his arms around me and kiss me like in some movies I had seen. An imaginary boy who would like me. Was it my neighbor Bizjan? I liked to lie down and think about him. Over time, such infatuations became monstrous, blurring my focus and leaving me imagining every boy I knew as a lover. I had a hard time relating my monster feeling to what was happening in the real world.

****

Persian New Year, *Nowruz*, starts on the first day of spring, the vernal equinox. Everyone starts preparing a month before. Cleaning the house and purchasing new clothes and gifts makes everyone busy during the last month of the year, *Esfand* (February 20 – March 20). But *Nowruz* of 1986 was different. Instead of cleaning the house, we covered the windows with tape and thick curtains: Iraq and Iran started bombing each other's capitals. There were at least two attacks every day, mostly at night.

The end of the year was also the end of the second trimester at school, which meant exams. After a couple of nights sleeping in the living room, away from any windows, and waiting for a bomb to hit our house, my parents decided to leave Tehran. We drove north an hour and half to Aunt Soghi's vacation house in the mountains. Exams were not scheduled every day, and my mother didn't have to teach every day either, so we traveled to the city only on the days we needed to.

Aunt Soghi's two-bedroom house was full of family members who had escaped the bombing. More than thirty people came and went day in and day out. Each night, sleeping arrangements were a story with a lot of laughing. One bedroom belonged to the men and the other to the women. Men who needed to use the bathroom in the middle of the night or who were famous for passing gas had to sleep in the small living room in between two bedrooms. The living room was actually only a foyer and the entrance door leaked the cold air in.

We held onto a pillow, a blanket, and a small space in the room starting in the early evening; otherwise, we might not get sleepwear or space. We slept like sardines in a can. During the day, crowding made it hard to find someplace warm and quiet to study, but I wasn't the only student, and together we all managed our study time.

On exam days two fathers carted us to Tehran. Despite the threat of air attacks, schools stayed open. We had to come back as fast as we could. After exams, we met at Vanak Square, a central point in Tehran, to caravan with the dads back to Aunt Soghi's.

One day when we arrived at Vanak Square, we heard that last night's bomb had hit a house right there. We went to see the scene. Half of one building and another building next to it were reduced nearly to gravel. I could see inside a bedroom in the half-destroyed building. It looked like my own. Had there been a girl my age there last night? Had the family gotten out of town? No one knew. With teary eyes, we walked back to the cars.

****

When my mother came home from school one day and excitedly said her school principal was planning a Caspian Sea trip for teachers and their daughters and sisters, I was curious to see if anyone my age would go, so I could have fun, too. I was skeptical. The teachers were nice, but I never had fun with religious people.

Although the villas by the Caspian Sea that we rented once a year through the labor department were now allocated to war refugees, our family still made an annual trip to the Caspian Sea. My parents booked a hotel right on the shore between Chaloos and Noshahr, two cities they liked. These trips were uneventful aside from my parents' fights. I was happy enough with my books and Walkman. I listened to cassettes my mother got on the black market for me; music was banned under the Islamic Regime. I loved to listen to new Persian music smuggled from mainly California, and my favorite Western band was the German duo Modern Talking. Walking on the beach or in town I had to hide my headphones underneath my scarf.

The school whose principal was planning this all-female trip was a new one for my mother. It was far from home, but she was much happier, especially because of the reasonable principal Ms. Moradi and her assistant Farnaz. They were both religious but nice, with the goal of keeping their teachers happy.

The trip north was on a holiday. One of the teachers had a vacation house and offered to accommodate everyone there. We filled a big bus. I sat next to my mother, very unsure. I had listened to her advice and brought conservative clothes even though it was an all-woman trip. I did not bring anything so forbidden as my Walkman.

One of the young girls, a few years older than me came to me a few minutes after we left and introduced herself politely. "Hi Shabnam, I'm Maryam. My mother has talked about you a lot. You want to sit with me in the back of the bus?" I said yes to be polite. She was pretty but her scarf was tightly warped up around her face covering her hair. I didn't think we'd have anything to talk about since I assumed she was religious. My scarf was always loose and showed some of my hair even in a situation where I was trying to be conservative.

She said she was studying for the college entrance exam, *Konkour*, aiming for dental school. She was studying twelve hours a day and this trip was her break. I knew *Konkour* was competitive and the questions in the test covered all four years of high school courses, almost 48 textbooks. To learn all that, one needed to add another 48 practice book to the study material and master everything to get to good schools. I could see how nervous she was. Even when on a break she was carrying a couple of books with her to study; she really wanted to become a dentist. Dental schools were highly competitive, and they allocated fewer spots to girls than to boys.

She asked me about my school. I didn't feel important after she explained her study situation. But had to report on my grades when she announced, "My mom said your grades are always great. You will be great at Konkour." So, I talked about my 8th grade experience only in bland, generic terms, "I am among the top three students in the class." I said proudly and continued briefly that I was practicing for a play. I was the chubby mouse who liked to eat all the time. I didn't mind to be called chubby and even liked it. It sounded cute. Maryam had offered me some nuts a few minutes before. She laughed and said it seemed like a perfect role for me. Especially with my big cheeks, I looked chubby in middle school, so she was right. We laughed together.

"Focus on your math, biology, and literature more than anything. You will do good at Konkour." She advised. I didn't want to think about it yet.

About twenty miles outside Tehran, we suddenly heard Persian music playing from the bus stereo. Maryam and I looked at each other with perplexed expressions as if we didn't know the song. No one knew how to react. No one trusted anyone else. Ms. Moradi came to the middle of the bus, holding her chador and started laughing. She started clapping her hands and asked everyone to clap and sing. Clap and sing a song we weren't even supposed to know existed? But two people did start singing, and the rest of us clapped with uncertainty. Within a minute, we relaxed and joined in. Every one of us knew the forbidden song by heart. The drive to the Caspian Sea—about five hours—went by so fast with so much fun.

The vacation house was a big one and accommodated all—almost 40 of us—comfortably. It was a block from the beach. To reach the sea, we passed a sandy path with honeysuckle bushes on both sides, especially aromatic in the evening.

We arrived in the early afternoon and tried to get situated. A few people went out to get cold cuts for dinner. Dinner was good, with a lot of laughter. I was still trying to digest the laughter, music, and the relatively free environment compared to what we had gotten used to after the revolution. A couple of my mom's friends asked her whether they should trust the principal and her assistant. Everyone was warming up but still holding back somewhat. At the end of dinner, Ms. Moradi announced a surprise.

She asked everyone to sit in the big living room and wait. First, music started playing and then: Here they were! Two girls dressed up in outfits looking like 1920s Persian ladies dancing into the living room. Everyone said, "Ohhhhhhhh."

They danced and danced and dragged others, one by one, to the dance floor. Ms. Moradi didn't dance; instead, she repeated, "There is no man here to watch you. Have fun." We did. The three-day trip was one of my great post-revolution, Caspian-Sea memories. We went home refreshed and surprised.

For a while, my mother expected to get in trouble because of that trip, but nothing happened.

****

Doing my homework in my room one fall Friday of ninth grade (Fridays are weekends in Iran), I could smell kabab, which my mother typically made on Fridays, reminding me how hungry I was. I was waiting to be called for lunch. As always, at the same time my ears were focused on my parents' conversation, alarmed for another fight. Sure enough, my mother screamed: "Am I the servant in this house? You get to eat the best part of kabab and leave the burnt parts for me? You don't even wait for us to join!? I am an idiot cooking food in this house. For who? None of you appreciate me anyway."

I walked to the kitchen and stopped by the door. My mother was washing her hands. There were a couple more skewers half-cooked on our small gas grill. She had turned it off. Crying, she passed me on the way to her bedroom and shut the door. My father said, "Why is she so sensitive? What is wrong with her?" He continued eating.

I looked at the table, at the tray full of rice, the bowl of plain yogurt, three bottles of Persian "Coke"– with a smooth sweetness, perhaps using cane sugar, three plates (two empty), and my father eating his food and cruelly mimicking my mom's facial gestures. I felt frustrated. They were both acting childish. Silently, I left the kitchen.

I knocked at my mother's bedroom, but she yelled that she didn't want to talk to anyone. I asked if I could take her some food and she said, "No! Let your father eat the food and fill his stomach. I am nobody here. He is the important one."

I gave up. I went to my room and closed the door, thinking, was that a good reason to fight? I promised myself not to fight with my future husband for idiotic reasons like this. I didn't know that when you are fed up, you can easily blow up, especially when the culture pushes you to be passive-aggressive. The word assertive has a beautiful meaning in Farsi dictionary, "someone who express his opinion," but culturally direct communication, listening with no judgment, and expressing feelings without hesitation never was encouraged. To be a good girl and to fit in, one needed to suck it up now and blow it out later out of control, turn it off and never feel it, or even worse, be polite to someone's face but complain and judge behind their back.

Either way, it was Friday lunchtime and I was hungry. *Chelow* kabab was my favorite dish. Before the revolution, we could afford to go out for *chelow* kabab. After the revolution and during the war, going out to eat was only for special occasions, but my mother made good *chelow* kabab. I always looked forward to it.

Kabab is yummy even when it's cold. An hour later I walked to the kitchen finding the table exactly the same.

My father had not put his empty dish in the sink. He was taking a nap on the sofa in the living room since their bedroom was occupied by my angry mom. I cleared the table and put some cold rice and a small piece of kabab on a plate.

****

As ninth graders, Negar and I were not allowed to go out alone. When we found out a new movie directed by Abbas Kiarostami was being screened in February 1987 at the Tehran *Fajr* (victory) Movie Festival, we looked desperately for a way to see it. We had heard of Kiarostami's documentaries because Negar's uncle was involved with the cinema industry and brought us the latest news. This movie had a social focus on a small town in northern Iran and used amateur actors. Negar's uncle had encouraged us to know Kiarostami's work better if we wanted to understand the social challenges in Iran. I had heard about him from my father too. Kiarostami was an open-minded, modern-thinking artist, and we were surprised the government permitted his movie to screen. We were afraid they would revoke the permission after the festival.

The movie's title, Khane Doost Kojast? (Where Is the Friend's Home?), alluded to a famous poem, *Neshani* (Address) by beloved Iranian poet Sohrab Sepehri.

"Where is the home of the friend?

Asked the rider at twilight.
The sky stood static.
The passerby bequeathed
the branch of light he held to his lips
to the darkness of sands
and pointed to a poplar and said...."

That made it even more desirable for us. Those days even breathing was being controlled by the regime and creativity was suppressed, so it was refreshing to think we could engage with art.

Tehran *Fajr* Movie Festival ran annually from February 1st to February 11th, which covers the days between Khomeini's arrival in Tehran to when they announced the victory of the revolution. These days were called *Dahe Fajr* (the victorious 10 days), and the government forced us to heavily celebrate them everywhere across the country each year. Tickets for the movies screened in the festival were pretty impossible to get. We weren't usually interested but because of the war and being repressed by the Islamic regime rules, Negar and I were serious to get tickets for this movie and see it. The movie theater was far away from our house and we needed to wait in line a few hours ahead. We couldn't go ourselves and our parents were not interested in waiting with us in cold winter weather.

When Negar's mother saw we were so desperate, she thought harder. She asked her father, Baba Karim, whom we loved as our dear grandpa, to go with us. Baba Karim graciously accepted. My parents generously agreed, too. We were thrilled. Friday morning, my mother filled a bag with tangerines and nuts and took me to Baba Karim's house. Negar had stayed there the night before, so they were ready for me. We needed to take three taxis to get to the movie theater. We got there nice and early and there were only about twenty people ahead of us. All bundled up, we waited until noon when they started selling the tickets. Finally, when we bought three tickets we were screaming, hugging each other, and laughing loud, celebrating our victory and making a scene in Abbas Abad Street in Tehran. Baba Karim had a big smile on his face. We loved him more than ever!

We went in as soon as they allowed us. Waiting for the movie to start, I was skinning tangerines and passing them to Negar and Baba Karim one after another one. I didn't want to return home and have my mother complain that we didn't eat them or question whether we spent money on junk food instead. Baba Karim finally felt full, laughed, and with a thick, cute accent said, "I didn't know you could carry a tangerine tree in your bag." We all laughed and then got totally absorbed in the movie.

The story was about Ahmad, an eight-year-old boy who lived in a village by the Caspian Sea. When he got home from school, he realized he had taken his classmate's notebook by mistake. He knew if he didn't return the notebook to his classmate that very night, the classmate wouldn't be able to do his homework and would be expelled from the class. Ahmad had no idea where his classmate lived, but he did his best and after he bought fresh bread for dinner to fulfill his mother's request, he searched all afternoon to find him. After a lot of struggles, he finally found him and returned the notebook. Late in the evening, he had to find his way back home, a village away, and do his own homework.

On the way home, Negar and I discussed how beautifully the movie showed Ahmad's determination. He didn't know his classmate well, and he could have been punished because of the action he took, but he still felt responsible. We thought that was something missing from our everyday life, being responsible for our actions. We thought the saddest part was that Ahmad's grandfather felt he had to punish his children and grandchildren to teach them discipline, which was a reflection of real life, more severe in smaller towns and subtler with less physical punishment in bigger cities like Tehran. Everywhere in Iran, punishment was considered a useful tool for kids to grow into good people, but the movie showed that kids had their own moral compasses.

When every movie was about war or religion, when every kid's cartoon was about an orphan child praying to God to bring her mother back, and considering the censorship on all art works and books by the regime, Kiarostami offered a new approach to cinema. Through art, without openly fighting with the regime's ideology, he showed society's concerns, the obvious conflicts, fears, and desire to love.

As an artist he didn't force an ideology on people like communism or the other opposition groups wanted. He just focused on ordinary people and their lives. Through an hour and half he pictured a great story to show how a little boy can feel helpless because of lack of societal support. The movie won the Bronze Leopard at the 1989 Locarno Film Festival. It also won the Golden Plate at the *Fajr* Film Festival.

Baba Karim napped in the cab on the way home. The poor old man was exhausted but still had a satisfied face from having created such pleasure for us. He was the hero of a day we would remember forever, a moment in our history that gave "a fresh breath to our dark days," as Negar would put it perfectly thirty years later.

****

One June day of my freshman year/ninth grade, I needed a break from studying.

My mother suggested we go out for ice cream to Tajrish Circle. Tajrish, a shopping area on the skirt of the mountains in the northern part of Tehran, was a favorite place for my mother and me to wander, especially for window shopping and mouthwatering snacks. My father disagreed. "Afternoons are the worst time to go to Tajrish. There will be no parking spots. It's hot outside. Why don't we just stay at home and rest?" To my mother, he grumbled, "You take advantage of her, suggesting ice cream to satisfy your own childish desires."

I felt bad that a fight was starting because of me and said, "Baba, I said I wanted ice cream. Can we go to Tajrish please?"

Grudgingly, he conceded.

I jumped to my room and carefully chose my white scarf to overcome the ugliness of my loose and long black mantow I had to wear to cover myself from shoulder to toe, thinking my red nail polish looked good with white and black.

In June we had an exam every couple of days but didn't have to attend school otherwise. The time between exams was a great opportunity for Negar and me to polish our nails, but we had to be careful to remove it perfectly for the exam day. If the school staff saw any remnant, our discipline grade would bring down our GPA. If *Basij* saw it, even worse. So, we made a ceremony of polishing our nails after each test and removing the polish carefully before the next one.

I had gotten a short haircut a few days before and had blow-dried my hair. Standing in front of the mirror, I carefully put my scarf on and brought a few strands out, making bangs on my forehead.

Tajrish Circle was always crowded by shoppers who enjoyed the mixed atmosphere of modern boutiques with a couple of Islamic headless mannequins wearing fancy dresses showing off their half beauty to the passersby and traditional spice shops with the barrels with the mound of colorful spices all lined up in front of each shop. In the southern part of the circle, inside the covered Bazar with narrow alleys, traditional grocery shops hung out beads of vegetables, decorated bunches of herbs. They set arrays of fruits on big-wheeled tables outside of their shop. No-one was allowed to touch the fruits. The shopper picked them up upon the customer's request with some stiff gestures that felt like he was giving his possessions away for free. Everything together made a lively picture, fun to watch. We never bought groceries from there. They were expensive.

As Baba predicted, we did hit a lot of traffic. At that time of the day, it took us almost 45 minutes— three times longer than it would have taken if it wasn't rush hour. It was hot inside the car.

My father's face was hardened. He made a frustrated noises: "Aaahhhhhh. I told you." Sitting behind my father, I looked out the window, afraid my mother would snap at any moment and scream at him. I knew it was getting close to the time my father needed to drink his Vodka too. That could only happen at home since alcohol was banned and not sold legally in the street. If it were late, he'd start yelling at us.

We passed the main round-about and got to the beginning of Pahlavi Street. The tall old Chenar trees on both sides of the street had brought their heads together to make a comfortable shade on this longest street of Tehran. We started to look for parking in front of our favorite ice cream shop, Ladan. Saffron ice cream with big chunks of frozen cream in was one option; chocolate, vanilla, or strawberry flavor were nontraditional options, "Italian ice cream." I was daydreaming which one I wanted to choose that day.

We were all looking desperately for a parking spot since my father's attitude was becoming intolerable when all of a sudden, we heard a voice in a megaphone behind us shouting: "Red Peykan, red Peykan pull over." A white SUV carrying four Basiji pulled close behind us. My mother and I immediately covered our hair completely. My father pulled over, although not all the way, and they stopped behind us.

Two women wearing chador in such a way that I had a hard time seeing even their eyes came to our car and opened the back door. They shouted at me to get out and directed me to the SUV. My parents jumped out of the car. The women pushed me into the SUV's backseat and jumped in with me. My mother stayed in front of the car in case they tried to drive me away.

The women started yelling: "Shame on you having red nail polish! What did you think!? You Western worshippers. You betray your own Islamic culture following the sinful Western culture. Don't you respect the blood of martyrs in the war? They are dying for us, and you worthless girls are thinking about red nail polish?" She handed me nail polish remover and cotton balls. I had heard they used poisonous chemicals in the nail polish remover. Scared and hesitant, I cried and removed my nail polish with shaking hands, wondering how on earth they had even seen it inside the car. She said my black hair against my white scarf had caught her attention. Most likely, while I was covering my hair she saw the nail polish.

My father talked to the *Basiji* driver, who seemed to be the leader of the team. My mother came to the window of the back door and begged the woman on my right to release me, promising I would never do it again. She was ready to cry, asking them: "Please release her."

Meanwhile a police car arrived and an officer warned my father to move his car, which was causing more traffic.

The woman next to me rudely told my mother to open the door. She got out and told me: "I know you go to school around here. If I ever see you like this again, you will go to jail instantly." I jumped out of their car, shaking, and took my mom's hand. The woman faced my mother: "It is all your fault you let your daughter be seen like this. You are careless parents promoting bad behavior."

My mother dragged me to our car and we jumped in. I was shaking while my mother said angrily: "Why did you have to polish your nails?" I cried quietly. They could have taken me to jail and given me lashes. I could have missed my final exam.

My father made a U-turn in the middle of traffic, and we went home with anger, our only ice cream the flavor of tears. We were all silent in the car, but of course my parents fought when we got home.

I went to my room to avoid their fight and to feel guilty I caused it, crying until I fell asleep. The humiliating tone of voice the *Basiji* women used stayed with me for a long time. Negar and I stopped the ceremony of nail polish wearing and removal between our tests. For a few days, I covered my hair under my scarf carefully. But soon it came out again.

****

Basij may have stopped me from looking cute in front of boys, but they couldn't prevent me from thinking about them. While we were dealing with our high-demand schoolwork, we never forgot to think about fun. As high school girls, we paid considerable attention to boys.

At the end of freshman year, we needed to choose a major. The options were math and physics, biology, liberal arts, or vocational school. I hated blood, so biology was out. Despite my love for books and literature I did not even think about liberal arts since it didn't promise a high-paid job and my parents wouldn't allow it. So, I selected math and physics because it was prestigious, with more promising jobs for the future. Plus, for girls, it was offered at only one school in our town, the one Negar was also going to attend. We wanted to become engineers to show everyone women could hold the same jobs as men.

Our high school was about 45 minutes away from our homes and we had to use public transportation to get there. On the way, we noticed boys going to nearby schools and picked nicknames for every single one of them.

Negar and I started taking a bus with a longer route just to see boys who took that bus. In the morning, the public city bus was basically a school bus since we were all students.

The bus was a safe little place to have fun and laugh far from the *Basij* and parents' eyes. Even if we didn't talk to each other, we reacted to each other's presence. Even though boys sat in front and girls in back, we caught each other's attention. Everyone wanted to get to the 7:00 a.m. Bus 107. Negar and I were lucky. We caught it almost at the beginning of the route. By the time we got farther south, past Gheitarie Park, the bus was full. The driver would shout at each stop: "You have to wait for the next bus." The boys at the bus stop shouted back: "We are late for school. We need to get in."

There were so many boys and they had only the front half of the bus. They pushed hard to get in; it was an everyday game. One day, the coolest boy, whom we had nicknamed Sean Connery, got his left leg stuck between the doors of the bus, and the angry driver started driving without opening the door for him to bring his leg in. The whole bus started yelling: "Bring the Sean Connery leg in!" We were laughing and shouting until the driver stopped and Sean Connery could bring his leg in.

Not every day was lucky though. One morning, I left the house a few minutes before my father, who had started a new consulting job in a private company. Negar and I jumped up to the back of the bus as usual. As the driver started to pull away, my father ran toward the bus, waving his hands asking the driver to stop. The driver stopped for him, and he got on and saw us. He shouted from the front: "Why are you two here in this bus?" He asked the driver to stop and told him the two girls in the back were on the wrong bus. We were disappointed as we climbed down. We were lucky the driver didn't tell my father we took that bus every day.

Theocracy can repress desires but it cannot kill them. We did what we could and we made good memories even under the darkness of Islamic dictatorship.

****

In early spring 1988 as I started the third semester of tenth grade, Iraq and Iran started sending ballistic rockets to each other's capital cities. Tehran was no longer safe; schools closed and we all stayed home. Each night, mothers prepared dinner as early as they could and asked us to eat it fast. They said, "Eat your dinner. Saddam (president of Iraq) is coming at 8:00." I guess they were making sure their children wouldn't die hungry. We were scared, and dinner before Saddam's arrival was not our favorite meal.

At night, my parents and I slept in the living room since it was away from all the big windows. The windows had thick cloth taped over them so the glass wouldn't shatter if broken. We went to sleep every night not sure whether we would be alive the next day. Although this wasn't our first time experiencing bomb attacks, the fear was almost the same and we never got used to it.

One night we were all sleeping but aware. As soon as we heard the hiss sound of the missile we all hugged each other. This one sounded so close. The loud hissing noise got closer and passed our house as we hugged each other tighter. Then there was a huge shake like a short earthquake. It rattled our house but the windows didn't break. My father ran to the kitchen to check for dust around our house and shouted that he didn't see any in our alley. By then I was crying and clinging to my mother like a crab. She was crying, too. In the darkness of the night, we didn't know what to do, and no one wanted to go outside.

In the early morning, my father walked out to see which house had taken the missile. It was a couple of blocks away, close to Dezashib street. Everyone in the house was killed. My father asked my mother to take me somewhere safe. Schools were closed, so we didn't have to stay in Tehran, but he had to stay to go to work. He had recently got a consulting job in a company to review their legal documents.

The only safe place we could think of was in the southeastern part of the country. Marjan, my older cousin, had been admitted to a college in Kerman the year before and had a small studio apartment there, so my mother and I flew to stay with her until the attacks were over. It was hard leaving my father, but I had no choice. A lot of people, including Negar and her family, went north. The northern part of Iran was safe, and people who had vacation houses escaped there. Tehran, the big, endless, and crowded city, was nearly empty, but still so many people were killed each time a rocket came down.

All schools in safe cities accepted students from unsafe cities. I enrolled at the only school in Kerman that offered math and physics for girls. The students were friendly, and I found a few friends who walked with me to school. It took a couple of days until I started understanding their accents. They talked slowly and rhythmically; I loved it. In a few days, I started using their phrases, bekhaz oonvar (move a few steps). I even picked up a little of their southern accent. My mother and Marjan laughed at me.

Marjan was always fun. My mother felt relaxed and even playful when Marjan was around. Marjan was always kind to me and had a close relationship with my mother that I envied. She could talk about boys and her naughty behavior to my mother without being criticized. It wasn't just because she was nineteen and I was fifteen. She had told my mother about naughty events when she was fifteen, too. I would never do that. I was aware of the consequence. Of course, she always had good grades while my grades were getting worse and worse. Still I enjoyed having a happy mother while we spent time with Marjan. I missed my dad and called him a couple of times per week, but there was nothing else I could do. He wanted us to stay in Kerman.

I was not obligated to complete my homework since I was a guest. I obviously preferred not to do it and preferred hanging out with Marjan and my mother. When we were tired of visiting historical places or shopping malls or friends, we made Turkish coffee. Iranian women love to gossip while drinking Turkish coffee and tell each other's fortune through reading the sediment in the cup.

When we finished the liquid but not all the grounds, we put the saucer on the cup and turned the cup upside down towards our heart. We left it to dry, then took the cup and read the pattern to see what the future would bring. Many people believed in it and trusted the fortune tellers who did this for a living, but we didn't. We did it for fun. My mother was not a fortune teller, but she could make up stories that made us laugh so hard that the neighbors would probably be wondering what type of fun these women had. Those were fun nights. It became even more fun when Marjan's friend Mina came over one night. She was in love with a boy and was thrilled to hear my mother describing a boy's face in her cup. With her eyes shining, Mina said, "Yes, yes! It sounds like him. Please say more. Oh, he loves me too! Would he offer his hand you think?" When my mother told her she wasn't a fortune teller, Mina denied it saying, "No Manzar *joon* (dear), you said everything correctly. I believe you." She didn't want to believe differently. Sometimes we look for signs everywhere desperately. We laughed and laughed, but she didn't mind. She was in love and just wanted to hear about her lover.

After a month, the missile attacks stopped and we went back to Tehran.

****

Our return ended a sweet reprieve from the tension between my mother and me. During the tenth grade, as math and physics got harder, my grades got lower. Math and physics were understandably hard but how about literature, history, and religion? I had no ability to focus on anything. I read one paragraph many times and remembered nothing. Instead I daydreamed endlessly. My thoughts traveled from anywhere to everywhere with no limit; in studying, my thoughts needed to stay with one concept, which bored me. Daydreaming about being a grown up and going to college somewhere far away from my parents, wearing sexy clothes, attending parties with boys, and having fun flirting with them made me much happier. My daydreaming bubble busted almost every time which was many when my parents started yelling at each other. Daydreaming became my survival technique.

I asked Negar for help. She planned study time together once a week. Whatever she taught me stayed in my mind but whenever I tried to teach myself, my thoughts jumped everywhere else.

The day I received my final grade-ten report card, I knew I was in trouble. My mother was waiting for it at home. From her standpoint, it was not just a report card, it was Shabnam's life and her lifestyle. It was Shabnam's whole self, her worthiness.

I had failed algebra and would have to pass an additional exam at the end of the summer in order to go to eleventh grade. This was a huge embarrassment to me and to her and a huge scandal if anyone in the family learned about it. On the way home, I was paralyzed from fear but trying to calm myself down by promising myself and practicing promising my mother to study hard for the exam. I played out the whole conversation in my mind – begging her to forgive, tell her she was right, affirming to her that I hadn't been studying enough. I was thinking about all the lies I had told her about my grades during the year, pretending everything was alright. I had promised myself to study many times too but I wasn't able to fulfill the promise to anyone. A lazy irresponsible student I was! I was ready to apologize sincerely and promise to make up for the huge failure in my life, algebra!!

As I was turning the key to the apartment door, I lowered my eyes and was ready to cry. I felt so little and worthless. I was also trying to make my mother feel pity by seeing how embarrassed I was.

She was standing by the kitchen door in the living room right where the entrance door opened. She saw my face. I didn't let her ask. Handing her my embarrassing report card, I quietly said, "I failed algebra, but I promise to study for it and make it up for the end-of-summer exam."

She grabbed the report card from my hand and all the muscles in her face spasmed. She made the emotionless, intimidating face I most hated and was most afraid of. Nothing could turn that face and that mind back to any pity for the embarrassed Shabnam. Next came screams. I knew the routine. She stormed to my room and I followed her, hoping for an appeal. She grabbed cassettes from the shelf next to my bed and threw them to the floor, breaking them all and screaming: "How can you do this to me? I trusted you, letting you have everything you wanted. I bought you all these cassettes and took you everywhere you wanted. I paid for tutors. I let you study with Negar. What did you do there? Look at her, at the top three of the class. You took advantage of my trust! Music, books, and friends are all distraction to you! How do we hide this from everyone?" I was afraid my books would be next, which I couldn't bear, but she was out of breath. I was crying and apologizing: "*Maman bebakhshid*!", hoping to stop her, but she didn't see or hear me. She walked out and closed the door, perhaps to avoid looking at the embarrassment of her life, failed Shabnam. I cried for the rest of the day.

I needed to study secretly to make sure none of my friend, besides Negar, who knew, or family found out I had failed. We didn't hire a tutor. I was lucky; our school offered summer classes to make up for the pause during the missile attacks, so everyone had to go to school every day. Negar offered to help me again. She made time on our breaks to reveal all the secrets of algebra and practice all the problems in our textbook with me. I couldn't focus on my own, but once she explained it I could do it.

I scored 17 out of 20 on the exam at the end of the summer and opened my way to eleventh grade. When I told my mother the result she said, "You should have gotten this grade in the first place."

****

Passing the living room on the way to my room one summer night in 1988, I saw my father with his glass of home-made vodka in one hand and a tissue in other. He was listening to melancholy, traditional Persian music and crying. I was not sure if I should pretend I didn't notice his tears or if I should react to them. I chose the former and casually stopped to ask if he had eaten dinner already. He didn't hide his tears. Wiping them, he said, "How can I eat? I just heard a big group of political prisoners was executed and buried in a mass grave who-knows-where." We were constantly hearing that the regime was killing political prisoners, many communist Marxists and many from another group that fought for a Marxist version of Islam that respected people's free will rather than following God's representative, called Mojahedin-e Khalq (MEK).

My father continued. "Family members were told only that their loved ones were dead. The executioners made sure no virgin girl was executed; they raped them first." According to Islamic law, if a girl dies a virgin, she goes to heaven. These "sinners" didn't deserve to go to heaven. "How do their fathers cope with this for the rest of their lives? You are my sweetheart. I want you to have a happy life."

I had tears in my eyes watching my father like that. Although I wasn't sure I understood everything he said, I didn't dare ask what rape was. My mother came out of their bedroom, crying too. She held me in her arms, wiped my tears with her hands, and then asked me to go to my room and focus on studying. I went to my room and closed the door. I felt confusion, hate in my heart, and so many questions in my head. Why couldn't a virgin girl be executed? Why did they refuse to give the dead bodies to their families to be buried properly, since being buried in an Islamic fashion was such important ritual? Why did the victims refuse to stop their political activities if they knew it was pointless to move forward? Did they choose to die and not live like my father? Obviously, I had no answer to any of these fundamental questions.

The next day at school, I pretended things were normal, but inside I could not put that question aside. After a couple of hours, it was heavy on my chest. I figured I could talk to Negar about it. Her family were open-minded, and I knew I could trust her even though she and her family were against the whole concept of revolution and believed that the country had been progressing under the shah's power. She knew a little about my father's Marxism and totally opposed it. We had our debates but our love kept us from fighting.

When I asked her why the regime refused to give the dead bodies to their family to be buried properly she had a logical but sad answer: "Because to the Islamic regime's eyes, the prisoners were sinners for fighting against God, and didn't deserve a proper burial ceremony." She was as upset as I was when I told her they raped the girls because they were not allowed to execute virgins. "Negar, what does it mean to rape them?" I asked. She whispered in my ear, "When a man forces a woman to have sex with her." I was still confused. I didn't know what, but something was missing in that equation. What I didn't know was the difference between intimate and forced sex, nothing like what I have read in books about cuddling and kissing about sex. That was all I knew about sex and no more. Without having any knowledge about it, the concept was foreign to me. I dismissed my confusion; clearly, rape was bad, and I needed to feel sad for them. I don't think I had ever felt so disturbed and horrified.

That summer, the long, eight-year war—more than half my life!—finally ended; however, it was under the worst circumstances. I'll never forget the day I woke up and heard the news that a commercial Iran Air aircraft carrying 290 passengers from Tehran to Dubai had been shot down by United States Navy in Persian Gulf through a missile attack. All passengers and crew of Iran Air flight

655 were killed in a matter of seconds in the blue sky of the Persian Gulf. We were going to school that summer to make up for the time the school was closed during the missile attacks. I walked to the main street pushing back my tears.

When I got to the main street, Negar was waiting for me. She was surprised to see me sad. "What happened?" She was curious to know. "Didn't you hear the news about the aircraft?" I answered stiffly judging her wasn't being sad. She lowered her eyes, "Oh yea, that's terrible." I was furious, expected a more serious reaction from her. "Terrible? It is not acceptable? It could be us. I can't take it anymore. I wish I'd died with them." Negar chose to be silent to my extreme reaction. We motioned a cab and got in. At school we had a quiet day. How far this war will go, everyone wondered.

Finally, concerned about the power of the U.S army and Iraq destructive chemical weapons, on 20 July 1988, Iran accepted United Nation Resolution 598 for a ceasefire.

Resolution 598 practice started on August 8th, 1988, ending the war between Iran and Iraq. Eight years of pointless war left both countries with millions of casualties. Is there ever a legitimate reason for a war?

****

For my future I had a clear image of becoming an engineer, a classy job that provided me good money, independence, and power I needed to live under my own rules and travel the world. It was a no-brainer. I wanted that job badly. I wanted the independence wholeheartedly. So I started eleventh grade with a serious plan to study even as I was secretly afraid I didn't have the discipline. On the first day of school I promised myself out loud in front of Negar that last year's failure would not repeat. Not only were good grades important, but now we were preparing for *Konkour*, the competitive college entrance exam at the end of twelfth grade. *Konkour,* a monstrous, comprehensive, nationwide, five-hour test that covers all subjects taught in four years of high schools. To get admission to a university, students have to take it every year until they are accepted by a school. To start studying next year would be too late.

Of course I would start now! How long am I going to listen to my mother's nagging: 'Focus on study. Stop your long phone conversations. Boys are not allowed in your life until you are married.' Am I not tired of my parents' constant fights? And, oh, the little black fish! Didn't she leave the stream and her mother and her boring life to experience something larger? I was supposed to explore the world.

Even thinking about going to college and having more freedom and independence made me feel overjoyed. I imagined one day I would have my own apartment full of books, just like Uncle Behrooz. A classy, sophisticated life full of travel was not too far away. I was getting closer and closer.

No way would I be married off—what my mother hoped for—just when I was gaining my independence. Every time she brought up suitors visiting my aunt or my uncle's house to ask for my cousins' hands, I abruptly said, "No suitor is allowed to come to this house. I will be an independent woman and will find the right man myself. I am not going through traditional marriage and I am not planning to get married soon."

My mother said, "Why should you be always so different from your cousins?"

My father understood.

But my mother knew I was different from my cousins. "Different" in that culture meant bad. I didn't fit in. I got bad grades, I didn't want suitors, and worse, I had started fantasizing about becoming a sailor girl to travel the world like the little black fish. It wasn't practical, but I knew with an engineering degree, outside Iran, it was possible.

I kept daydreaming about my romantic future and continued reading my books, especially poems. That year I read and memorized poems from Iranian modern poets such as Sohrab Sepehri, Ahmad Shamloo, Nima Youshij, Fereydoon Moshiri, and Siavash Kasrayee.

Between the books my father had kept, through his friends, and from underground markets my father had found them all for me. He recited some. I did not like the smell of the alcohol he exhaled, reciting passionately, but I loved the poems, and his passion was inspiring. The themes of these poems were life, freedom, humanity, and love.

Our favorite one was "Arash Kamangir" by Siavash Kasrayee. It tells the story of an Iranian legend, an archer who became a hero by sacrificing his life for the country.

Here is a small part of that poem:

"...Yea, Yea, Life is beautiful
Life is an everlasting fire-temple
If you lighten it, you'll see the flames dancing in every border
And if not, it will be quiet, and that will be our fault
The Iranian army was so worried
Two by two were mumbling
Children standing on the roofs
Girls sitting in the alleys
Mothers standing beside the doors sadly
People were like a wild sea
It was windy, angry
And a man like a pearl was born out of the sea

It's me, Arash
He began like this to talk to the enemy
It's me Arash, the free army man
I'm ready now, ..."

I wanted to go far. I wanted to be Arash or the little black fish.

To focus I tried everything. Weather permitting, I sat on the balcony and studied, imagining everyone was looking at me to force myself to focus. It worked better than not focusing at all. But as we entered the fall deeper, cold weather removed that option. I was back to my cave, the room full of ruminating thoughts and the apartment full of the potential for my parents' constant fights.

I closed my book, sat there, and listened to my mother screaming at my dad one evening. "It is none of your business that I do my prayer. That is my belief. Did I ever complain about your stupid beliefs? Why do you think you can make fun of me all the time doing my prayers?"

My drunk dad laughed hysterically and said, "Your stupid beliefs are from 1,400 years ago! You jump up and down like a monkey and say words in Arabic without knowing the meaning of them, repeating them every day. That is totally stupid." He laughed more.

Their bedroom door slammed shut and I knew we wouldn't have dinner. My mother would not come out of the room until morning.

A little later I went out and saw that my father had heated up leftovers. He had his drunken laugh and sleepy-looking eyes that I hated. He said, "What do you want to eat?" I answered I was not hungry and needed to study. He said, "Yes, study. It's important to become more educated. You should become an independent woman and not a stupid one like your mother, talking to her God." I turned my back on him. I felt bad for my mom. Her prayers were personal and caused no one harm.

I knocked on my mom's door and then opened it since I knew she wouldn't answer. The light was off, and she lay in bed crying. Her migraine headache must have attacked again. I asked if she had taken any medication. She said she had. I asked if she could eat a little. Still crying, she said, "I am not hungry. Don't worry about me. I am used to this shitty life and this stupid man. Go back to your room and study. Become an independent woman who doesn't have to live with a stupid man." I wiped her tears, handed her a tissue, and kissed her cheek.

Back in my room I didn't bother to try to pick up my studying again. Instead I focused deeply on reading poems. That night, I read Sohrab Sepeheri's poem "*Neshani*" (Address) over and over until I fell asleep:

"Address

where is the home of the friend?
Asked the rider at dawn.
The sky stood still.
The passerby bequeathed
the branch of light he held to his lips
to the darkness of sands
and pointed to a poplar and said,
"Before the tree,
there is a garden lane greener than God's dream
where love is as blue as the wings of fidelity.
Go on untill that alley which emerges from maturity,
then turn to the flower of loneliness,

two steps before the flower
remain at the foot of the eternal fountain of earthly legends
where a transparent fear overtakes you.
In the flowing sincerity of the space, you hear a rustling
A child you see
has climbed a tall pine, to take a chick from the nest of light
and you ask him
where is the home of the friend?"

During wintertime, I didn't study for *Konkour*, thinking I still had plenty of time. Spring came, and I barely passed eleventh-grade final exams. That embarrassed me because my friends, whose home situations were no better—some were worse—than mine still earned good grades. I made my mother angry and my father concerned. Denying my inability to focus, I called myself lazy but told myself I could make it up.

I also started asking around if there was a way I could get admission to a sailing school outside of Iran. Perhaps it was a fantasy I created to escape from the pressure of *Konkour*, but I felt so much excitement thinking about that lifestyle. In Iran back then, it brought a good smile to everyone's face who thought I was crazy asking for such an unattainable, masculine job. Perhaps they all said to themselves, she will be alright and will grow out of this craziness.

****

In early summer, my parents' fights got worse and worse until one day my mother made the decision to leave home for her brother Hassan's house, which kicked off a lot of unnecessary real estate transactions—all within a few months. Over the years, she had left my father a few other times. Her brother's house was her shelter. After a while Uncle Hassan would convince her that it was better for her to go back. By the time my mother reached the point of leaving the house this time, my parents had gone months without speaking to each other unless it was a verbally violent fight, cursing each other loudly and amusing all the neighbors. Even if our neighbors had gotten used to my parents' fights, I had not!

It was me and my dad again. I cooked, and I ironed his shirts, but I never cleaned the house. I hated cleaning. He was patient with my cooking skills.

I stayed in touch with my mother. We had short conversations on the phone. She was serious this time. She reassured me; I am getting divorce to live a free life. I cannot tolerate this monster anymore. You and I will have a calm life together."

I was skeptical of having a calm life with my mother. She always yelled at me and my father. My father didn't yell at me but nagged all the time and criticized me.

Our apartment was spacious and had a great view to a big orchard at the end of a dead-end alley. It was gone almost as soon as it went on the market. They split the cash since it was in both their names.

My mother found a small unit she could afford with her share of the money. It was close to her brothers' and sisters' houses. She assumed I wanted to live with her and offered me the one bedroom in that small unit, but I was tired of her punishment for my poor grades. My father was softer on me. I didn't tell my mother about it. She was excited about her new life. My father was not.

He called Uncle Hassan and arranged a visit with my mother at her brother's house. My mother later told me my father had apologized for his bad behavior. She didn't believe him, so she walked away toward a bedroom. He followed her, begged her to come back, and promised to behave respectfully. He admitted he was tough on her and said he was willing to make any change to make life better for her. He even promised to stop drinking. She didn't believe him because she had heard it all before, but Uncle Hassan's heart felt so soft that he asked my mother to give my father another chance.

We found a condo in Yousef Abbad neighborhood, far from my school but close to my mother's siblings. Three of us moved there mid-summer of 1989 before my twelfth-grade year.

****

A couple years after the end of the war, people felt a little more comfortable spending money and even going abroad for vacation. My mother was one of them, which left me the freedom to experiment a little with independence. Turkey was trendy and cheap and didn't require visas for Iranians. That summer, Uncle Mohsen, who had fled to America at the beginning of the revolution, planned to fly to Istanbul from the United States and reunite with his family after more than eleven years. It was a few weeks after we had moved to our new condo. My mom, all my aunts, Uncle Hassan, and a few cousins all planned to go to Istanbul for a month.

I signed up for *Konkour* preparation classes, giving me the best excuse to stay home and let my mother go to that dream trip she was planning for. In my mind, home without mother's discipline was calm and I liked it. She was disappointed I was not going but satisfied that I was serious about studying since my eleventh-grade report card had not been very bright.

My father happily agreed with my mother's plan for the trip. He was still behaving. If it had been a few months earlier, there would have been another big fight. This time he was calm and encouraging.

Going to summer *Konkour* preparation classes was so much fun! Negar and I found a way to take the same bus even though we didn't live close anymore. We wanted to be together as much as we could. A few boys who were taking *Konkour* preparation classes close to our classes took the same minibus. Unlike the city buses, the minibus was so small that the government had not thought of separating women and men in it. We were all sitting and standing together. Negar had a bright green purse. When the minibus got closer to where I needed to get on, she tried to hold the bright green purse out the window to signal me. It was hard for Negar to get through the crowd to do this, so one of the boys, Mehran, started doing it. He was tall and masculine. It was easier for him.

If I was lucky and the minibus stopped, it took a few minutes to get to the back where Negar and her crew were waiting for me. Passing all the people and inhaling their smell of sweat through crazy sudden stops was an everyday adventure. I was getting better every day and got to a point that didn't even notice the underarm sweat or garlicky exhalations of people. Well, Mehran was at the back to give me his seat.

Since the crowded minibus didn't stop every time I raised my hand, Mehran started trying a new strategy. When he saw me from the window, he shouted: "Stop, I am getting off." But this was just to let me get on. That is how our story started. He was good-looking and he liked me. The more I talked to him the more I liked him.

Mehran and his friends were students at the high school across the street from ours. We talked and laughed every day going to class and coming back. The back of the crowded minibus was a safe place for our fun time without fear of the *Basij*.

I started feeling sad that I could be with them for only half the trip. After a couple of weeks, Mehran started getting off at my stop. We walked in small alleys shaded by tall trees and covered by sounds of the creeks with their running current between Vali Asr and Yousef Abad. Since my mother was in Turkey and my father never asked me to get home by a certain time, Mehran and I walked hand on hand and whispered love noted to each other's ears for hours, forgetting we could be caught by the *Basij*. It felt like we fell in love.

CHAPTER THREE

1989 - 1990

One day early in October 1989 I was walking home from school with Mehran. It was a crisp early afternoon in the streets of Yousef-Abad, my middle-class neighborhood. Many four-story buildings sat next to each other on both sides of the one-way roads, with a lot of trees and creeks under them. The creeks, usually on both sides of the road, remained from the old days when this part of town was a little green village. Narrow sidewalks filled the space between the little paved creeks and the building entrances. Tall, old trees lined the road and the sound of running water made it feel like a garden compared to other, more urbanized parts of Tehran.

We were having a quiet, romantic conversation but not even holding each other's hands when we saw a big white SUV labeled *Basij* driving towards us. We panicked inside but continued walking and pretended not to see them. Mehran reminded me of the fake ID he had made me from his sister's library card, stamped with carved raw potato and ink.

The car drove fast towards us and stopped suddenly, tires squealing. My heartbeat fast and my face felt hot and red. I quickly adjusted my scarf and covered all my hair. Two *Basiji* men jumped down and walked toward us fast, looking at us hatefully. The taller one demanded: "What are you doing here? What is your relationship?"

Mehran, hesitant, said, "She is my sister."

The *Basij*i looked at me with a big frown. "Shame on you! Who is he?"

Shaking, I said, "He is my brother." We were terrible at this.

"You are lying!"

"I have my ID card." I brought it out of my backpack and handed it to him.

To the shorter one he said, "You take her back and ask her questions."

Once we had been separated, the shorter one asked, "What is your father's name?"

"Hossein." This was my father's name. I didn't know Mehran's.

"Your mother?"

"Mina" I knew this one. I had been at their house and she had been kind to me.

I was scared, and mad at myself. Are they are going to take us to jail and call my parents?

Mehran and I had been taking advantage of my long commute since my family moved to Yousef Abad. The bus ride was about an hour, and my 10-minute walk home from the bus stop turned to half an hour or more as we wandered through the afternoons. At age 18, we took the relationship seriously without knowing what each of us wanted from life. It was a pure infatuation that felt like deep love. I loved it when he recited the famous poem of Fereydoon Moshiri for me. He always worried I would leave him. He recited,

"...Without you
On a moonlit night,
My thoughts aflight,
I visited that alley again.
My body,
transformed into eyes,
Craved to actualize,
Another meeting with you, in vain..."

Almost all Iranian lovers for generations had memorized this poem. It described how the lover who left forgot the heartbroken partner.

Romance in Iran in the 80s was taboo, especially for teenage girls, and had to be hidden from parents, neighbors, family, and *Basij*. If anyone saw us, we were in trouble. Depending on who saw us, the degree of trouble varied. If it were family members, my mother would find out within minutes and I would be in serious trouble. Not only that, family gossip would start immediately. In their eyes, I would be a lightheaded, flirtatious girl who didn't deserve a good husband or a good family life. If *Basij* saw us, we could go to jail and receive lashes on top of our parents' punishment.

Parents, neighbors, and family members opposed romance outside of marriage because they believed girls should remain untouched. The Islamic rules permitted cleansing society of sinners, and vested *Basij* with the authority to arrest the sinners to teach them how to become faithful Moslems. *Basij* could arrest people on the street or inside their house. They interfered with the most private parts of a person's life. There was no relief from the tyranny of the dictatorship.

Standing next to the *Basij* car, I felt desperate and tried hard to hold back my tears. I was terrified of jail and lashes. On top of that, since my mother was ignorant of Mehran, her punishment waited for me upon release from jail.

Then I looked up, and in utter disbelief, I saw my father.

My father hated the *Basij* and often tried to intervene when he saw them with young girls. His white hair and his age sometimes helped convince them to let the girl go. This time it was, magically, his own daughter.

When he saw me he started walking faster. I saw an angel with big wings coming to rescue me. He asked what happened. The guy who was questioning me said we had lied, saying we were siblings, and they were proving it to take us to jail. I was shocked. He was not finished with his questions with me and had already made his decision. But with the arbitrary rules, he did not need any evidence to take us to jail. He could do it if he felt like doing it. The taller guy, not older than 23, who seemed to be the leader, came over. My father took him aside and talked to him. After a few long minutes, my father came back and said to me, "Let's go." He took the fake card and started walking. I followed like a robot.

Too scared to look back at Mehran, I asked what they would do with him. Angrily, continuing to look ahead, he said, "They will release him. You should be grateful I am taking you out of this mess. Do you know what you were getting yourself into?"

I did not answer. The light and bright feeling of relief from his rescue did not last more than a few seconds as we neared home and I started thinking about my mother's reaction. I did not expect much better from her than from *Basij*.

But as my father turned the key in the lock door, he said, "Do not tell your mother anything about this." Anger twitched in every muscle of his face. "We say we happened to arrive home at the same time if she asks." The fact that my boyfriend was a secret from my mother but not my dad was an upside-down family set-up compared to other families around us. Fathers in that culture were typically the dominant and disciplinary figure of the household.

The next morning when Mehran showed up at our usual meeting place he said *Basij* had released him after he listened to all their condescending advice. He didn't talk much about it. He would have felt shameful admitting anyone had power over him.

****

Although my senior year was the most important year of high school, with *Konkour* looming, I almost stopped studying. I thought constantly about going to college, getting a professional job, and becoming an independent woman, but I could hardly focus or study. Night after night, I stared at my homework and daydreamed about how I wanted to live as an adult. It was as if I thought ruminating and angry feelings could change the current situation. I wanted to become independent and live on my own rather than under my mother's nonsensical rules.

I escaped to writing in my diary and reading my favorite poems and novels about freedom and liberation. I had to read them secretly from my mother of course since only *Konkour* study material was allowed, not Fyodor Dostoyevsky, Leo Tolstoy, Victor Hugo, or Roman Roland.

I felt bad about my grades but still had a lot of fun with Mehran, Negar, and other friends who were our partners in crime. The boys attended the boy version of our girls' school across the street and we shared algebra and geometry teachers—a rare exception to the rule against men teaching girls.

Our desire for romance, gossiping behind those teachers, *Konkour* anxiety, and other common things drew us close to each other. We had adventures in the mornings before school started. We all (sometimes seven of us) squeezed into a car that one of the boys secretly took out of the garage while his father was asleep. We rode around, listened to music, laughed at nonsense stories, and made memories. We got caught by school staff and parents, not mine fortunately, and luckily never again by *Basij*, but we never stopped having fun. The more we could bend the Islamic rules the better. As rebellious as it was, by bending those rules, we were only trying to live like normal teenagers in democratic countries.

****

My mother's co-worker asked if she could bring her son for a matchmaking visit. With her traditional values, my mother was thrilled. She said the boy was handsome and seemed to have a good handle on money matters; he drove a BMW. But I was furious. The year before, when she mentioned her principal was asking for my hand for her only son Abbas, I had told her I did not want an arranged marriage

Fed up, I again declared loudly that no one was allowed to come to our house as a suitor. As a modern girl, I would find my husband myself. I did not want to marry a closed-minded boy who followed the clichés, obediently asking his mother to find a virgin girl for him.

When my father heard my complaint that day, he yelled at my mother: "Leave her alone. What is this bullshit? She needs to focus on school." She didn't follow up with the BMW driver's mother. I felt relieved.

Around that time my mother, frustrated yet again by my father's behavior, left the house staying at my uncle's, and during her absence one night, my father allowed me to invite Mehran for dinner. I made tomato omelet, a popular but casual French-influenced dinner plate in Iran that is easy to make. The three of us had a good chat. Mehran seemed to feel comfortable and began talking about his parents' marriage.

His mother had married for love, outside her religion, and had been cut off from the family. She was a sweet and understanding lady, a beautiful housewife with her life all about her family and nothing outside of that. She had told me stories about being great at gymnastics in her youth, and with a sigh she said, "Those days are long gone. We have now an Islamic government. There is not much fun left for girls. Comparing all the opportunities I had back then, I feel bad for my daughters."

She was more than fifteen years younger than her husband. They had fallen in love when she was eighteen. Mehran's mother came from a Jewish family, and they opposed her decision to marry a Muslim man. She said she missed her father but didn't regret her marriage. The result of their marriage was four kids.

Of course, as part of the discussion that night, my father asked about Mehran's plan for college. Mehran, the only son of the family, wanted to take his father's business over, for which he felt he did not need to go to college. But he politely answered, "I am studying for the

Konkour." He knew my father liked to hear he had plans for college.

****

When my mother saw my semi-final report card with many failing grades, her face turned red, her frown grew tighter and tighter, and she started shouting. I stood close to her, paralyzed and hearing her words from far away. She said I was lazy and irresponsible. Throwing my report card on the dining table, she said I was grounded and could leave the house only with her for urgent matters.

Then she yelled even louder, so the neighbors could easily hear, "No more gatherings with friends, you hear that?"

I went to my room, closed the door, and cried for the rest of the day. How could I live without Mehran, Negar, and my other friends? She didn't call me for dinner. My father didn't come after me. I had made everyone upset. Was it the pleasure of romance that distracted me? But Mehran didn't get bad grades. My other friends with boyfriends didn't get bad grades. My mother was right: I was a lazy and irresponsible girl. I felt helpless.

In twelfth grade, after the semi-final exams, seniors did not have to be present at school. For the couple of months before final exams, we could go if we wanted to do group studies, but with my mother restricting me from any activities with friends, there was no school for me.

After a couple of weeks, on a beautiful spring day when things had calmed down a little, my mother allowed me to accompany my father to a bakery walking distance from our house. Every day at 10 a.m. they had fresh donuts ready. Excited, with a bag of fresh and hot donuts in hand, I opened the apartment door and called out happily to ask my mother whether tea was ready.

But she stood by the kitchen looking serious. Her face muscles quivered. Then I saw it: my diary, in her hand. My heart dropped and fear paralyzed me again. Shaking it, she shouted: "You have no idea about life! You think this boy cares about you? You are wasting your time and your future on him! You think about him instead of studying and getting ready for *Konkour*? Look at me, trusting you, letting you go to a faraway school. How idiotic of me. You are wasting your life and damaging our reputation. Did you think what would happen if someone saw you with him? How would people judge us? You let a worthless guy take advantage of you. And you have no respect for me." I was paralyzed. I knew I could not complain about her crossing my very private boundaries. Iranian mothers cross any privacy boundaries with their children, especially with their daughters. In her mind, she was being protective. But of course now she wasn't the only one who knew about my secret boyfriend; our neighbors could hear her hysterical yelling. It didn't matter who knew and who didn't anymore. She yelled: "Go to your room and study now. I will get this stupid thought out of your head." Then she started in on my father, telling him it was all his fault, too. He was too easy on me and that caused me to disrespect her.

I went to my room crying. I remembered being a first grader when my mother sat next to me after school at the dining table with the ruler in her hand, telling me to do my homework correctly, using the ruler to punish me when I didn't. I was tired of her punishments.

I thought I would die if I couldn't see Mehran. I already missed him a lot and didn't know what he was doing. Was he already with another girl? But he said he loved me. Having a boyfriend wasn't the reason I wasn't doing well in school. I had plenty of time at home and I still couldn't study. I was not thinking about Mehran when I read novels and poems. Was I dumb? I knew one thing, imprisoning me at home was not the solution. I learned better in group studies, but my mother was so angry and even if I wanted to communicate my thoughts and opinions, being deafened by her anger, she would not hear them. I had lost her trust.

Still thinking about Mehran, I found a way to communicate with him through friends by excuses such as needing study material from them. My mother took me to the friend's house to exchange study material and brought me immediately back home. Mehran and I exchanged love letters along with study material. I knew better than to hide them in my room since even during the time I took a bath she searched my room. I shredded them into small pieces and hid them at the bottom of the big kitchen trashcan.

****

One night from my room I heard someone calling "Shahram," a boy's name, in the middle of the street. The voice was familiar. I was right! It was him. I checked out the living room quickly. My parents were busy watching TV. I came back to my room, closed the door and ran to the window to wave. He waved back with a big smile: victory! After that, he came to the street a few times a week, standing under my bedroom window. "Shahram" became our secret code. I ran to the window and waved, believing none of the neighbors saw us when in fact they watched closely to see what was going on. The buildings on our street were lined up close. His shouting could catch any parent's attention to come to the window to see what's going on, but my parents sat in the living room in the back of the house and couldn't hear. My mother would be furious if she found out her daughter was flirting with a boy like that. She would have sat in my bedroom every night, staring at me to make sure I didn't do anything wrong. I never cared what the neighbors thought!

****

Following my high school area of focus, I was trying to get into engineering colleges. I knew I wanted to be educated and have a career, but math and physics were not turning out to be my path. I did not get good scores for *Konkour* and was not admitted to college that year, so I had to stay home and start studying for the next *Konkour* the following May. *Konkour* was competitive. The ratio of acceptance was almost one to ten and for good schools, forget it! It was impossible except for genius students. I had hoped for a smaller college outside of Tehran but didn't happen either.

I lost my self-worth and developed an ugly self-image as a lazy, low-IQ student. I thought I could not learn anything because I was not good at math and physics. It seemed engineering at smaller colleges in smaller cities sounded like my only choice. Although I was attracted to sociology and literature, liberal arts had no promising, high-paying job opportunities so it was not important. My heart didn't believe this, but my brain did. I certainly needed to be financially independent to pursue my dream of independence.

A well-paying and prestigious job would make a bright future. Culturally, whoever could make more money was considered more successful. It didn't matter what your heart wanted. People still followed the older generation's habit of surviving after World War II. Indeed, the Islamic dictatorship and eight years of war put the Iranian nation back several generations to only focus on basic needs. Basic needs including biological and safety needs are not about what the heart desires. To fulfill the basic needs means to have a culturally accepted spouse, a safe home, and good food on the table. That was the recipe for a stable life. Love didn't have much room to wiggle. Romance didn't make a stable life. The Farsi proverb says, "Romance won't bring bread to your dinner table." It even applies to pursuing a career of your passion that doesn't promise stable income. Anyone who focused on fulfilling the basic needs was a wise person. It didn't matter if only the face value of their life looked admirable, those wise people had respect because their efforts were spent fitting in and creating the picture perfect family.

To my mother, to survive, there was only one God to worship, one way to love, one way to study, one way to eat, one way to marry, and one way to think. If I did not comply with that one way, I was not good enough, or on a lot of occasions, I was judged for my improper behavior. I always felt I was inadequate, but subconsciously, I knew I needed to find my own way. The more I observed, the more frustrated I became with the cultural norm. During that summer, I had to accompany my mother to family gatherings and take part in their non-intellectual discussions.

An afternoon at Aunt Nasrin's, baking with my mother and her sisters, illustrates the social pressure we all felt to conform. That day, the subject was Mahin *khanoom* (Lady. Mahin), Uncle Hassan's second wife (he had divorced the mother of his three children to marry her, making her a frequent target of gossip). She had replaced her bedroom furniture set only six months after buying the previous set. Her habit of spending a lot on furniture was a favorite subject, especially when all four sisters were together.

While Aunt Sara busily formed the dough into small cookies, she complained, "She always gives it away to her family for free. She loves to show off."

Aunt Nasrin added, "She never shops at inexpensive stores either. Not only that, the more she spends, the better she feels." Mahin claimed to spend her own money, inherited from her first husband. "She complains our brother doesn't spend enough on her."

The conversation continued until everyone was satisfied that she was an absolutely selfish person with no respect for my uncle or his family.

The next day at home, I heard my mother talking to Mahin *khanoom* on the phone, complimenting her for her thoughtfulness. I was puzzled! My mother explained to me that Mahin *khanoom* had cooked a large amount of food and distributed it to the family members due to a religious commitment she had made. She was going to bring us food too. If people prayed for something and God granted it to them, they either made a blood sacrifice, like a sheep or a chicken, or they could make food and distribute it to others to thank God. My mother was happy with that and thanked her a lot. Although I didn't believe in religion at all—I was my atheist father's daughter—I still thought that for religious duties it would be better to distribute that food to less-privileged people rather than to my mother's relatively wealthy family. I was being judgmental, too.

There were so many paradoxical concepts in that world that I never understood: Go to school because it's classy to be educated but wait for a man to offer a hand for marriage. Get married, become an educated housewife, and raise your children without using your education. In the case of an open-minded husband you could have a job, but you still had to be a full-time mother and housewife who put fresh dinner on the table every night and let your husband have the last word—unless you knew how to manipulate him. Through fights or through diplomacy both wife and husband were determined to prove each one was better than the in-laws in every possible way. That summarized one's life purpose. I needed a way out of that.

In Iran, going to college in a different city or getting married were the only ways to leave your parents' house. I wanted a world bigger than the walls of the house that limited me to this routine family life. Routine family challenges weren't attractive to me. I wanted different challenges. I wanted to learn about the world out there. I had ambitious dreams, but I did not know how to realize them.

Back then, until you finished college, you didn't look for a job. Parents were responsible to pay for all the cost for their children until the sons had a professional job or the daughters got married. So, I could not apply for a simple job or take any job without having a degree. To become independent, I had one option: college.

****

To celebrate her admission to one of the best colleges to study software engineering, Negar had a party in the beginning of fall of 1990. The party was also close to my 18th birthday in November, so she planned to have a big birthday cake. Her achievement motivated me for a better future. All my high school friends got admission to college. Like magic (and probably with my father and Negar's mom's influence), my mother allowed me to go to the party! She said she would drop me off and pick me up herself. I was still grounded and had had little contact with my friends all summer.

For the party, I had a short white dress to wear with a red ribbon on the waist. My mother had sewn that dress for my cousin's wedding that summer; it was perfect for Negar's party, too. My parents were not strict when it came to clothes, and I loved that I was also allowed to have a little eye make-up (I would wear *mantow* to cover myself on the way to the party).

When I arrived, to my surprise, I saw Mehran! It had been almost six months since I'd last seen him. His big black eyes were glowing. Tall, handsome Mehran had a big smile on his face. We hugged each other tightly, and the smell of his One Man Show cologne felt so familiar and sexy. He kissed my neck and said, "I love you." He had not changed. Negar had invited him as a surprise for me. Her family was more open-minded about teen romance than mine.

I missed my friends. I missed talking with them about books, future plans, and our dreams. I was worried whether I could still talk about my dreams with my friends since they had been accepted to college (Mehran would be going to Tehran Azad University for mechanical engineering) while I hadn't. I was nervous but happy to be with my friends anyway.

There were a bunch of us kids, boys and girls and even alcohol. My mother had no idea about that. We were taking a big risk by breaking the Islamic rules and my mother's rules having a party with boys and girls together along with music and dance. If *Basij* heard the music on the street, they were allowed to break the door down and come in. The punishment for the host and the guests could be jail, penalties, and at least twenty-five lashes—especially for alcohol. The party was at Negar's grandparents'. Their house was on the third floor of a building in a small alley. Her grandparents had put cash aside for bribes in case the *Basij* showed up. Yes, laws forbade alcohol, but it was at almost every party. Negar's uncle and aunt, who still lived with their parents, had their friends over, too. They were a few years older than us and provided the alcohol. But I never drank. I did not have good feelings about drinking because of how it affected my father—and us.

That night, Mehran and I danced to almost every song holding each other's hands. We enjoyed all the delicious food Negar's grandmother had made. Stuffed pepper, *kashk e bademjan* (made with eggplant and whey), Salad *olivie* (a combination of potato and chicken salad) and so much more. After dinner, Negar brought out the gigantic cake she had ordered for my birthday. We had a dance ceremony around the cake with a few songs, passing the knife to each other before I cut the cake. Every minute was so much fun. Talking, laughing, dancing, and being silly was so much pleasure, but the night was so short.

Around eleven p.m., when Negar's grandmother said my mother was downstairs to collect me, I knew I needed to run down so she wouldn't come up. I knew she was curious, but if she saw boys, alcohol, and Mehran, everything would turn into a pumpkin. It was so hard for me to say goodbye, but I had to hurry away. They promised me to end the party soon, so I wouldn't miss much more. With heartache and tears in my eyes, I ran down the stairs.

****

Imprisoned at home for almost eight months and feeling helpless, in late fall of 1990 I gave up on my hope of a future with Mehran. I wrote him a letter to end our relationship. I cried for a few days but soon I forgot about him. One night, I came out of the building after my *Konkour* preparation class ended and was going to get into my father's waiting car when Mehran appeared. I felt so scared. My father jumped out of the car and angrily asked why he was there. Sadly but calmly, he said, "Mr. Shahmohammad, your wife got what she wanted. She separated Shabnam and me." He turned his face to me and with tears in his eyes said, "Not only didn't you stop her, you followed her advice. I should have known you didn't love me. I hope you never enjoy your love life." He left, and I cried all the way home. My father was silent.

I grew out of touch with my friends, including my dearest Negar. I lost my community and my comfort zone. I was mostly at home but still had no ability to concentrate on anything. I constantly blamed myself for how dumb I was and kept trying to force myself to focus, but I got nowhere. I had no interest in my study material.

Konkour preparation classes were three days per week in the early evening. My mother dropped me off at the door most of the time and picked me up promptly to make sure I was not being naughty on the way to or from class. One day she was not available, so I took the municipal bus instead. I liked the little bookstore right by the bus stop. I loved all the bookstores. They were my favorites. I snuck into that little store whenever I could, which was not often since my mother usually watched me enter the class building.

That day a small green book caught my attention. It was the first time in my life I heard of such a thing, meditation. Something that helps to focus! I was desperate to focus. I walked in and bought the book, and that night I read the whole thing. It was a completely new concept to me. I learned there were ways to overcome distraction. It made me hopeful, but its methods, like sitting and looking at a candle and not thinking, never worked for me. I needed a different solution.

CHAPTER FOUR

1991 - 1993

One night at a sleepover with my girl cousins—the only people in my mother's circle of trust and therefore the only ones I was allowed to visit—I ended up talking to Farshad, a distant boy cousin I had never officially met. Farshad, twenty-five, and his sisters, both in their late twenties, all lived at home as was the tradition for unmarried adult children. He seemed open-minded and considerate. We both had read books by my favorite author, Samad Behrangi. I got so excited talking about books. I had a short skirt on, sitting on the floor in his bedroom. He pulled a blanket off his bed and handed it to me to cover my legs and said, "Your skirt is short and you might feel cold." It seemed like a sweet gesture. We talked about Behrangi's most popular book, The Little Black Fish. He liked it, too, and always dreamed of exploring more of life. By the end of the conversation, I liked him. The next morning, he joined us for breakfast, and when I was leaving he asked if we could stay in touch. His attention to me melt my heart.

Farshad was also planning to study for *Konkour*, which, that summer of 1991, I knew I had again failed. He had been busy with a construction project for his father but now that it was finished he would focus on studying. He said he learned best through group studying. We had a lot in common.

So, I started attending the same family gatherings he did. It was easy because his sisters were my cousin's friends. Unlike in the past, I started liking family gatherings!

Farshad was tall with dark hair and dark eyes and talked fast, with a reassuring tone of voice. He had finished his associate degree in computer science and was planning to get a software engineering degree. He had helped construct a beautiful building in an upper-class neighborhood in Tehran, Pasdaran, where he and his family lived. His father owned the land. Farshad had designed and managed the construction of the building with modern architecture and interior design. He had done a great job; everyone was proud of him, and I saw him as capable and responsible.

Aunt Soghi had a close relationship with Farshads's mother, Pari *joon* (dear). I had met her during the family gatherings before. She was a kind and happy lady with a beautiful voice singing old songs along with dancing and laughing at the mostly all-women gatherings.

Farshad's father, Mr. Zarin, seemed different from everyone else. With his ocean-blue eyes and charming, musical Isfahani accent, he convinced you to believe something you never believed before. Before long though, I observed his own beliefs changing based on his audience's opinions.

Farshad was the father figure at home since Mr. Zarin was distant, despite his charm. Farshad was protective of his mother and his sisters. But he was his father's only son and had to help the family business. That business seemed to change continuously and remained unknown to me.

His older sister, Tara, was an emotional and kind-hearted girl, always making sure everyone was comfortable in gatherings. She was good company for easy laughter and jokes. On the other hand, struggles in her romantic relationship conspired to make her unhappy. Tara's mother didn't agree with her choice for a husband, the boy she loved dearly. When her mother seriously disagreed with her choice for marriage, Tara became depressed and attempted suicide. Farshad, who was watching his sister carefully, caught her fast enough and immediately took her to the hospital.

After that night of turmoil, Farshad convinced his father, and without telling his mother, they helped Tara to secretly marry her dream man, Farid. When her mother found out, she said she never wanted to see Tara again and threw her out of the house.

Farshad said his parents fought all the time. That was a common ground between me and Farshad: our parents' violent arguments, a fact I hoped would help us to create a peaceful environment due to learning how not to behave.

Najva, Farshad's other sister, was a nurse and was engaged to Saeed, a doctor at a hospital where she used to work. They were getting ready for their big wedding in August. My cousins and I accompanied her on a lot of her wedding shopping trips. This way we would end up at their house for the night, and Farshad and I could spend time together. Even though we had not told the others our developing romance, they felt the closeness between us. We were focused on each other and spent a lot of time in his room talking—with an open door.

Wedding expenses are the groom's responsibility in Iran. Saeed was a newly graduated medical doctor and did not have much money. Najva needed to find ways to convince her rich father to pay for the wedding she dreamed of, a fancy one. There was one way to soften her father to get the money: flattery. She told her father how pleased and awed people would be by such an elegant ceremony. She said they would admire him for it. Indeed, when it came, it was a dream party. Mr. Zarin looked satisfied and proud.

****

Soon, Pari *joon*, Aunt Soghi, and therefore my mother, figured out Farshad and I were attracted to each other. I was happy and playful and had forgotten all the drama of school and Mehran. Surprisingly, my mother reacted positively and even helped me buy a present for Farshad's birthday without my father's knowledge. Everyone in her family was positive about Farshad, and my mother was pleased that I was attracted to one of her relatives. They certainly looked at it as a promising and serious relationship. Unlike with Mehran, my father was the last person to know, my mother told him briefly about Farshad and I being interested in each other and therefore we needed to interact with his family more often. My father was not happy to hear that surprise.

Before long we were invited to Farshad's parents' home for a dinner as a normal family gathering. As soon as we arrived he called me to his room to show me the latest poem he had written for me. It was romantic and touching. He said, "I knew I was talented in poetry but, more poems have come to my mind since meeting you." My heart melted. He wrote many poems for me in those days.

Farshad shared many of his dreams with me. Our conversations went on and on effortlessly. I was already walking towards utopia with him when he said, "Shabnam, you and I can be a role model couple who love each other and help others. We can spread love and bring peace to our families. We can do so much together, better than our parents." He wanted us to go beyond the ordinary lives of our parents and make a better world. I squeezed his hand and reassured him, "We can."

Farshad's parents lived separately in adjoining apartments in his new building. When we arrived, Mr. Zarin invited my father to his unit. The rest of us had a fun time in his mom's apartment, talking, telling jokes, and laughing. Najva, her fiancée, Farshad's uncle, his wife, my mom, and his mother seemed like a perfect gathering. Only Tara and her husband were absent. This was so rare to me. I never felt happy and comfortable in family gathering. Farshad and I were walking on cloud nine to be together in a fun and safe environment.

When my father and Mr. Zarin walked over for dinner, my father's face was full of stress. I knew what it meant and what was next, his sharp critical attitude. Why did he always want to be angry? What was wrong with him? For once I was having a great time with family.

The fancy dinner followed the Persian tradition of presenting several different dishes: *Sheereen polo*—basmati rice, butter, barberries, orange peel, almonds, pistachios, sugar, saffron, cinnamon, and cumin served with sautéed chicken; *Kashk e Bademjoon*—sautéed and mashed eggplant with liquid whey protein and topped with fried onions, chopped walnuts, and mint; *Ghormeh sabzi* stew—sautéed herbs, (parsley, leeks or green onions) seasoned with dried fenugreek leaves and turmeric and mixed with kidney beans, pieces of lamb or beef and dried lime; and *Gheime bademjoon*—beef stew mixed with golden sautéed eggplant, cooked tomato and split peas, turmeric and cinnamon, and thin fries.

Mr. Zarin complimented my family and me, saying how happy he was to meet my father. He had also sensed Farshad's and my affection. "My son is so important to me. I want the best for him," he said. "You see this beautiful building? He built it all himself." His blue eyes focused on me as he continued: "All I have in my life belongs to my children, especially my son. All I want for them is a bright future. I'd do anything for them." Pari *joon* had a satisfied smile; she also approved. My father was silent and respectful, but his nodding and smiling, with one arm on the dining chair like he was about to get up, were forced. Seeing this confused and worried me. Less than an hour after dinner, my father suggested we leave, and we did.

He exploded as soon as we got in the car. He shouted at my mother, saying the family was an unsuitable match. "Zarin's words are ninety-five percent lies. He will have no support for his son and his future. He is smoking all his money away through opium."

As he was shouting his alcohol-soaked breath filled the small space inside the car, and he drove crazily. I immediately felt nauseous. We were scared we would get into an accident. I was silent. He said, "Farshad is twenty-five and has done nothing worthy except this building. He has not done his mandatory military service and will not be able to get a job in any organization. His father is going to bribe the government to buy out his obligation. Who knows if he can. Farshad cannot continue his education because of that either. Zarin is lying!"

It seemed unreasonable to pick on Farshad's family style and his father's addiction to opium (I had not known about the opium until that moment). Couldn't he see how happy I was with Farshad and his family and how different Farshad was from his father? "You are building a dream on a mirage," he told my mother. "This is a confused boy with no plan for his future. You are looking at his father's money, but your daughter will not see even a penny of that. You idiots think money brings happiness."

Even though it was not the first time, it was still hard for me to hear the words coming out of his mouth, so insulting to my mother and me. My father's anger always made a thick wall between us, stopping me from thinking about his opinion when it came to judging people. When we got home, I ran to my bedroom and slammed the door. I knew I had my mother's support this time. I also knew my father gave up upon seeing my tears. I cried and promised to get better grades, he accepted my promise over and over. I cried and asked to learn skiing and he gave up despite the great expenses the sport had, disregarding my mother's disagreement, I cried to go to a friend's house, he took me there ignoring my mother's argument. I could get anything I wanted from him by crying.

****

Throughout the summer, I spent a lot of time in family gatherings to be with Farshad. I wanted to spend even more time with him. I started daydreaming that we could study together for *Konkour* and then go to school together and plan an amazing life. We were both tired of not having privacy at home, frightened of *Basij* outside, and certain of our heavenly love. Two months after we met, in late August, he proposed, and I accepted happily. He was the path to my bright future! His family came to our house with flowers, cookies, and gifts and officially asked for my hand. My aunts and uncle Hassan were there too. Everyone was happy. My father didn't express his disagreement while they were there and everything went well.

My role models were the little black fish and recently Jonathan Livingston Seagull, who flew much higher than other seagulls and enjoyed his few friends who shared the same ideas. Farshad was going to fly high with me.

Finally, I would escape my parent's house and my mother's unreasonable discipline. Marriage would grant me freedom. I would create my own lifestyle. An ambitious but ignorant nineteen-year-old with dreams of sailing around the world, I thought a partner who had read Samad's books would share the same values.

We had a lot of family approval for our marriage. His mother and his sisters were happy since I was a familiar face and well-behaved in their presence. Uncle Hassan approved. My mother, of course, loved the idea of me marrying her distant cousin, especially with her sisters and brothers' approval. Perhaps she also felt if I married I would calm down and she wouldn't have to deal with me being naughty. My father's resistance seemed so unfair that I switched my loyalty to my mother. Her punishments and my fear of her became distant memories. Now she was helping me build my way to heaven, to escape her.

I begged my father. I cried and promised him to create a great future. Under the pressure of my tears and my mother's talks, within a week he gave up and accepted it. All he asked was that we remain engaged for a long time to get to know each other.

I was happy.

After we officially announced our engagement, I got to meet Farshad's father's family. They were religious, so to go and meet them, even inside the house, I had to dress conservatively and put a scarf on my head to cover my hair inside the house when visiting them. I did not like that at all. I was used to covering myself outside, but not inside. It frustrated me, but I reasoned it would be only once a year. I could do this to respect them.

On another day though, getting ready to go to his friend's house, I stood at my closet to select a dress. Farshad stood behind, watching me. I showed him a short black skirt and said, "If we have the car to go to Amir's house, I can wear this underneath my *mantow* without pants."

His face darkened. "You have no proper clothes whatsoever. You have silly, careless clothes unsuitable for a woman like you. You need skirts that are proper for an engaged woman."

I silently put the skirt back and took my pants out of the closet. Tired of my parents' constant fights, I decided to show him respect, make him feel comfortable. I wanted a peaceful partnership. If changing my dress code would make him happy, it would clear the way for the more important values we believed in. We could explore life beyond ordinary even with a conservative dress code.

I wanted to believe he was open-minded, so, unlike a lot of other girls, I did not hide from him my romantic history. One day as he sat on my bed and I cleaned my desk I came across my diary. I told him the story of how my mother had found out about Mehran. He listened silently; it was the first he was hearing about Mehran. I felt good being honest and not secretive.

But that night he told me about all the girls he had liked or had any relationship with. It made me so jealous, and I regretted revealing my secret to him. I was disappointed at him and myself. Why did I not think about the consequences? But that wasn't the end. Soon he started forcing me to watch my behavior with other men. He said if I had had a boyfriend before, which meant I could be flirtatious and cross boundaries again. To make him feel comfortable, for a while I spoke only with women when we were in social gatherings. I avoided friendly talk or jokes with his male friends and communicated only with their wives. But that wasn't me. I wanted to talk to everyone freely. I liked Saeed and Farid (Farshad's brothers-in-law) as if they were my own brothers, and since we spent so much time together, we were all close. Although in the gatherings men sat and talked separately, we had some co-ed events like ping-pong, dinner, and car rides. Eventually I forgot about Farshad's sensitivity and joked and was friendly with

Saeed or Farid until Farshad's angry face reminded me of my "sinful behavior."

Still we felt passionately toward each other and trying to preserve my virginity until the wedding night was difficult. I would have given up if he had, but he was committed. His traditional mindset awakened his religious conservatism. So, in early September, he suggested that we register our marriage. By then we had known each other for just three months. I didn't oppose the idea. I felt I was in love with him, we could have sex, and stay together at nights.

My father wouldn't like to hear that, but I knew I could soften his heart. If my mother disagreed (although she supported our marriage), that was another story. I told her about our new decision. My mother easily agreed.

Now I had to tell my father, and I was nervous. At 19, I felt so much like an adult and was so sure of the decision that nothing could stop me.

I asked my mother to tell my father. That afternoon we all sat down in the living room. My father's look was questioning and at the same time submissive or maybe sad. I felt he knew what we were going to say and was resigned to it.

My mother smiled, threw her hand in the air dramatically and pointed at me clumsily. "They want to get married!" she said. My father leaned on his elbow on the armrest, hunching his back. He nodded. He didn't shout. He didn't get angry. He just nodded. I started crying. I begged my father to agree and promised him to make the best out of that marriage. I promised to become an educated and independent woman through that marriage.

Finally he said, "I hope you get what you want." Then he stood and walked out the apartment door. I cried for a little while, but then I felt I did get what I wanted. I loved my father, but I was sure he was wrong about Farshad.

We had a simple ceremony in my parents' house. Our immediate families attended and my Uncle Hassan registered the marriage. We had to bribe the officiant since without having completed military service Farshad was not allowed to marry. We planned a reception one year later and delayed getting a house so we could study for *Konkour*. We would alternate staying together at our parents' houses, without the responsibility of a household.

****

The next day we traveled with Farshad's sister Tara and her husband Farid to Ramsar, a beautiful northern city along the Caspian Sea. With cash we received as a wedding gift, we stayed in the fanciest hotel in Ramsar for a couple of days. My mother had told me to keep my virginity until the reception, but I was not going to do that. When we checked into the hotel I was a little nervous. Kissing was easy and fun, but did I know how to have sex? When we got to our room, I told Farshad I was scared. He hugged me and promised me to be gentle. He was so happy to hear I was scared; until then he had not been sure how far my relationship with Mehran had gone. Well, it didn't take much to figure out how to have sex. It hurt at first, but it was a lot more joy than I had imagined. Tara and Farid were frustrated that we never wanted to get out of bed until noon. After that, we had a few intimate and passionate weeks including a couple more trips to romantic Caspian Sea shores, walking and reading poems at the beach.

We soon started to study for *Konkour*. We stayed at Farshad's mother's house three nights per week and my parents' house the rest of week. We planned to study all day and have fun in the evenings. It sounded good at first, but having fun to Farshad meant spending time with his family members or friends every single night. Men played cards and women talked, mostly gossiping or chatting about the newest brands of clothes and makeup. As an only child used to entertaining myself with books, I was not up for this. It was too much. However, to make him feel comfortable, I justified his plans and convinced myself his ideas were the best. The mental effort this required left little time or energy to discover my own thoughts or opinions.

In a few weeks I asked if we could have some quiet time, "only me and you." His reaction was not what I expected at all: "Try to get to know your new family better. Reading is for single people. You are going to be responsible for your own home soon and have more important things to focus on, your married life, me, and my family." I was stunned but didn't argue. Instead I started reading when he was not around. I started hiding my thoughts from him.

On top of this deception, I had to perform in front of Farshad's parents. One night at the dinner table, an off-white Louis the XV style fancy French dining set that they were proud of, per my request his mother started telling a story about Farshad's childhood. Farshad's father started interrupting her, coming up with a different version of the story. After every sentence, in a formal way he asked me, "Shabnam *jan* (dear), doesn't my version make more sense?" I didn't know what to say. I sat next to him. Pari *joon* offered me the rice platter and ignored her husband completely. If that had been the end of the story, bad enough. But Mr. Zarin sarcastically commented that in old days food went first to the man of the house.

His mother turned her angry face towards me. "You see Shabnam *jan*, I have lived with this idiot for thirty years. He ruined my life." I was uncomfortable and crushed. It had all begun because of the conversation I had started in an attempt to bring Farshad's parents closer together. I assumed discussing their son's childhood would bring happy memories.

Farshad's parents' relationship had been deeply broken for more than thirty years. Farshad had asked me to find a way to bring them back together. He wanted me to be the angel to create emotional closeness for them. He believed their only daughter-in-law could be loving to warm his parents' hearts to trust each other again. When it didn't work, I was a complete failure in Farshad's eyes.

"You did not use proper wording to get their attention positively. The way you asked made them more sensitive. You need to be careful of what you say." This made me feel bad—even scared.

With Najva, I got them a photo tree and put the parents' and the three children's pictures in it. We gave it to them one night after dinner. Pari *joon* said she loved it and took it to her room. Later I saw she had taken Mr. Zarin's picture out.

One day, Farshad asked me to clean his mother's apartment to impress her and show her my love, hoping to warm her broken heart from her broken marriage and her dark relationship with Tara. When my own mother wanted me to clean the house, I always found a way out. I hated cleaning, and cleaning someone else's house, especially in-laws, was culturally considered degrading. I was frustrated that Farshad would demean me this way, but I did it.

When Pari *joon* came home, she didn't notice, so Farshad said, "Shabnam wanted to help you so she vacuumed and mopped the floor." She glanced at the floor and said, "Oh, thank you Shabnam *jan*. You know I was thinking about you today. I want to spend more time with you to transfer my experience and everything I have learned to you to help you to become a good housewife."

Her advice was traditional and against my values. She wanted me to focus on keeping my husband happy. She spent hours giving me advice. That cleaning day she told me how proud she had been when she finally delivered a son after two girls. A son! Her husband and his family were happy and she was proud of herself. I scratched my head and thought about their behavior towards each other. I was disgusted she considered having a son one of her major life victories.

My parents' marriage was no better; I did not want to emulate it, either. I wanted a modern, understanding, peaceful, and intimate relationship with my husband, but we had no good role models, and every day brought a new drama.

Our plan to prepare for *Konkour* was not going well amidst all the turmoil; it left us without energy to study.

My mother noticed I was not happy anymore. I tried to tell her about my problems as little as I could but she read my face. Since I was still officially living in my parents' house and not at my husband's, culturally they had the priority over my husband to rule me.

To protect me, my mother started creating new rules. She said, "You no longer stay overnight there." If I went to Farshad's parents' house, I could stay for only a few hours and must come home at night. We were not allowed to stay together overnight until we had our own house. When I was at their house, my mother wanted me to avoid any offer to help in the kitchen since she thought they were taking advantage of me. Culturally it was classier if the daughter-in-law acted like a formal guest in her in-laws' house. It would build respect for me. Not only did I help and wash the dishes to keep peace with Farshad and make his family happy, I even cleaned their house again, but I did not dare to tell my mother or she would restrict my attendance at their house even more.

Farshad was not happy with the new rules, but he tried to keep his relationship with my mother as there was no hope for positivity with my father. His disapproval of our marriage set the wrong starting point in their relationship.

My mother became angry at my mother-in-law. Pari *joon* had never learned to drive and started asking my mother to drive her to a lot of events, feeling entitled because she was the mother-in-law. Our house was not close to their house and it was inconvenient for my mother to chauffer her around, but if she refused, Pari *joon* became upset. It became a burden quickly, and they became sarcastic and even sneaky toward each other.

My marriage and my in-laws were the hot new family gossip. My mother and her sisters were angry at my mother-in-law, who had been a sweet distant cousin until the marriage. They blamed me: "Why do you follow your husband's rules? Say no to him. Don't make the same mistake we did." They told me how naïve I was. Although they never said no to their husbands directly they fought, yelled, screamed and cried when they didn't like their husbands' behavior. I didn't want to fight. Their criticism, which was the best advice from their standpoint, confirmed I was not good enough and could not take care of myself.

My marriage created more family drama than I thought. My mother and aunts excluded Pari *joon* from trips and picnics that had included her in the past. My mother wanted to avoid giving her a ride and dealing with her sarcasm.

One day my mother-in-law found out about a day trip they were taking without her to Kashan, a central city in Iran famous for rose gardens that made rose water. I was going to stay at my in-laws that day. I rang the bell, and Pari *joon* opened the door and started yelling at me. I was so scared and upset. Farshad tried to calm his mother down. Later, though, he told me it was unfair and unethical for my mother to exclude his mother from activities they used to do together. Remaining silent, I sheltered myself under my fear and did not see any reason to have a conversation. I couldn't believe how things had changed from the friendly relationship they had before our marriage to hatred a few months after our marriage. I felt I was at fault. I didn't manage the in-law relationship well.

Things got worse as time passed with no sign of planning for our reception or looking for a house. My father invited Mr. Zarin to our house for a serious conversation. My father thought our living situation created instability. We needed to take our marriage under our control under our own roof. He asked Mr. Zarin to help his son, as he had promised, to get a house. Mr. Zarin agreed but did nothing, which gave our parents a new reason to fight each other.

My own parents' fights were more frequent than ever, and often on the topic of my marriage. Pressed between these two worlds, I was far from my independent dreamland.

Farshad was angry all the time and tried to minimize contact with my parents and his father. We saw each other less, and the distance created resentment. When I went to his house I got an angry hello. "Let's go to the room" he said. Closing the door, he started: "Why can't you stop your father from calling my father? I fight with my father every time I see him. I don't want money from him. I want to get a job myself and manage our finances myself. I don't want my father's money."

In tears, I said, "Then get a job. We need to live together in our own house. This situation is terrible."

"You can't tell me what to do. I have to take *Konkour* first. You just come here to fight. We don't study enough."

Crying harder, I said, "Yeah, it's all my fault now. I am tired of this."

He left the room and let me cry. In an hour or so I went out, washed my face and tried to talk to him nicely. We went back to the room and he immediately started undressing me and kissing me, saying "You are mine." I swallowed my sadness and got fully involved in sex before I lost the opportunity of what I thought was Farshad's love. Problems could wait until later. I didn't want to lose him. Any little positive attention from him felt great.

Perhaps our high sex drive gave us a way to make up for disappointments. Perhaps sex was our only way of intimate communication, only physically. We had not learned how to create emotional intimacy.

One of the biggest complications in his family was Tara's marriage. We had to hide the time we spent with Tara and Farid. She wanted to come to her parents' house and be with us. We managed to have her there when her mother was out, but sometimes Pari *joon* came home earlier than expected. Once, she entered quietly, found Tara in the kitchen, and started yelling and screaming. When Farid heard the commotion, he tried to leave from the door behind the building but Pari *joon* caught him. She slapped his face. "You worthless creature! You stole my daughter. Get out of my house." Of course, next in line for her abuse were Farshad and me because we had let them in and because we accepted Tara's husband among us. Farshad asked me to be silent and respectful to his mother.

I was in the middle of their family dramas. Farshad told me if I loved him, I would support him which meant would do anything he asked without complaining. If I didn't agree, he would show frustration.

All the dreams of liberty and independence were buried under my stress and anxiety. I was not doing one right thing to make anybody happy. My husband, his parents, my mother, my father: everyone was unhappy with me. I was not happy, either, but to avoid drama I pretended I was.

The emotional intimacy I craved had no infrastructure in this relationship. The harder I tried, the less intimacy I created. I learned to be careful about expressing my likes and dislikes to my husband. I bitterly figured out I was better off to keep my emotions to myself. If he did not agree, he challenged me with insults and anger like I was all wrong.

The circumstances after getting married were far worse than I anticipated, and I had no desire to study. Farshad felt no better. We were both drained by all the conflicts. Each drama created a new drama, and I was sickeningly worried about going to college.

****

I took *Konkour* for the third time, knowing I'd do worse than ever. Farshad was not hopeful either. He started looking for a job. We hoped to make a better environment in our own house away from our parents' interference. He thought my parents made everything worse and I thought his parents did.

In Iran, the tradition is that the groom and his parents provide a place for the new couple to live and pay for the wedding. The bride and her parents furnish the house. Of course, it depends on the financial status of each family to provide the best they can for the new couple, but at any level in society this part of the process is usually stressful and creates family conflict.

My mother bought smaller kitchen stuff and sheets but was waiting to see our apartment before buying furniture.

My parents constantly reminded Mr. Zarin of his obligation.

We thought it would be easy for Farshad to get a well-paying job in construction management since he had good experience taking care of the construction of his father's building. Soon he figured out his experience on a project that he finished costlier than expected was no good for commercial projects that needed connection with contractors and vendors with fair price. He needed experience about how to build a building on budget and on time. He then developed hopes that his father would help him invest in construction so he could have his own business. But when he asked for money to invest, his father said there was none.

Farshad could not apply for any organization since they required proof of his military service. He thought he could bribe someone but even that was expensive. The best would be if he could find a businessman willing to trust him and give him work. We were desperate and agitated. Of course, my father reminded me that he had warned me this would happen.

Farshad's uncle had a small business distributing kitchen appliances. Seeing us in despair, he offered to bring Farshad along and teach him to do the same business. To begin, he offered a small monthly payment. It was not even close to Farshad's dream job, but he swallowed his pride.

With this small income, we could just manage our non-rent expenses if we lived independently. Because Mr.

Zarin had told Farshad he didn't have money, Farshad told me he didn't want to get any money from his father. Things were becoming more and more complicated.

After so many calls from my father, Mr. Zarin finally conceded to borrow money for us. Farshad gave up his resistance and accepted it. In the midst of all this, Mr. Zarin decided to throw a big reception party. I was shocked and without thinking and without my normal respectful tone of voice, I said, "But *Pedar jan* we don't need a big reception! We need that money for rent."

"This is not about you, Shabnam *jan*. It is my pride. I must have a big reception for my only son." He was silent for a few seconds. "A big reception will make everyone admire me, and that is good for your reputation as my daughter-in law. I am borrowing money for this reception. It is a good investment in your future." I felt angry and helpless and annoyed by him and by his son, standing there submissively.

I was not allowed to get a job. The culture, my parents, and my husband would be against it. With Farshad's little job and the money his father finally gave us, we started planning. We squeezed everything we could and planned in a way that could keep a portion of money to pay rent for a small apartment in a middle-class neighborhood called Shahrara in Tehran. The apartment was on the fourth floor of a building with no elevator, so it was cheap. We planned to move in right after our reception at the end of summer.

The whole process of reception was so stressful. Neither of us wanted to have it but Farshad's parents' only son and my parents' only daughter had to have the best of best ceremonies. I hated them all! With all the fights and gossip, they still wanted to show off to the rest of the family.

Planning wasn't easy. There was not one thing we could agree on. Farshad wanted the best menu and I wanted something moderate to save some money. We fought. My mother and I ordered a modern-looking sofa and loveseat, but when I took him to the store to see it Farshad said it was not formal enough to invite high-class guests like his father's rich family members. We fought, and I canceled the order. He asked my mother to buy formal, classic furniture and curtains—nothing modern. I told him he was putting too much pressure on my parents, but he said, "Look at my friend's wife. She brought the best furniture and her parents are not wealthier than yours. Your parents have only one child. They should be able to do it." We fought.

A few days before the reception he complained I hadn't cleaned our apartment well enough. People who came to see our place the day after the wedding would be disappointed in me. We had both worked hard, fighting constantly, to prepare the apartment. Standing in the kitchen in my parents' house, I got so angry that I threw a glass of water at him. I was lucky he was fast and moved his head. The water splashed on the wall and the glass shattered. I did not expect that. That was not me. I never threw tantrums, but I guess I was fed up. I started screaming at him. He walked to the door and left the house. I sat down and cried until I realized I had to clean the mess before my parents got home.

****

On the day of our wedding reception in September of 1992, Farshad and I started fighting as soon as he picked me up from the hair salon. The tradition was the groom picked the bride from the hair salon along with photographers, who video-recorded the drive to the venue. Ribbons and flowers decorated the car. When they arrived, the bride and groom would enter the venue together and welcome the guests.

The photographer took the video and pictures of the decorated car and the groom, and then came upstairs to the salon for the next part of the video. As instructed by the photographer, I opened the door slowly with a smile, expecting my flower bouquet and Farshad's smile in return. Instead, he started frowning. "Your neck is low cut. It is too open. How are you going to cover it?" I was shocked. It was not low cut. This was not the first time he had seen my wedding gown. Besides, the first part of the reception in the venue was in a salon with only female guests. A partition would separate the room into two different areas for men and women. The Islamic government did not allow any venue to throw parties with men and women together unless women covered themselves from head to toe. It was the second part, where men and women would party together at his parents' house, that he was worried about.

As a bride, I expected to hear how beautiful I looked. I felt sick to my stomach and decided to avoid his comments for the rest of the night. The photographer was shocked and asked us to re-play that part so she could take a video, this time with friendlier attitude. The whole night we either ignored each other or fought. During the reception, I mingled with others to distract myself. I guess by then fights had become a natural part of our lives.

Everyone asked where we planned to go for our honeymoon. We had no desire to plan a romantic trip. However, I had started planning a different type of getaway. I began asking people to join us at Caspian Sea two days after the reception. A bridal shower is normally the day after the reception, and I couldn't skip that since it was in our newly furnished apartment. The day after the bridal shower was perfect to escape and spend time with others. Farshad's sisters, their husbands, his cousin, and my cousin planned to come. Farshad, being angry and stubborn, didn't want to go. I figured I could go without him and he would be okay since I would be with his sisters. But he said he would not allow me to go.

Two days after the reception, at 7:00 am sharp, my cousin Marjan rang our doorbell with Aunt Sara, ready to go. They came upstairs and my aunt was surprised we were not ready. Farshad didn't want my aunt to know about our fights, so he had to come along. It was always all about creating a good picture in front of others and hiding our fights.

I was upset until then, but a big smile came back to my face as soon as I saw everyone at the bus station. I started talking to everyone and laughing with them and having fun like a normal twenty-year-old. The more fun I had with others, the more furious Farshad became, accusing me of being empty headed. Still, we did not let others know about our fights, which helped the trip to be fun with laughter, singing, dancing, and being silly for three days.

When we came back, Tara and her husband stayed at our place since we arrived late and our house was closer than theirs to the bus station. The next day at 6:00 a.m., his mother rang our bell and as soon as we opened the door, she ran in with a white face and started screaming, still catching her breath from four flights of stairs to get to our apartment. She had found out Tara and her husband had been with us, but she did not know they were in our house at that moment, hiding in the bedroom. She started screaming at us for accepting Farid, an enemy.

I had a hard time following her words through her screaming but was shocked when she told Farshad: "You have no understanding of a family life and as a husband you have no control over your wife. You are taking your wife to a trip with that bastard [Farid], and even if they sleep together you don't care."

We tried to calm her down and worried what the neighbors would think. I made her a cup of chamomile tea, brought it to her, and hugged her. Meanwhile Farshad was assuring her Farid had not come. Trying to have a lot of sympathy in my voice I said, "*Maman jan*, please don't bother yourself. It is not good for your heart. It was only Tara." We did not know who told her the news but there was enemy among us for sure. She finally believed us, calmed down, and in half an hour left.

Tara meanwhile had to prevent Farid from jumping out of the bedroom with all his anger at his mother-in-law to defend himself. He had heard every word Pari *joon* said. After she left, he burst out of room and we had to calm him down. That was much easier compared to the previous scenario.

Pari *joon* was becoming less and less stable. But she denied her emotional ups and downs and would not accept professional help. She thought we needed professional help and she understood life deeply. She wanted us to listen to her advice to be able to create a happy life. Calming her down, listening to her screaming and cursing, became part of our life, not even mentioning that Mr. Zarin had been the one to tell her Tara was with us on the trip to the Caspian Sea. He gave away those secrets to make his wife mad at us. He denied any of that of course! He played a role of a good guy, getting information from us and revealing it to his wife to damage her relationship with us and make himself look better to his children.

****

When all the bitter and sweet ceremonies were over and we were settled into our house, we decided to start studying for *Konkour* although by then we knew Farshad couldn't get into college without military service. He still hoped he could bribe someone to get ahead, a popular Iranian mindset and strategy under the totalitarian government structure.

We started studying, but we fought almost every night: too many social gatherings, my interactions with men, Farshad's sarcastic comments, me not being a good wife, and now financial problems. He wanted to throw parties and invite family and friends over to impress them with his hospitality through good quality food and snack, even if he had to borrow money to accommodate the gathering. I was against spending money that way and felt we had barely enough for our day-to-day life.

I felt nauseous for three weeks thinking I was always stressed out. We had only missed one time protecting our sex between me dropping pills and getting ready for an IUD. There was no way I could be pregnant. With my mother's suggestion, I went to the lab for a test. The day after my mother and I went back for the results. When my mother smiled and said, "What if you are pregnant?" I didn't answer pushing back my tears. I wasn't ready to be responsible for another human yet. I wanted to go to school. When we entered the lab in a downstairs kind of basement of a building lit with so many white soulless florescent lights, my mother went to the front and asked for my name. She grabbed the piece of paper. She opened it in hurry and almost screamed: "You are pregnant!" I was about to collapse. I was only 20 years old. I panicked. That was not my plan. What happened to all my becoming an independent woman idea? My mother grabbed my arm and took me to the car.

She was looking at me with smile during the whole drive, but I was silent looking out the window. Once we got to our apartment, I ran to my bedroom and hid underneath a blanket and started crying. Farshad came home a few hours later and received the news from my happy mother. My father arrived minutes after Farshad. He already knew—my mother had called him and told him the news. Farshad was shocked to see me upset and complained to my mother about my childish behavior. My mother told him; "It's okay, she will feel better soon. She is shocked." Only my father came to comfort me. With a lot of empathy in his voice, he put his hand on my shoulder and said, "Don't worry." Tears were wetting my pillow, and I said, "I am sorry!" I was really sorry. I was hardly able to speak but I told him: "I will try to do my best to go to college." Farshad—happy to become a father—came over and said he would help me to go to college. I had a hard time believing that.

By the next day I was not crying anymore but I was still in a state of shock. Farshad reminded me that I needed to be realistic and feel happy and blessed. I was not happy but it was easier to keep my emotions to myself.

I had a hard first trimester with a lot of morning sickness. I could not eat anything except bread and plain yogurt. I lost weight and felt weak. A couple of weeks after I got the results, still feeling sick, Ramadan started. Farshad wanted to fast every day. He needed to get up before sunrise to eat and then fast until sunset. The night before the first day of Ramadan Farshad asked me, "Would you prepare food for me tomorrow before sunrise *azizam* (my dear)?"

I preferred to deal with morning sickness than with his accusing words and behavior, so I did it. I didn't want to be lectured about what a loving housewife should and must do. I gagged every morning as I prepared his food for him, and still did not get a lot of approval from him— there was always something wrong with my food. "You are so spoiled. Your mother didn't teach you anything about real life. Your father raised you by reading unrealistic books, and they never asked you to take responsibility. It is now time you learn how to live real life." Through his criticism, he believed he was trying to help me to become realistic.

I started believing that I was spoiled so I had to make up for it. Pregnant and helpless, I was scared and had lost all my self-worth. I did not want to argue. I gave up. I did not study for *Konkour* that year. I was figuring out how to be a good housewife, avoiding harsh criticism from my husband, and learning to become a good mother.

****

I had an ultrasound after the twelfth week and learned we were having a girl. Farshad and I were both happy. My parents were happy to have a granddaughter. I was a little nervous to share the news with Farshad's parents, though. When I got to their house, Pari *joon* opened the door. They knew we had come from the doctor's office. Pari *joon* with her curious but concerned expression asked, "So?" Mr. Zarin appeared, too. With a big smile I said, "It's a girl." Pari *joon* turned away and she said hopefully next one would be a boy. Mr. Zarin said, "Shabnam *jan*, don't worry, this is just the first one." I looked at Farshad and he motioned me with his eyes to say nothing. I was mastering how to pretend and swallow my frustrations, especially in front of family members. I only said thank you. It got better when Najva and Saeed and Farshad's uncle and his wife came over for dinner that night. When they heard the news, they shared my happiness to have a baby girl. Najva especially was excited to become an aunt. She whispered to me that she couldn't wait to tell Tara. I told Najva about her parents' reaction and she asked me to forget it since they were traditional.

I was almost six months pregnant when one of my old friends had a small wedding. They made it small so they could have it like a normal wedding with men and women all together dancing and celebrating. When she saw me sitting silently, she came over and asked me to join her on the dance floor. Farshad stopped her. "She is soon to become a mother, and dancing with other young and especially single people isn't be appropriate for a mother-to-be." Then he turned his face to me like it was my fault that my friend had asked me to dance. He said, "You need to focus on important matters in my life, not silly things like dancing." My friend's face turned red. She went back to the dance floor, unable to tolerate my situation. My mother sat next to me, shocked and silent. I was devastated about what I had done to my life.

During the last few months of my pregnancy, I found a lot of time to myself when Farshad was at work and read a lot more books. I finished two long novels. I enjoyed every moment of my reading time. Reading was like going back to my natural being, especially since both these stories had protagonists who were both strong and independent women. Annett's life story in L'Âme enchantée gave voice to my dreams and thoughts. In the bourgeoisie style society of 19th century France, she bravely refused to marry the fiancé who was controlling and possessive, and yet kept the baby from him still out of wedlock when she found she was pregnant. These books reignited my dreams.

I did not know much about myself, but I knew I did not want to accept the traditional clichés and walk the same path other women did before me.

CHAPTER FIVE

1993-1994

I was not even twenty-one when my child was born. For sure, I was not ready to be a mother and I still needed to learn a lot.

Having a baby so long before I expected to made me think hard. I wanted to build a mature and supportive relationship with my child. I did not want to say no unreasonably. "No" was the first word I learned from my parents when I was one year old, because I had heard that word the most. I thought that was sad! I did not want to be a fearful figure who used unnecessary discipline. I wanted my daughter to think and to ask questions without fear. But that was all I knew! I needed to learn a lot more about democratic and non-fanatical motherly behavior, but I was young and had no good role model. I was scared and insecure, but I hoped we could figure it out together, a mother-daughter team.

Despite my fears of childbirth, I had a fairly smooth natural delivery; the worst part of labor, with serious pain, took only two hours. Parnian was born around noon on September 29, 1993. My mother and her father chose her name, and I liked it too. Parnian is a Persian name that means floral pattern silk. I wanted to make sure my daughter had a Persian name and not an Arabic name. Many Iranians are prejudice to use pure Persian names since Arabic words were forced to our language over the invasion of Iran by Muslims 1000 years before.

She was so little that a pillow from her carriage was bigger than her entire body. There she was my precious little daughter.

According to the hospital rules, no one could accompany me in the delivery room. Worse, they took Parnian away from me a few minutes after she was born. I was transferred to a recovery room alone and after a couple of hours transferred to another floor. My mother joined me in the elevator and asked how I was. She said, "Everyone is waiting for you in your room downstairs." I asked how Parnian was and whether she was crying. The nurse who was transferring me on the gurney said hospital policy was to keep the baby in a baby's room for the first 24 hours since they were not yet immune to viruses and bacteria. I looked at her in disbelief. I could not have my baby with me right away. There had been no preparation or training for this process; every step was learning on the job.

In the room, Farshad, his mom, Najva, Aunt Sara, and my mother surrounded me, asking questions about the delivery. I was desperate to hold Parnian, but my mother wanted me to stay still on the bed and rest. Luckily, a couple of hours later, I found myself alone in the room. I stepped down from my bed and slowly walked down the hallway to find the newborns' room. They only allowed me to look at her from behind the big glass window. Was I ready to be her mother? It was a whole new lifestyle, scary. That innocent, quiet doll-like baby, wrapped in a pink blanket. She reminded me of my baby dolls I owned not too long ago. I loved my baby dolls, especially the two that looked like newborns.

It was hard to believe she was mine, a real baby.

That night, to prepare to nurse her, my body developed a fever, and I was shivering, but they wouldn't bring her to me or let me go to her. It was a tough night.

Finally the next day they brought her to me. She made nursing easy, learning how to latch on quickly. With her little mouth getting tired so quickly, she did not eat fast, and feeding took an hour every time. She was so little and I was worried and wanted to make sure she was fed properly. I had to try different positions to make sure I didn't fall asleep while I was nursing her. Later, when I came to the States and saw nursing rockers, I thought that was surely an ingenious invention that did not find its way to Iran.

Two days later my doctor released me. I was excited and scared to begin this new chapter of my life. I was getting ready to leave when the pediatrician walked into my room. I felt happy. With his kind face and calm tone of voice the day before, he had made me feel secure about my baby. So now, I was shocked when he said they would have to keep Parnian a few days because she had developed jaundice.

I was upset but had no choice. My mother had tears in her eyes, too. She hugged me and reassured me the baby would be fine. My dad's face was sad; he avoided eye contact with me, never being able to bear my tears. Farshad stood there continuing his conversation with my uncle—perhaps about a new business idea—and didn't even notice my sorrow. The motherhood path already felt bumpy. With a broken heart, I left.

Our apartment was on the fourth floor with no elevator and I was still pretty weak, so I could not visit Parnian every day. We did not have a phone line at our home either, so I couldn't even check on her. I kept feeling a lump in my throat and wanting to go get my baby, but I had to trust the doctor's decision. I could not stop thinking about her. When my mother, who did go every day, finally brought her home, I forgot about my pain and my stitches and jumped from the bed. My heart warmed when I took her into my arms.

She was quiet. She did not cry even when she was hungry. I woke her up every three hours to feed her, worried she might starve.

We had so many visitors. Some came in the first two days after I came back from the hospital, and because I didn't have Parnian with me, they promised to come back. The visits should have been short, but Farshad was always thinking of appearances. As soon as guests said they were leaving, Farshad insisted, "No, no I won't allow you. We

have a little extra food, let's eat it together. Please stay!"
He had to prove he was a family man and had a happy
family. This continued for a couple of weeks after my
delivery, usually including a two-course meal, entrée and
dessert, which he of course did not prepare. Instead, he
went to the kitchen and whispered to my mother to add
more meat to the stew or add an extra course to make sure
guests felt respected. While I was in bed getting used to
the new routine my mother took care of the countless
guests and at the same time taught me how to take care of
the baby. My mother lost about 10 pounds during those
weeks. I felt bad not being able to help and was mad that
Farshad only added to her burden, but I was so sleep-
deprived and exhausted that I could do little.

Guests gave me an avalanche of advice: I could have
four or five ladies all jammed into my room, sitting on the
side of the bed, sometimes all talking at once. My uncle's
wife, Shokouh *khanoom* , and her daughter-in-law visited
on the fourth day I was home. Without asking me,
Shokouh *khanoom* grabbed Parnian and started kissing
her cheeks! I did not want people kissing my newborn
like that. She barely had any shots yet. Shokouh *khanoom*
put the baby back in her crib and sat at the side of the bed
closer to me. I knew new advice was coming. She started
whispering: "Don't listen to these doctors. They are
young and know nothing about babies. Listen to your
mother and your aunts. We know better."

Just then Parnian started crying. I tried to politely
interrupt my aunt so I could comfort my daughter, but

Shokouh *khanoom* grabbed her instead and asked if I had sugar water. I freaked out without showing it. I calmly said, "No, Shokouh *khanoom*. I don't give her anything but my milk. I can feed her." I didn't give her water for the first three months, as her doctor had recommended. I added sweetly: "Thank you!"

But she turned her back to me with my baby in her arms and said, "This baby is thirsty and needs water. Sugar also helps her to gain weight. She is too little."

I wanted my baby back. My mother came into the room when she heard crying, since Parnian so seldom made a fuss. She took Parnian from Shokouh *khanoom* and handed her to me. She was not hungry; she was complaining about having too many visitors.

Persians make guests happy even at the price of our own comfort. That part of the tradition was one I followed seriously. I was not supposed to show my frustration since it would make me look spoiled.

Things weren't easy and were not becoming easier, but the story had a good part, and that was cheerful Parnian. She brought peace with her. A couple of weeks after she was born and the visitors had all come and gone, her father and I almost stopped fighting, and we finally had a few fairly peaceful months together. The hormonal changes in me and my new role as a mother made my behavior a lot more compatible with his mindset. I focused only on my baby, which was how he thought a wife should be.

****

For the fourth time, I started studying for *Konkour*. It seemed I had plenty of time to prepare, but I had a lot to learn. Studying gave me a good excuse to bail out of family gatherings at Farshad's parents' house. I did not know how much I needed the quiet time until I got married and felt trapped by nightly get-togethers. I wanted less and less while he wanted more and more. The baby and studying gave me the best excuses to stay home.

I still could not focus on my course materials and still hated studying but getting time to myself was so peaceful. I could daydream about everything I wanted. I did not have to gossip or engage in superficial conversations. I did enjoy time with the family every now and then, just not too often. I wanted to read more books and daydream about building a community of people around me who talked the same language about those books and poems—and liberty.

That fall, every time I rocked Parnian to sleep, covering her with her soft pink blanket, I sang a lullaby by my beloved singer Mohammad Nouri, "*Jaaneh* Maryam," (Dear Maryam) to give her a message to dream big.

> "*Oh dear Maryam, open your eyes*
> *call my name*
> *the air has become bright*
> *the sun has risen*

it's time to...
go to the wilderness
Oh, dear Maryam
Oh dear Maryam, open your eyes
call my name
let's go
let's leave the home
shoulder by shoulder, together"

I was singing for both of us. We were growing up together.

With the hope and love my daughter gave me, I felt I had a chance to grow up once more, with her, and build everything in my life the way I wanted. Each night I lay on the floor beside her, dreaming about a better future for us.

During those few months, I established a strong mindset for my future, what I wanted for Parnian and me. I could study better than in the past, too—I seemed to have more focus. Parnian became my study buddy. My dreams came alive again, and they had no place for Farshad. I could not fit him into the picture. I thought of Annett from L'Âme enchantée. She chose freedom over a traditional marriage. There was a man in my future picture, someone caring and kind who accepted me for who I was. He was somewhere, and he was not Farshad.

****

Parnian was growing up fast, a happy baby. Everybody loved her. Her grandparents, her aunts, my aunts; even my two young boy cousins, who were always distracted by their toy cars, wanted to play with little Parnian.

My mother looked for any excuse to babysit and give me a chance to study more. By then, we were all worried about my educational status while my family responsibilities were getting tighter.

I was home one afternoon, still in my PJs, when the doorbell rang. I looked out through the window and saw my mother's car. Feeling a little worried and suspicious, I buzzed open the door. When she walked in she announced, "I thought of cooking Baghali polo tonight and I know it's your favorite food." Baghali polo was made with rice, dill, and fava beans, usually served with chicken or beef shank. They recently had bought a VHS player and got Western movies from friends or the underground market. "Let's go. We can call Farshad to come after work."

I loved the idea and quickly cleaned the kitchen, changed Parnian's and my clothes.

When we got to my parents' house I called Farshad at work and told him the plan. In a cold tone, he said, "OK."

When he arrived a few hours later, he sat down and talked to my parents for a while. Then he said he needed to lie down and went to my bedroom. He didn't show his anger in front of my parents. I always felt he was a little scared of my father and watched his behavior in front of him. He called me to the room, and when I saw his angry face I felt scared.

"Now that your parents have a VHS, don't think you can come here all the time and watch stupid movies. You are a wife and a mother. Set your priorities. You are becoming out of control. How dare you call me and give me plans for what to do."

I just cried. We stayed in the room until my mother called us for dinner. My parents noticed my puffy eyes but said nothing. Dinner time was silent and over soon, and we asked my mother to take us home. I immediately got Parnian ready for bed while Farshad slammed our bedroom the door. I waited in Parnian's room until he was asleep. I felt angry but knew that showing my anger did not take me anywhere useful.

I was falling right into the clichés of family life I had always hoped to avoid. My mother and I had hoped I would become an engineer and get a high-paying job, but Farshad wanted a full-time, obedient housewife. My mother, who would do anything to help me get educated, started to sense the prison I was living in. By then I had learned to look beneath her criticism for her positive intention. "Look around. Everyone—all your friends and cousins—is going to school. I'll take care of Parnian. You must get admission to a school, any school, even a crappy one." She was right, but I hated to be compared to others. Our relationship was evolving, but it was still complicated. I had never felt comfortable sharing my feelings with her, but I started understanding and accepting her support.

My father, angry and dissatisfied with my situation, tried to be cooperative. It must have been hard for him to watch his only daughter trapped by values he and I did not believe in.

Sometimes Farshad confronted my father's ideas. One night at the dinner table, we were talking about my cousin Shiva, who had just finished college and gotten a job as a radiology therapist at a hospital. My father said, "I am proud of her. She is now useful to society and financially independent. It helps her build a better life." Looking at me with a hopeful but sad expression he said, "I know you will go to school. This year you have more time to study."

My heart clutched. Farshad hated those comments. As his face became more frantic, I felt a heavy weight on my legs and arm muscles. I was scared. He did not like the conversation and the fact that my girl cousins were all getting jobs. Feeling paralyzed, I dove deep into my thoughts.

I came back up when I heard Farshad's bitter voice, fast and nervous. He looked at me but spoke to my father. "The first step is she needs to pass the exam. If she gets admission to any school she will have four years to study. By then I will make enough money for all of us and she won't need a job."

"Financial independence is for a woman's freedom regardless of her husband's income," my father said through clenched teeth. "It gives her dignity. Even her mother was financially independent. She needs to do better than the older generation."

I went to check on Parnian in the bedroom. She slept peacefully, blissfully unaware of the tension in the dining room. That was a better place for me, to be with her. I was so afraid their conversation would turn into a fight with my short-tempered father, but after I left the table there was silence.

After dinner, Farshad came to the room. I sat on the side of the bed holding Parnian. He stood close to me. "Your father brainwashes you. He thinks he is doing you a favor. No, he is ruining our marriage, interfering in our husband-and-wife relationship. You need to stop him when he talks nonsense."

I had zero tolerance for his disrespectful comments. Even though my father was not emotionally available and was lost in his personal pain, he was important to me.

"I will manage our life," I said coldly just to end the conversation. "Don't worry about my parents interfering." I resented his very existence at that moment. I wished I could change my whole life and live without him. I had to get into a college, any college! It was getting late and everything except Parnian was getting worse in my life.

****

Parian was born in September, which gave me almost nine months to get ready for *Konkour*. As the test approached, my mother gladly came to our house directly from school to collect Parnian and keep her overnight. I felt lonely at home, but I knew college was the only way out of the prison, so I studied those impossible subjects of math and physics the best I could.

So many things got in the way of my focus. For example, religious ceremonies with Farshad's fundamentalist relatives. Not only did we have to attend, I had to wear chador and say all the prayers prescribed. I didn't want to swallow all that. I'd fought with my mother ever since I was old enough to say no to religious ceremonies. My mother and her family's religion was moderate. Two of my aunts wore *hijab* to cover their hair, but this was ceremonial. They prayed five times per day, and they liked to attend religious ceremonies, but this was cultural. The ceremonies were fun get-togethers for them. My mother never forced me to practice Islam. She merely said, "Come on. It's fun and we get to see everyone." But I stayed home to read my books. To me my books were the right companion not people going to those ceremonies gossiping and showing off.

Farshad's relatives were not moderate. The most important holiday was the 10th day of *Moharam*, the first month of the lunar calendar. That is the day Imam Hossein, the third Shia Imam, was martyred at the battle of Karbala in Iraq 1400 years ago. During the first 10 days of the month *Moharam*, Shia Moslems mourn Imam Hossein. Parades filled the streets of Tehran every evening and on the morning of Ashura, the tenth day.

Mourners gathered at a mosque for sorrowful, poetic recitations chants of Ya Hussain (calling Hossein).

I wore chador, carried Parnian, and stayed on the road for hours along with other women to watch the parade of men marching and mourning. Then women and men separately went to huge venues for food. It was a long wait until all the prayers were done and dinner was served. Parnian was little and got tired and fussy. All the babies cried. They were all tired. I wanted to cry with them. I was frustrated and felt out of place.

Before I got married, if my mother asked me to join her at one of her ceremonies, I laughed at her: "Of course I won't waste my time." What happened to that Shabnam? I was jealous of the pre-marriage version of myself. I had thought I was in prison back then. Not only that, I had to pretend to my mother that I liked those ceremonies to avoid her advice to confront my husband. I had no idea about the concept of assertiveness, knowing only passiveness or aggressiveness. I chose to be passive, a defense mechanism to avoid fights.

If I were invited to a ceremony for a female group Quran reading, I went only to avoid family judgments and the disdain of Farshad, who would call me a spoiled girl. I dutifully put on a polite face to show a picture-perfect family. Cooking, cleaning, hosting guests, taking care of a baby, and building relationships with friends and family members who he cared about were the requirements of the job. A degree was not required but nice to have.

After years of studying the Quran and Arabic as mandatory courses at school under Islamic government rule, I hated sitting around and reading it aloud. Some women could recite it like a poem, which sounded beautiful. But I lied and said I was shy. Not only would I have read it poorly and invited judgment which would have gotten back to Farshad, I didn't believe in it and could not bring myself to say the words. I had to pretend and participate in religious conversations after reading each verse, too, with appalling ideas such as its being perfectly fine for Ibrahim to have had a mistress only to have a child. I wanted to scream; I don't believe in anything you say! Leave me alone! I lied to everyone, myself included. I hated myself and felt trapped by my commitments.

****

Maybe because I never had the mindset to chase Parnian around the room to feed her, she soon learned how to eat on her own. Once she could control her hands and arms, I let her feed herself while in her highchair, and we laughed and played at mealtimes. I could clean the mess she made, but she needed to taste the happiness of being capable. I never shared that thought with her father of course. He was fine with her eating on her own but didn't know why I was doing that.

Without a role model for modern motherhood, I turned to books about how to raise a resilient and confident child.

Not many democratic parenting books had been translated into Farsi, but the few books I found, such as How to Behave So Your Children Will Too by Sal Severe, were thought provoking. Learning about democratic parental relationships gave me such a good feeling. I longed to live in a society that embraced that parenting style.

My husband mocked it: "She is raising her child by the book. A child needs to be raised normally, not by Western books with no sense of our culture." I had stopped arguing with him about my beliefs long ago, but secretly I did what I thought was correct.

****

The months flew by and I took *Konkour* feeling unsure about the result.

Back then, the names of people who were admitted to different schools were listed and published in a special edition of one of the national newspapers in September. The special edition came out early morning, a couple of weeks before school started.

The night before the results were due we spent the night at my parents'. I woke up so many times that night. Early that morning, my mother carried Parnian while she and I walked across the street to the magazine kiosk. A line of men and women waited for the distribution truck. When it came, I was still feeling pretty hopeless about finding my name. I sat on the ground, laid out the newspaper and started searching. There it was. I saw it. It was my name! I read it twice, maybe three times. I touched it with my fingers, not trusting my eyes. I was not mistaken. There were not two Shabnam Shahmohammads. I had been accepted to the physics department of the Azad University!

My happy tears were not the only ones, and we didn't notice the ones who left quietly because they didn't find their names. My mother had her happy cry, squeezing little Parnian in her arms. No words were needed in that moment. We gathered ourselves and hurried home to give the good news to my father and Farshad. I walked upstairs as fast as I could. When I opened the door they both stood right there, as if they had heard me. Still in disbelief, with teary eyes, I told them. I was beyond myself. Farshad said congratulations with a smile. He seemed truly happy for me, so I blocked all the negative thoughts I had towards him. I knew he was nervous about the result of his own exam, which would come in a few days.

My father didn't hide his happy tears. He hugged me and patted me on my back without words. I was so happy to have finally delivered on the big promise I had made to him. I desperately needed his approval, and I had never received it like this. My school admission was promising and leading me to the right path for a better future, one my parents wanted for me too.

Physics! I am not joking. Physics! Didn't I hate it? Physics and Shabnam? I thought they were mutually exclusive! It's amazing how we humans can justify our likes and dislikes under different circumstances to the point that we can fool ourselves. Sometimes we embrace the dislike just to open our path! Even as a housewife, I needed a weapon to prove to my husband that I was educated enough to understand the type of milk I was buying for my child. Before applying to schools, when I mentioned to Farshad I wanted to choose business or English language as one of my majors, Farshad had taken the form from my hand and started working on it himself. He said, "We don't have time for you to go to school for a major that is wasting time. You need to study something with a good name. You need to be practical."

What difference did it make when he wouldn't consider letting me get a job anyway? With my passive behavior, I accepted that he chose only engineering or science majors for me. I just wanted to go to school.

A few days later Farshad got his result for his exam, and although he was accepted for a bachelor's in computer programming, he could not find the magic person he hoped to bribe. His studying was wasted and he lost hope. At twenty-seven, he refused to leave us for two years to take care of his military duties. He should have handled it long before. So, he continued working with his uncle in his small business.

We still had many money conflicts, but when he managed to pay my school tuition for the first semester, I became hopeful that we could build a good life together.

****

In the fall of 1994, I started school two days per week. I was in a new world back among many other girls close to my age, and I immediately and happily started to build a new community, enjoying my freedom from Farshad.

One morning a few of us were walking to a 7 a.m. class. Nasrin, an olive-skinned girl with cute round cheeks and a big smile said, "I hate waking up early in the morning. I hate the sound of the alarm clock."

"I have a natural alarm clock," I said with a laugh. "She wakes me up early every morning."

Farnaz, another girl with her beautiful oval face and a perfect natural nose said, "What type of alarm clock is that?"

I smiled. "I have a one-year-old daughter."

They looked at me in disbelief. "Whaat?" Then we started laughing together. They asked me to bring her to school one day.

They were all single, from families that had not forced them to get marry young. Even though the majority would end up becoming housewives, education was important to them. Still, a number of girls, like me, wanted to have a voice and make decisions for ourselves. Our numbers were growing.

At school I joined a research group in chemistry class that would give me the opportunity to present the result to the class too. I was eager to use my potential. I needed to grow. I loved to be busy like that instead of with constant family gatherings.

A couple of weeks after school started, I came home one night to the wonderful smell of roasted chicken. My heart filled with happiness. Farshad had picked up Parnian from my mother's house and made us dinner. Our apartment had a good-sized kitchen with two big windows. I opened both windows for fresh fall air, maybe to share my happiness and hope with the wind too. The smell of food mixed with the breeze that came through the window; it was the aroma of hope and a better life. We had a cute little wood table with four chairs. Excitedly, I set the table. Farshad took the chicken out of the oven. Parnian was ready in her highchair, and we started to eat.

I was talkative, and when Farshad asked how school was, I began to explain everything that had happened during the day. Casually, he said, "Don't take your classes so seriously. Attend the minimum and as long as you get a passing score, you will be fine. Just get the damn degree. Don't waste much time on it. That is what I did when I went to school."

I didn't get the point and continued talking happily. I was too pumped up. Too much dopamine. I said, "My chemistry professor chose me to prepare a presentation, an extra activity, for class for next week. I have to start working on it."

It must have been hard for him to see me shining while he had to bury his dream of becoming more educated and getting a professional job. His face changed. "You are taking this too seriously. You don't need extra activities and extra interactions with your chemistry professor. Why did he choose you among all other girls?"

"I volunteered. It was my choice."

Done with his dinner, he stood and walked to the living room. "Be realistic. You are a mother. Spend time with your daughter instead."

My balloon of happiness popped just like that and all the dopamine in it was wasted on the floor, to be mopped up and trashed.

I felt for Farshad, understood his insecurities. But I could not ignore my passion for exploring a new life.

CHAPTER SIX

1995 - 1997

The fundamental differences between Farshad and me were becoming intolerable. I censored myself around him and wanted to spend less and less time with him.

A few months after I started school, his cousin offered him a job managing his business on Kish Island, in the southern part of Iran. It was a great opportunity, at least financially. Luckily, they did not have accommodations on Kish Island for all of us there, and our apartment had a few more months until the end of the lease, so I would have to stay in Tehran with Parnian, almost 18 months old now. I encouraged him to accept the job not only for the money but because I welcomed the breathing room. I did not feel comfortable with him at all, especially in our intimate time. I had lost all the passion and desire for sex but hid even that from him. I never complained. I pretended, and made myself available to him whenever he asked for it, but all I thought was, *Is he done?* Wearing so many different masks to avoid his disdain drained me. I hated him for who I had become.

I spent a couple of nights per week at my parents' and a couple in our apartment, with or without Parnian. On those special evenings, I relished the solitude. I read or listened to music. Alone, I could focus on my philosophy and sociology books, subjects I always loved.

It was also sweet when I had Parnian with me. I sat studying and she sat in the middle of the dining table playing with my papers and throwing them around, giggling and making me laugh. She dropped papers and pointed to have them back, and as soon as I returned them, she immediately dropped them, laughing. I loved our games. Just the two of us with a Shabnam closer to her real self. Those nights were innocent. There was no pretending like I had to do in front of my husband, my parents, or other family members. She was the cutest and the most innocent thing ever in my life. I didn't have to pretend to her. Our mother-daughter time was precious.

****

At school I enjoyed great philosophical conversations with Mina, a strong, hard-headed girl who had finished a degree in sociology and now wanted to study physics. All I wanted was to spend time with her, to talk and learn. She knew so much about sociology, psychology, and philosophy. She had read so many books she sounded like an encyclopedia. Our conversations were dreamy. She introduced me to Plato's argument book series. She taught me about women's desire, about democracy, about how people thought in the West, about where our society fell—almost at the bottom of freedom chart—compared to the rest of the world. I wanted to know even more.

I secretly read Plato's argument series after finding it on the underground market. It was risky. I had to trust the street booksellers in the middle of the city close to Tehran University. They whispered to people walking by, "Old books, forbidden books." When I asked for a book, I had to wait while they brought it from secret storage. Then I had to quickly put the book in my bag, pay for it, and scurry off.

I hid the books under the sofa when Farshad was home. One night he sat on the floor, resting against the sofa and playing hide-and-seek with Parnian. She put her head on the floor, making believe she was hiding. Spotting something, she curiously dragged a book out. Farshad took it from her and his face twisted into anger, making me nauseous. "You are so self-absorbed. You think you are Socratic?"

He tossed the book aside. "You live in the sky. Come down here and live with us."

There was silence for the rest of the day, until later he said, "I chose the worst mother for my daughter. You are worthless." I never answered him, and I never forgot the fresh feel of his sharp words.

Thank goodness for Mina. She helped satisfy my curiosity about the big question of what life is about. Our friendship was joyful and fulfilling and I could not get enough of that.

We sometimes went to the house of Mina's sociology professor, Professor Hamidi. The first time we entered his apartment, the style and furniture looked familiar to me. It reminded me of pictures I had seen of the Paris apartment-living style in the 70s. Books were everywhere. Tall, dark, cherry bookshelves covered the living room walls. A small, round dining table in front of one of the bookshelves had books stacked on it. Four chairs, placed in the corners of the small living room but belonging to the dining table, filled the whole room. It was busy and lovely, and I had a good feeling there.

Hamidi had been educated in Paris, and his wife still lived there. They were a model of Jean-Paul Sartre and Simone de Beauvoir's romantic style.

Since I was still learning and could not contribute, I mostly listened to the stimulating, intellectual conversations. Professor Hamidi started and continued with questions. Once he looked intensely at Mina's beautiful, lively, wide-open eyes and quietly asked, "Mina, do you think there is such a thing as too much freedom? Jean-Paul Sartre thinks humans are condemned to too much freedom, and consequently have too many choices. Is that a bad thing, do you think?" A half smile played on his lips.

Smiling, Mina closed her eyes, but my mind reeled. Too much freedom? I hid everything from almost everybody. Where was too much freedom? Could I have some?

After a few seconds, she said, "Do you mean I have the freedom to become a physicist rather than a social analyst? Is that a choice I can make? And even if I become a physicist, I still have a choice to become a homeless person? Which one is the real Mina? Which one represents the existence of Mina?"

Professor Hamidi listened intently. He took a draw on his pipe and exhaled it slowly. I loved the smell and the atmosphere. I was confused and deep in my thoughts but listening carefully. Professor Hamidi said, "How do you know whether you are using your full potential?" He paused, then said, "We all have choices all the time. Our choices are limitless. It all depends on how we select them. What is important to know is humanity's unlimited freedom should be used to build morality. It is hard though. Make sure you read Sartre's "Existentialism is Humanism" lecture."

I felt ecstatic but puzzled. Thinking aloud, I said, "Too many choices? If I have unlimited choices then I should be able to select some good ones, but how do I do that under the Islamic regime? I know I have made poor choices in my life so far, and I could do better." It was the first time I had admitted this.

"Read, read, and read more, Shabnam. You'll see in every step of life, there are more choices than you think. I promise."

The discussions were awakening and satisfied a deep need in me. It felt like home to my emotions.

I learned more about Jean Paul Sartre and Simone de Beauvoir and the concept of existentialism. Their modern thoughts and ideas, as well as their interesting and unique love relationship, long-term lovers and partners who never married, fascinated me.

I started matching my new knowledge to older thoughts from other books. When Annette, the protagonist of L'Âme enchantée, chose to keep her baby but called off her engagement and had a child out of wedlock in 19th-century France, she chose freedom for her soul over becoming an object in her future husband's life. She observed how empty other wives' lives were despite their beautiful dresses and houses. They had empty hearts, a judgmental attitude toward others, and had to endure the existence of their husbands' mistresses. She took a different path. Not an easy path, but a path that suited her dignity. Learning from her, my favorite character back then, I didn't expect an easy path to freedom, but I wanted to walk that path. It was, after all, the same path taken by my first heroine, the little black fish.

Mina and I talked about women's rights on our long walks after our classes every day, usually on Pahlavi Street. It was the longest road in Tehran with tall, old trees and narrow creeks with fat rats hovering around. Walking under the shade of the trees was always a pleasure. One day, we got to talking about sexual desires.

Mina said, "One important right for women is enjoying our sexual desire, but it is not encouraged in Iran. We are told to be shy and not to expect pleasure if we want to be rated as good women according to society norms."

What she said lit a lot of lights in my head. I had never talked about sex as an adult before. With a wondering tone of voice, I said I had enjoyed sex until I was upset at my husband all the time. Now I understood why Farshad was so surprised when I was not sexually shy at first. I suddenly understood a lot of comments from other women complaining about their husbands wanting to have extramarital sex. Wives were supposed to be available for their husbands all the time but were not allowed to enjoy it. Being shy about sex and during the act of sex was a proof of goodness for a woman. I was glad that old school of thought never reached me. I was glad my mother never taught me anything about sex.

Since our classes were girls only, I got to know only girls. Farnaz, who always looked serious, asked interesting questions about philosophy, didn't gossip, and became a good friend. She had her own curiosity, encouraged by her mother, who thought progressively for her era. Farnaz and I had long walks and talks, and she stayed over at my apartment sometimes. We listened to music and studied together, which was helpful since I hated studying physics, especially alone. She was independent, searching for freedom and happiness, too, and we shared a lot of values. Those friendships were my treasures and helped keep up my spirits.

One night Farnaz and I sat at the dining table with the windows open, enjoying the fall breeze. From my cassette, recently smuggled from California, came the sound of the latest from Ghomeishi, a popular Iranian singer. Farnaz was being trained by Mrs. Parisa, the famous voice instructor, who was working secretly since women's voices were banned in Iran. In a beautiful voice, Farnaz started singing along.

Caged birds are used to loneliness
All their life they sit alone at the corner of the cage
They don't know what travel is
They don't know what is homeless lover
They don't know how easily the free bird would fall in love in the rain
Whoever scatters grains for them
they would think that person is their God
they have no lover all their lives
There is no difference when you don't see and you don't know
It's sorrowful when you know and see

I told Farnaz I felt like that caged bird. I said that while Farshad was not a bad person, he was possessive and wanted to dictate my life plan, which was different from the plan I had for my daughter and myself. Talking to her helped me to articulate my thoughts.

I said I wanted to be more than Mrs. P, our first floor neighbor whose life was all about controlling her husband.

Farnaz said, "She has a small world. You know more. You can live better, Shabnam. Now that you live apart, you need to think and decide for your future. Think about it. What is the best for you and Parnian? No one can give you direction," she said. She got me thinking, hard.

We found books about philosophy and sociology—translated or written by some great Iranian authors—to read and talk about. More freedom shone through the publishing industry in the era of Mohammad Khatami's presidency compared to the years before, and we took advantage of that. Before the revolution, Western philosophy, sociology, and classic novels were all translated with good quality. After, even The Great Gatsby was censored. We looked for and found those old copies on the underground market. Every book Farnaz and I bought was a gemstone to add to my secret treasure box. We discussed them walking to school or on those endless nights at home. I dreamt of being able to read books in English one day, all those books that had not been translated to Farsi.

Farnaz had heard about a new English school using a novel method. Since first grade, I had gone to many English schools, but they taught grammar only. I still had no clue how to speak or understand a text in English. This school covered all four language skills: reading, writing, listening, and speaking. The only drawback was that it was four days per week, 1.5 hours per day. Learning English was a door to the world beyond the closed geographical borders of Iran. Farnaz decided to sign up. I wanted to go with her badly but the time commitment was too much, considering it was far from my parents' house and I would have to hide it from Farshad and lie about a reason for needing money.

Farshad often called midday just to see if I was home at my parents'. I told lie after lie. "I took Parnian to play with her friends." "I stayed at school because a difficult exam was coming up."

What were a few more lies? I registered for the English class. Parnian's clothes and toys suddenly become more expensive. Since there was no credit card and therefore no credit card statement, I got away with it. I went as far as saying my English class money went to charities. He was suspicious but didn't have the tools to prove anything, and since he was making good money, he was less careful with it.

I was becoming an expert in subterfuge. It took a lot of energy to keep my lies straight, but doing so took me to where I was heading. I missed a lot of the English classes, especially when I had to go to Kish Island to visit, but I attended as many as I could. It was slow progress but it was progress. I was finally learning correctly!

Farnaz and I had some deep philosophical conversations with one of our physics teachers, Professor Bashiri. Tuesday evenings after our analytical mechanics class with him from 7:00-9:00, Farnaz and I usually went to my apartment, walking partway before taking a cab. Professor Bashiri lived close to my apartment, and once we saw him walking, we joined him, and then so did a couple more students. Tehran has cold winters but it didn't matter to us. Bundled up in big coats, we talked and walked.

He recommended books to read and told us to ask questions and not be shy.

Perhaps emboldened by this, I asked how he felt when he played tar, a traditional Persian string instrument he had built himself. I didn't play any instrument, but Farnaz played *setar*, another Persian instrument, and I had enjoyed watching and listening to her play many times. Professor Bashiri said it was one joy when you built a *tar* and played it but it was a greater joy when you played your own *tar* with a group of musicians and felt the harmony, became one. This experience gave him the capability of loving everyone and loving life. It took him to a world higher than daily routine.

Oh, I longed for something like that. I didn't dare sign up for a music class, though; I had enough secrets to hide. It was enough that Mr. Bashiri confirmed what I had suspected: Life was bigger than my small world, which I needed to expand.

Everyone was talking about the presidential candidate Mohammad Khatami and his ideas about democracy. But he was a mullah like the rest of them. Even if he had good intentions, which I doubted, he wouldn't have the power to correct our broken Islamic constitution. I argued that we shouldn't even bother to vote because it got us nowhere. The regime needed to go away.

"Shabnam," Mr. Bashiri said, "we are going to choose between worse and the worst. It may not be a good choice, but it is still a choice. We need to vote even if it makes things only a little better for us." I couldn't argue against that but had my doubts and continued thinking about it. It disgusted me to participate in a mullah's election.

We talked about the meaning of life, of humanity, of freedom. It fed my soul. We usually walked more than two hours, so engrossed in our discussions that we did not feel the time or the cold. Our subjects were not condoned by Islam. If the school's security department found out about our sojourns, we students could be expelled and Professor Bashiri fired. To be safe, we never talked about those subjects at school, only outside of school. He trusted us and we trusted him. I hoped nobody saw me walking with him—even in a group—because that would be scandalous, a married woman speaking with a man who was not her relative. It was usually dark, but a group of people on a busy street drew attention. It was risky, but the joy of it was bigger than my fear.

Once, Bashiri said, "The opposite of love is not hate, it is indifference. As long as you hate someone, you still have some feeling for that person. You still have strings attached to him. When you are indifferent, it is like that person doesn't exist in your life anymore." At that moment, I realized Farshad was long gone from my life. I had no feelings for him anymore, good or bad.

Still I had to visit him on Kish Island for a few days every month, which took me away from school and my friends. He shared his apartment with four coworkers, so sometimes Parnian and I stayed in a hotel, and sometimes his coworkers cleared out for us. Either way, Farshad always picked us up from the airport. He put me straight to work cleaning their apartment and cooking a lot of food with all the groceries I had carried from Tehran. That was what a good and loving wife did.

On his way out, he said, "Are you comfortable here in the apartment working? I'll take you to the hotel after work. You should be done by then, right?"

"Yes, Farshad *jan*," I sweetly lied. The sound of the door closing behind him was the best music to my ears. He was gone for a few hours.

I made sure Parnian enjoyed her visits. When my chores were done, we spent hours at the playground or on the white sand beaches of the Persian Gulf while her father was at work.

The island was a tax-free zone, and retail prices were reasonable. It had many big shopping malls, each with interesting architecture, which attracted many tourists and businessmen and women. Farshad asked us to join him during the evenings at the store he managed. He said he missed Parnian.

To pass the time at the store, which sold decorative crystal trinkets, gorgeous and shiny, one night I started helping customers. The beauty of each object sparked a discussion with interested customers.

Before I knew it, Parnian had run fearlessly out of the store. I flew around the mall looking for her, stopping by every store and looking in. Finally, the salesperson from next door walked toward me with her in his arms. I ran toward them and grabbed her. Victoriously, oblivious to my worry, Parnian held out a giant piece of candy. When I told her she should not have run off, she turned away and started singing.

I wrote her name, the store's name, and the store's phone number on a piece of paper and taped it to her chest. But after just a few words with another customer, I looked up to see the piece of paper on the floor by the store entrance. Abandoning my customer, I ran after her. Another neighbor who knew us returned her this time. I put the name tag on her back where she couldn't reach it. I wasn't truly worried; since we knew the other shop owners, she was safe in the mall. Plus it was an interesting adventure for her; the small store was not the place for her to be entertained. Farshad of course did not see it that way. "You are a careless mother. Why do you let her go loose?"

I didn't go back to the store. It was a lot of work for me to run after her, and I hated to lock her down and micromanage her. All I wanted was the visit to be over so I could fly back to Tehran, to my world. In Tehran I felt confident and alive.

****

I still felt passionate about sailing, and at school I heard about The Environmental Aquatic School and National Association of Aquatic Techniques and Science. I planned to visit the campus immediately. Since I hated physics, my passion for sailing turned my thoughts turn toward switching to something nautical. I got to know one of the sailing school graduate students, Farah. She was in charge of the association, and I met her at the campus. She was sweet, communicative, and active. She wore her head scarf tight, covering all her hair, unlike mine. From this I knew she practiced Islam for her heart, not the government. I told her of my interest and the possibility of a major change. I asked whether I could get involved with any activities at her school. She said I could help with association activities. It was one of the happiest moments of my life. I could figure out later how to hide it from Farshad.

A couple of months after I started volunteering at the association, Farah offered to pay me for planning for the annual conference. I felt like a grown up with a job for the first time in my life. I was working in an environment that was all about ocean and sailing and I was getting paid? The dream of becoming a sailor surged like an ocean wave.

Getting to know professionals in the sailing industry, I started building a network, taking careful notes about everyone I met in a little phone book. Naturally, I had to hide this treasure, since most people I got to know were men. Farshad would be livid if he found it and might force me to quit school altogether.

I signed up for a computer class—DOS. Farshad would be opposed, of course. Sick with fear he'd catch me, I signed up anyway. I had to build my skills any way I could.

My parents knew little about my activities aside from the facts I was going to English school and volunteering for an association. They saw me spending a lot of time outside of the house and coming home happy each night. They saw how my life was unfolding by exploring the outside world. They supported me with no comments, taking care of Parnian and letting me be. My father opposed hiding in general and knew I hid a lot of my life from my husband. But he said nothing. He helped care for Parnian; weather permitting, he took her to the playground every afternoon to let her play with other kids. His nickname was the best grandpa in that park. I felt so lucky to have my parents.

Then Farshad called home two days in a row while I was out. I lied, saying I had been out with my friend Farnaz to buy fabric to sew a dress for Parnian.

It didn't matter. "You are out all the time. Farnaz is a single girl and a distraction. You need married friends who will be a good influence."

On the phone we did nothing but argue, unless I grew distant and avoided any answer that would heat things up more. He must have sensed my distraction and it must have made him insecure. I was passive aggressive, agreeing to his demands but never meeting them. One day he told me to learn to drive. "My parents need a lot of help and you are the one in Tehran who can take them to their doctor appointments or shopping." The next day he said, "Forget about driving. You would only go off to do your silly things, taking your friends out for fun instead of helping my parents."

****

Eventually, perhaps influenced by my distant behavior, he decided to quit his well-paying job with not even a penny in his saving account. He had spent all his money taking people out and buying them gifts, buying friendships. That satisfied him.

In February of 1997, he came back to find a job in Tehran and to be close to his family. We rented another apartment, close to my parents.

He started spending time with his uncle and his family almost every night again. I stayed home with Parnian. I wanted to have time to read and learn, but mainly I did not want to be around him.

I had to quit my job at the association. I had to quit English school. I felt I was in prison. I started secretly studying books related to ship design and shipbuilding. I hid them among my college books, covering them with newspaper. Many were in English, so I bought English cassettes. I ironed his shirts in front of the TV while listening to the courses, always on alert to shut them off and hide the tapes behind the TV stand as soon I heard his footsteps on the staircase.

I made a mess of books on the dining table so my sailing, philosophy, and sociology books would not stand out. It looked like I was into physics and studying hard, but in truth the only books I was not reading were my schoolbooks. One day, he started asking questions about my friends at school and their marriage status. As I was trying to answer his questions, calmly and carefully, he plucked a little phone book from the mess of papers and books. He started flipping through pages. All he saw were family members' phone numbers; how relieved I felt he had not picked up my other phone book!

But suddenly he grew suspicious. "Where are your school friends' numbers?" Of course they were in my secret phone book.

"They are in my mother's phone book." After all, I had lived in my parents' house while he was gone. I don't know how I came up that lie so fast, and I don't know why he didn't poke holes in it, but although he was dissatisfied with this answer, he dropped the conversation. Maybe he did not really want to know the truth.

He controlled my dress code ever more tightly, criticizing everything I wore. Thanks to the new reformist president Khatami, it was now okay on the street to leave some hair out and wear a scarf loosely. I could get away with it with the *Basij* but not with Farshad.

From his standpoint, I deserved to be shouted at and reminded of my sins all the time. He rubbed his finger on the TV stand and showed me dust. "You're distracted." I was distracted. I was resisting him dragging me back in history.

For decades, people had bought sheets and curtains from the store, pre-sewn and ready to use. My grandmother perhaps sewed all her sheets and curtains. But Farshad told me to learn how to sew the sheets and curtains instead of buying them from the store, saying I had never learned how to live economically. "I sent you too much money from Kish. You got spoiled."

Parnian was three and a half. I had signed her up for a painting class close to home, and she loved playing with colored pencils. Her teacher was a sweet young woman aware of the colorless authoritative environment, trying to teach little children about a colorful life which seemed far from reality under the Islamic dictatorship. She looked at her students' paintings for clues about their family life. She explained "Look at the image of you and Parnian hand in hand smiling in her painting. She is comfortable with you." That was advanced psychology back then, and she was smartly using it to help her students. Parnian seemed happy with her colorful paintings. She loved to run to me and my parents to show us every single thing she painted. We looked at them carefully and told her we loved the colorful pictures she created.

She ran to her father one night with a painting. He had come home that night with an angry face and been silent most of the night. She looked at him with big bright eyes. "*Baba, Baba*, look how pretty it is. Do you like it?"

He glanced at it and said, "Yes *azizam*, what have you painted here?"

Looking at it, Parnian thought for a few seconds and said, "It is a picture of you, *Baba*."

He tossed the picture aside, put his hands on Parnian's little shoulders, and yelled that there was nothing in that painting indicating it was him. "You have no idea who your father is! It's my fault for leaving you, going to Kish. Trusting your careless mother."

Parnian started crying. I grabbed her from him shouted at him, calling him unreasonable and fanatic. I took her to her room, wiping her tears, telling her the painting was pretty. "Baba is not angry at you, *azizam*. He is angry at something else."

Farshad grabbed his coat and walked out. I wished he wouldn't come back.

I had put up with this behavior since day one. By lying and being passive, I was condoning it, not standing up for my rights. I did not understand the consequences of my conflict-avoidant behavior. I was so naïve. I married Farshad to escape the environment full of fights created by my parents, and I ended up with conflicts myself. Like the old saying goes, "The lesson repeats itself until it is learned." I stood up to him that night, but I still had a long way to go to truly resist him and build the lifestyle I wanted.

****

About a month after he returned to Tehran, a cold night in March 1997, Farshad arrived home, bringing my parents. I looked from him to them for some explanation, but all I saw was seriousness, with no hint of what this was about. We sat down in the living room and endured an awkward silence for a few long moments. He finally said, "I asked your parents to come here because we need to make an important decision tonight." Of course be "we" he meant himself and by "need to make" he meant "already have made."

"I am going to complete my military service. You and Parnian will move in with my father (to supervise us) in a small town." His father had spent all money from selling condos and had no more. His mother had left his father with what little money she had saved and lived outside Tehran, too. There would be no tuition money for college. We would break the lease on our apartment.

"Your staying with my father helps us financially, and it helps him. He should not stay alone; he is getting old. You will help him."

He wanted to keep me away from all my activities, imprisoned under his opium-addicted father's watch? I asked my parents to leave, and they did, looking sad. I imagined they wondered how they could stop this.

But Farshad had finally gone too far. By proposing this plan, he pushed me over an edge I had seemingly been waiting for. At the moment he wanted to squelch me down the most, I finally found the courage to switch from the wrong path I had taken. My parents would take me back. They were fed up with his behavior, too. Then I would create a better future. I will make up for all my mistakes.

Without a word, I took Parnian to her bedroom. We both wore pajamas. Without changing clothes, I put Parnian in her bright green coverall and slipped into my own coat. Farshad's lay on the sofa smoking, eyes closed. I stood before them with Parnian. "We are going to the park," I said.

He did not open his eyes. "Go to your parent's house," he said.

It felt like he didn't want to watch us leave, like he knew it was the end. I walked out. Closing the door behind me felt like freedom. Out!

I walked to my parents' house two blocks away. My mother opened the door, surprised to see me there so soon after they had left. My father came to the door, just as curious. I entered and closed the door behind me. My mother grabbed Parnian, and they stood there, silent, reading my face but waiting for me to say the words.

"It's over," I said simply.

There was a silence for a few seconds. Looking at my father but talking to me, in a confident, quiet voice my mother said, "This is your house. It always has been."

Although he remained silent, relief was on my father's face. Ordinarily, when married women came home in Iran, fathers sent them back to their husbands; a divorced woman created scandal with every step she took in her life. But my father had not accepted my marriage in the first place. He saw clearly how fanatical Farshad had been all along. I was blind. Of course my father never wished to see me go through a painful divorce, but he must have known it was the only path to freedom for both me and Parnian.

In those few seconds and with those few words and the love expressed on our faces, we created a new bond among the four of us. Without saying it aloud, we promised to be in this together.

Parnian needed to sleep. My mother carried Parnian, and I went to my old bedroom. My bedroom. It felt like home like never before. I lay down on my bed, listening to my mother singing a lullaby for Parnian. I knew I had made the right decision.

A few minutes later, when my father called Farshad to let him know I was staying at their house that night, Farshad asked my father to come over for a talk. He did, and listened to Farshad patiently, empathized with him, and told him firmly what my decision was. When he returned, all he said was that Farshad felt devastated.

I felt nothing but certainty and relief. It was not just our different values; it was his inability to take on the responsibility required to build a family. He was not capable of it.

****

I stayed in my room for a couple of days, refusing to answer any phone call coming from Farshad's sisters.

They wanted to soften my heart. I did not feel like explaining myself to anyone. I stayed in my solitude and left my parents at on the frontline to inform family members. It must have been difficult. Everyone felt a need to step in and give advice, since this separation and our pending divorce made no sense to them: Farshad didn't beat me, he didn't cheat on me, and he was not a drug addict. What was I thinking? I hid behind the closed door, thinking, oh, people. Oh, Persian culture. You don't get it.

A few days later my mother sat on my bed playing with Parnian. I sat in the chair behind my desk next to the bed. Without looking at me she said, "I made a mistake encouraging you to marry Farshad. I, of all people, understand what a bad relationship is. I have lived most of my life being in the wrong relationship with your father. You should not repeat my mistake. You have a life ahead of you. I will help you with Parnian. I will support you as much as I can."

Silent, we sat without looking at each other, but in the silence I could feel the beginning of a new relationship.

Nowruz, Persian New Year, was coming up. March 21st, the first day of spring, is the first day of the solar calendar, Iran's official calendar. Nowruz is usually the beginning of a two-week holiday including a lot of family gatherings. I was not looking forward to that and felt happy when I came down with laryngitis and lost my voice right on the first day of the New Year.

I did not need advice. I did not want to listen to anyone trying to change my mind. I did not need anyone to remind me that Farshad could legally take Parnian; divorced mothers had no custody rights. They could keep residential, but not legal, custody of daughters only until age two and sons until age seven. If the father decided the mother should not visit her children, he could enforce it with legal support.

Despite the fact that my parents and I provided all her care, the law would never give me custody of my child. Farshad was the default. His father was next in line. If neither one were alive, the paternal family can determine the child's fate. Failing all of them, the mother may have a voice. Farshad may have refused care for her, but she was legally his.

I stayed far from the Nowruz celebrations that year.

Between leaving Farshad and the *Nowruz* holiday, I had not attended any of my classes at school. A few of my friends from school called to let me know a woman had shown up looking for me. It had to be Najva, Farshad's sister, so I didn't return to school that semester. The only way to follow my decision was to totally isolate myself for a while.

****

After a few weeks, my divorce decision was no longer headline news among the family members. I started to come out of my room and the house, I started returning to some of my routines.

One of the first things I did was learn to drive. My father patiently (!) taught me, and I passed the test. I appreciated that he was doing anything he could to help me walk my new path.

After the New Year holidays, when offices were back to work, I returned to my part-time job at the association, but I needed to make more money than Farah had work to pay me for, so I looked for other opportunities.

My father smoked a lot, deep in his thoughts, but surprisingly, he didn't drink that much. He felt responsible for Parnian and wanted to make sure he was available for her. I had overheard him talking to my mother a couple weeks before. He reminded her that no one had listened to him when he tried to warn us. "What are we supposed do with a young woman and a child in this house? I don't know if she can get her degree. I doubt Shabnam can take care of her life independently. What about when we are not around?"

I was crushed. Tears rolled down my cheeks. My father, who always told me to become an independent woman, had given up on me.

After that conversation with my father, she seemed more intent on reminding me to study harder for my college courses. "You focus on studying. I'll take care of Parnian."

I don't know what my mother told Aunt Sara, her sister, about her concerns, but one day out of nowhere she called to say her friend, who owned and managed a private school, wanted to see me; she had an opening to fill. It was not an interview; she hired me on the spot as a part-time, middle school sociology teacher. I accepted it to avoid offending my aunt and to reassure my parents about my future. But it was not the job I had in my mind.

The National Association of Aquatic Techniques and Science conference we had been planning was in May of 1997, on Kish Island of all places. Farah and I flew there to take care of the administrative work for attendees. I had also prepared a wall presentation about different types of fishing boats in southern Iran with the help of Captain Babaee, a retired naval officer who had organized the seminar.

As I stepped down from the airplane at the Kish Island airport, I noticed the breeze and inhaled deeply. It felt so different from all the times I had come there to visit Farshad. This time, the air smelled like the bittersweet scent of Turkish coffee and freedom mixed together. Both were my favorites.

****

My father, with his law background, helped me to apply for the divorce I had no legal right to. I could apply, but it would go nowhere without Farshad's agreement. On the other side, he could have decided anytime, unilaterally, to divorce me.

Over the course of the next few months, Farshad and I had many bad fights. He saw picking up Parnian an opportunity to try to talk me into going back to him (though not because he understood what caused me to leave), so I did not let him come up to my parents' condo. He had not changed. "What do you think people think of us or of you? People look down on divorced women." It was sad watching him try to change my mind, but I refused to engage. We never had two-sided communication anyway. Neither after our separation nor before did I feel I could speak freely. I was hurting, but I had no regret. I felt more sure of my decision every day.

In June 1997, the presidential election brought reformist Mohammad Khatami into office. My parents and even I voted. Mohammad Khatami offered a little freedom by giving permission to publicize more movies, plays, books and even music (Women were still banned from singing). Libraries became more active and many recreational art institutes began offering music and painting classes to children and adults. There were cultural conferences, and the annual book festival in Tehran offered more titles. People openly embraced opportunity. Economically, however, Khatami mainly followed in the footsteps of the former president, Akbar Rafsanjani. The aftermath of war was still hitting the economy badly and corruption had only gotten worse. Lessons I learned more about in the coming years.

I started raising Parnian more freely, by my standards as before but with no fear of her father now. I signed her up for social activities, art classes, and dance classes to keep her active and happy. I read her any type of book I wanted, The Little Black Fish among them. I made sure to plant the seed of freedom in her heart.

Khatami's more open leadership only took the country so far, and it certainly didn't trickle down into Farshad's mentality. Unfortunately, Parnian soon learned to watch what she said around her father. It was impossible to avoid hiding and pretending in that society, but it was worse with him. One way or the other, subterfuge became part of our lives. Everyone was careful. No one could escape. Everyone needed many masks to present herself properly for different people. With all these conflicting versions of ourselves, inner peace didn't seem achievable.

My father and I made many trips to court and endured its bureaucracy while Farshad stalled. My father didn't allow me to go there alone. Court was stressful: women with sad faces, hoping to escape addicted husbands who beat them; mothers crying because they were not allowed to see their children after the divorce. They would go back to the unfair judiciary system to ask for their motherly right and would get nothing. They looked miserable, but they still kept a little hope by coming back to the court.

Finally, one day my father and I were sitting on the bench at the end of the room waiting for my first hearing. I knew Farshad would not show. Each woman called had only a couple of minutes to present her case. Most were crying, which took half their time. The judge, usually a cleric in Iran's court, yelled at them: "Speak clearly! I don't understand what you're saying." If one managed to speak a little clearer, she said, "For a year he hasn't let me see my children. He divorced me because of that new woman. How am I to blame?"

Harshly, the judge explained the law: She had no legal custody. All she could do was submit another request. They would serve it to their husband's house, which would take a few months. If he showed up for the next court date, he might allow a visit. It was terrifying.

They called my name and we walked to the front. The judge asked if my father was my lawyer. I gathered all the politeness I could and said, "No sir, he is my father. But he would like to answer the questions."

"If he is not your lawyer, he cannot speak for you. What is your problem?"

What was my problem? All of a sudden, I felt insecure and small. Meekly, I said that Farshad did not have a job or income and that he was stopping me from continuing my education.

"That's it? Do you hear yourself? Go back to your husband. He will find a job soon. Do you want to lose your daughter? A child belongs to her father. Look at these women. This will be your future too." He looked at his secretary and asked for the next person. He was finished with me, and my father took me out of the room. It was obvious Farshad had no capacity to raise a child by himself; he had admitted as much to my father and said he was scared of losing his relationship with her. He would not take Parnian from me. She and I were safe with my parents.

We went back to the drawing board: My father, to make sure we took the right steps and saved money, consulted his lawyer friends. They suggested a different approach.

To put pressure on Farshad I could request the dowry he had never paid. I never wanted it; I was not an object to trade. But now it was our only recourse. According to the law a wife was entitled to her dowry and could request it any time, and her husband had to pay. If he could not, the judge created a payment plan. If he still refused, he could go to jail. I knew Farshad had no money. Since he refused to cooperate, we filed an official dowry request— a conditional one. I would waive the dowry if he agreed to divorce. I received my official divorce in March 1998.

CHAPTER SEVEN

1997 – 2000

With Farshad out of my life, I felt free and was more active than ever. My volunteer job at the association helped me build a network. To pursue a career, I made phone calls and appointments to speak with different people in the field about my dream job: sailing officer. Women had started entering engineering jobs but still in that culture the job was associated with masculine personalities. No one could imagine a female sailor.

In fact, women did not hold professional positions in sailing at all. I was serious though. Maybe I could get out of the country. My heartbeat went up talking about sailing on a ship, going to the middle of the ocean, and landing in different countries. It was exciting to imagine a lifestyle free of clichés. My heart was begging me. What if I could do it? I reached out to anyone who could possibly give a hint of what to do.

A couple of people took my words seriously. One said I should send letters to sailing schools and request their admission requirements, but I didn't even know how to find such schools. The internet was new and not so vast as now. I searched, but the result wasn't clear. One person suggested a sailing school in Belize, which one of the smallest and farthest countries in the world, and expensive. Other people politely dismissed me after hearing my wild thoughts. It was frustrating. I wanted to build a life full of adventure for Parnian and me.

Among the association members I reached out to that summer, one, "Captain," seemed to be in his early forties. He had a mature face, and he paused before he answered questions. He was thoughtful and listened to me attentively. Although he appeared serious, a sharpness in his deep blue eyes traveled to the middle of my heart, and reassurance in his masculine voice made me feel confident. I was comfortable answering his questions about my personal life, but I was hesitant to confess my crazy idea of becoming a sailing officer. After a couple of sessions at his office discussing membership questions, I saw he thought deeply and put things in perspective, so I tossed my idea out there.

"Captain, have you traveled a lot? Are there opportunities for a woman to become a sailing officer? I have always dreamed of having your job. I want to go see the world."

With a kind smile he said a few countries did accept women for commercial crew sailing trainings, but it would be a few hard years away from Parnian. "What will happen to her education?" he asked. "I had to stop sailing because of my kids. I got an office job to stabilize their status. What if you got another job, something related to the sailing industry?" He said another job might at least involve business trips, since they were international.

"Start with something here and go further. You seem capable and motivated. With your English classes, computer classes, and part-time job, you're already ahead of other young women. Plus, you are studying a good major in college. You will be an independent woman soon."

Or course, he had no idea about my bad grades at school, but still, he saw my work and thought I was capable. Was I? It was hard to accept his compliment, but I liked it. I had never heard a compliment like that before. His voice echoed in my mind, reassured me. A few days later I asked whether he was aware of any openings for such a job. He suggested I work as a quality systems analyst on a project related to sailors' qualifications. It sounded great, but how? I had no idea what a quality systems analyst did.

He explained the department of sailors' qualifications was part of the sailing and ports affiliation agency. This organization was mandated by an international sailing organization to establish quality management standards. The concept of quality management had found its way to Iran just recently, by international mandates and as a result of Iranian companies wanting to be more competitive internationally.

He said I would have to learn the standards, analyze companies' processes and procedures, and diagnose the gap. "You will help them write procedures to follow the standards fully." Then an auditor would evaluate what I had done and whether the companies had met the standards. Captain gave me documents to study.

He said he could recommend me for an internship at an engineering consultancy. It was exciting, but I said I doubted I could do the job. He said the internship would teach me. He leaned on his desk, looking at me intensely, decreasing the distance between us. "You can do it. Don't doubt." I felt enchanted.

I called the senior executive, Mr. Mardan, of the company, Tavana, introduced myself and scored an interview, but I was nervous. What if he didn't like me? I had no background. I studied the documents (all in English) Captain gave me but had no idea what they were about. They were complicated.

Mr. Mardan was a young man, tall and chubby with green eyes and a big smile. I instantly felt comfortable. He started asking questions about my background and education. I caught his interest with magic words: "I am a physics student." With that on the table, his questions became easier. Tavana was a small company and it would be an unpaid internship. He said I would have to help with anything, including administrative tasks. I was happy just to enter the industry.

It was not an official internship related to school, but the more hours I could spend on the internship, the faster I would get to a real job. That school year, I didn't go back to teaching. My parents were worried and my aunt angry about that, but I hoped to get hired at Tavana. Mr. Mardan hadn't promised to hire me, but I would try my best. I didn't want to lose the opportunity.

In October 1997, Iran beat Australia in the qualifying game for the World Cup for the first time since 1978, before the revolution. At the end of the second game marking Iran's eligibility for the World Cup, people poured onto the streets to celebrate. I was walking to my parents' house after a class when the game ended and I got caught up in a huge parade in Valiasr Square. Inside cars, walking on foot, on top of city buses, people shouted, danced, and waved their hands. No *Basij* could manage that crowd. I stood on the sidewalk watching people. Somehow, I didn't want to be part of the crowd. Instead I observed: People were so repressed that they went off the rails, celebrating beyond reason; it was pandemonium. There had been nothing like this demonstration in Iran after the revolution. Men and women, young and old happily waved at each other, beeping their horns and making any noise they could. But the powerful demonstration made me sad. It didn't matter. Religion still ruled the country and until it didn't, no one would be truly free.

The next day nothing remained of the excitement; instead trash littered the streets, and city bus seats bore scars of graffiti and rips. People went back to the bitter reality of their lives. The government and press were silent on the matter. Mullahs went on repressing people. People forgot they might have power to change their destiny. Repression so damaged people's consciousness that waking it up was not that easy. This regime was not going away. Iranians were in a big, invisible cage, and women were in smaller cages built by their husbands. I escaped the small one but breaking out of the bigger one required more work and preparation. I needed work experience, a degree, and English skills to be truly free.

In early fall of 1997, I started the internship eager to learn and progress. Every inch of my body wanted to excel.

It was a brand-new, small consulting company with only a few employees, so it was easy to get to know everyone quickly. Free-spirited Neda, our admin, was fun, assertive, and a deep thinker. She didn't behave diplomatically or conservatively, as other women in my life did. Her behavior helped me envision a different way to be. Her son, Ashkan, was Parnian's age. Soon, we started to go out after work with our kids, becoming close in no time.

Soft-spoken, smiling Shakeeb was the lead engineer who had graduated from a prestigious school and was a friend and schoolmate of Mr. Mardan. Shakeeb seemed like a kind grandpa despite his young age.

Kamran was another young industrial engineer who started at Tavana a few weeks before I did. He was caring, polite, and reserved. His thick black mustache appeared before him, entering the small office in the morning.

A third young industrial engineer, Reza, started a few weeks after me. Reza was confident and brash, always joking.

To my surprise, the three men accepted having a woman on their team. The atmosphere was a bit formal, but Neda broke the ice. At lunch times, if we sat silently or spoke formally, she told funny stories that helped us let down our guard. She made it fun. Soon, even during work hours, jokes and laughter flew around the office. We became a little family. Reza and Kamran taught me the basics of industrial engineering, which helped me understand the quality management standard structure. They answered my many eager questions without hesitation, making sure I was prepared for upcoming customer meetings. When for the first time, in the hallway of a car manufacturing company, Reza told me you go to that meeting and I have to attend another one, I panicked. "But Reza, I cannot do it without you!" As he was stepping away, he turned back, waved his hand and said, "You know everything you need for this meeting. You will be ok. Don't worry." I surprised myself by knowing the requirements needed to be disused, managing the meeting, and making a list of action items at the end. It was a meeting with purchasing department manager and his team. I put the confident mask on and explained how they need to write a manual for their transactions to cover ISO 9001 quality standard requirements and then explained how they needed to execute the manual phase by phase until it reached the final edition that could be approved by top management as the first version of their department manual. They listened to me respectfully and even asked questions. I was so proud of myself. Reza's reaction was, "I told you. I knew you could do it." I was learning how to make a cultural change. Perhaps being a woman made them to listen to me however they didn't do any of the homework I had assigned to them.

Because of their kindness, I felt safe to share my divorce status with everyone in the office, and they supported me emotionally when I was involved in conflicts dealing with Parnian's father.

Within a few months, in early spring of 1998, Tavana hired me as a part-time quality analyst on the sailors' trainings and qualifications project. My parents were happy but skeptical; they wanted a full-time job for me. But I was sure I was on my way, and enjoying every step of the journey.

Shakeeb knew more about quality management standards than anyone else, but it was still pretty new to everyone; no one had a lot of practical knowledge. We were fascinated by its systemic approach. In a country in which businesses and industries were all like little islands with their own kingdom, it was a new avenue to connect customers and businesses at all different levels. We joked about implementing quality management systems in our personal lives. We would commit to provide the requirements that we promised to the people around us as our personal customers. We enjoyed learning the concepts of continuous improvement, root cause of the problem, and corrective actions. These concepts were like cute newborns in our culture; we almost didn't know what to do with them.

It was much easier for me to learn through watching others and discussions than by reading textbooks. Soon, I could participate in discussions and even work on some actions on my own. The subject of quality systems management falls under systems engineering and could fit under a business major. It was cake compared to the abstract theoretical physics and math I still hated at school.

Still cautious and scared of *Basij*, my work friends and I nevertheless threw parties in our houses with music, dance, and booze (though I still didn't drink). Almost every weekend we were at someone's house for another party. We added friends of friends to our Tavana circle of Neda, Reza, Kamran, and Shabnam. Parnian and Neda's son the same age, had a grand time playing with each other. Sometimes uncle Kamran would sit Parnian on his laps and carefully painted her little nails with red nail-polish. Reza was good at joking with Parnian and making her laugh, like belly laugh that made everyone else laugh. We became a close circle like family together.

When it was my turn to have a party, everything was going well. Music blasted from the stereo. My cousin Nima prepared his guitar to play later. A few friends danced in the middle of the living room, and I ran to the kitchen for more glasses.

There, I found my mother, furious. She had heard my friend Hossein had gone out to get more alcohol. "You gather all these low-class people who drink and dance and don't do anything else." I was lucky the music was blasting in the living room. Of course she hated alcohol because of my father's violence. I didn't like it either, or never drank myself, but people expected it at parties. To calm her, I promised no one would get drunk, but her anger did not affect me much. I was financially independent, proof that I could manage my life despite her lack of faith in me. She could no longer control me.

My father, however, came home completely drunk that night, late, after everyone had left. My mother had recently made a pilgrimage to Mecca, Saudi Arabia, and had become more strict in her religious practices, for example wearing her headscarf inside the house. My father hated it of course. When he arrived that night, my mother was doing her nightly prayers. He started picking on her, mocking her practice, a favorite mean-spirited drunken game. I quickly escaped, going to check on Parnian, who slept peacefully. My mother finished her prayer, and, still seated on her *sajadeh* (small prayer rug), she said to my father, "Shame on you. I am an idiot wasting my life with you. I am the unluckiest woman in this world who had to live a nasty life with the worst guy on the earth."

My father laughed hard, the drunken laugh I hated. He yelled and cursed back. Then my mother yelled at me for having low-class friends who drank. Parnian woke crying and I tried to calm her. I am pretty sure neighbors did not appreciate the noise either.

****

Standards documents, particularly those related to ISO 9000, the international certification at the time, were mostly in English, which Captain, having been educated in Belgium in a college that offered all the courses in English, knew best. Because of his expertise and my strong motivation to learn English, we worked together on those tasks. Our conversations were mainly work related, but he also asked about my progress and encouraged me. He asked about Parnian, and his interest in my daughter touched my heart. Despite his serious personality, we spoke easily together.

In the heart of winter that year, one late afternoon, already dark outside, we worked in his 9th floor office filled with fancy white furniture. After a while he asked about my life and Parnian as usual. Farsi has formal and informal pronouns, and business conversations in Iran used the former, especially at the management level. But Captain had already started using the informal you in our conversations, and I liked it. I babbled happily, warm in his familiarity.

"You are doing great, girl," he said. He was happy for me. A man was glad I was making progress in my life. Farshad had wanted to stop me, and my father was critical or concerned. Captain's words reassured me. There was something special about him, the softness behind his serious eyes that I was drawn to, the strength behind his kind and encouraging heart.

When I got up to leave, he stood to open the door for me. In his small office, his chair was not too far from the door. But he didn't open the door. Instead, he leaned against the wall and looked at me intensely, saying nothing. I stood by my chair. I didn't move, but my heart beat hard. I returned his intense look. A strong current buzzed through my body, vibrating my heart. I wanted badly to take those few steps between us to find myself in his arms and kiss him. There were a long few seconds of silence.

I finally managed to say, "I have to go." I took slow steps towards the door, and he opened it. I said goodbye and rushed out, totally confused. I had never felt like that before.

****

A couple of months later, we were on the phone discussing work one afternoon. Then he said, "Maybe we should go out for a coffee sometime." Oh, how I wanted to hear that offer.

"That would be great. I go to English school every evening from 5 -7 but I can skip it anytime when you have time. Just let me know."

Next time I called him for work I hoped he would follow up, and he did. We planned to meet in a quiet coffee shop in the second floor of a shopping mall in an upper-class neighborhood of Tehran, where it would be safe to sit and talk and not worry much about *Basij*.

We met on the street outside the shopping mall on a cold, drizzling March day. Walking with him toward the coffee shop felt like I was walking on clouds. The impact of his presence was so different from anything I had experienced. As we walked, he spoke about his son's interest in soccer. He looked at me and asked if I were cold. He didn't wait for my answer, or perhaps my smile was my answer. He put his arm around me, with a smile, looked closely into my eyes, and continued walking.

We sat at a corner table in the furthest place of the coffee shop and talked for hours. I don't remember what we talked about but I vividly remember how I felt, in love. There was a smoothness in the air that I was inhaling and a softness of a velvet fabric on the chair that I was sitting on. My body temperature rose and heat came into my cheeks. He pushed his cup aside and reached across the table for my hands. At that moment of my life, everything was gentle. Did we think where we were going from that start? No. Everything was beautiful, and scary thoughts of the future would have damaged the moment.

He offered to drive me home when we left the coffee shop, and I asked him to drop me a few blocks from the house. He pulled over in a narrow quiet road and said he had a great time. I looked at him without being able to talk. He pulled me over and touched his lips to mine for a few long seconds. I was powerless in his arms. When I got out of the car I could hardly keep my balance, as if I were weightless.

At that age, I was still building my values. I could be judgmental when it came to morals and ethics. When I observed a man mistreating his wife, I judged him harshly for not respecting women's rights. But with Captain, I slipped. I did not see myself as a person crossing my own moral values. He was married, but I fell for him anyway, blind, headlong, heedless. I was 26, divorced, with a 5-year-old daughter. He was 39, married with two children. I should have been scared to step onto such a fraught path, but the pleasure of being with him was so profound that nothing seemed scary or sinful.

****

After a few times meeting in coffee shops, kissing, or holding each other on quiet park benches; driving aimlessly around the city, he suggested a day trip to his friend's vacation house outside the city. At that point, the fantasy of making love with him was almost unbearable. It needed to become reality.

It was spring but still cold with snow on the ground. The road to the house passed through the middle of the village, and our appearance as strangers attracted attention. People were religious and conservative; seeing us would make them think of the exact sinful act we were about to commit. They could create trouble—anything from slashing our tires to breaking into the house to attack us. At least that's what Captain thought, and anxiety overtook him.

The house was cold. Captain had to light the wood fireplace, which was difficult because the wood was damp. He grew frustrated, and I had no clue how to help. He asked me to watch out the window. Being caught with me would destroy his family life.

He gave up on the fire and found a thick blanket instead. As I watched outside through the corner of the window from behind the curtain, I felt his touch on my neck. I let the curtain go and turned my face to his. He pulled me into his arms and took my breath away with deep, passionate kisses. As he started undressing me, he suggested we go under the blanket. Before I knew it, we were both undressed and he was having orgasm. Just like that! Not only had he used no protection without asking if I was on birth control, he seemed oblivious to my pleasure or lack thereof. Still shocked and confused by the speed of all the events happening, I said, "It's a good thing I have an IUD."

He laughed. "I didn't think about it."

I didn't push to continue, although I was disappointed. Instead I justified his inconsiderateness, told myself he was nervous.

We were nervous about every sound outside and soon decided to leave; it seemed best to end the date despite how much we had both looked forward to it. It was clumsy, but I tried to understand the situation. He apologized for putting me in an unsafe situation but not for ignoring my sexual needs. Feeling sad to cut our time short, I said, "Don't worry, I understand. Our safety is the priority." Although I was thinking about the orgasm I had been fantasizing about for a long time, what did I expect from something so secret and forbidden?

I was still learning about life and shaping my personality, deciding what I wanted to do with my life. I was exploring different roles at school, at work, as a mother, as a daughter, as a friend and—the newest and most complicated—as a secret lover.

He had followed the cultural norm, building a stable, prestigious life: higher education, marriage, children, good career. He had become an important figure in his field, family, and community. He had achieved all the traditionally expected milestones. He had built a traditional family structure that excluded words such as divorce, career-oriented wife, or non-virgin wife. But, he was curious about my personality and desires, which at the time meant the world to me. I saw him as like Sinclair Lewis's character, Babbitt, who identified himself by his family and community's traditional values, yet longed to experience the bohemian life through his love affair with Tanis. Lewis understood the human contradiction of wanting the excitement of a nontraditional life, following desires that seemed unruly but smelled like freedom, but being unwilling to forgo the security of tradition. Captain, like George Babbit, wanted only to take a sneak peek and get back to his secure, prestigious comfort zone, repressing any thought of whether it was actually fulfilling.

****

College was not going well. I had no desire to study and no ability to connect with physics or math. In the office I was learning, gaining confidence, while in school I was hopeless. I stopped attending class, using the distance between the office and school as an excuse. But how long could I hide my disastrous educational status from my parents—and now my boss?

Physics was not the way, but I needed a degree, so I started thinking about changing my major to business. It meant dropping out of physics school to take *Konkour* again, and if I were accepted, it meant starting college over. I might have been able to transfer about 20 credits to a new school, but there was no guarantee I would even get in.

Only my school friends, especially Farnaz, knew how badly I was doing. She listened to my concerns but didn't agree with dropping out. But four years in that school with no major progress needed to be over. I needed to act.

Captain proposed focusing on school—putting everything else (work) aside for a while to finish. When I confessed how much I was suffering and failing at thermodynamics, quantum physics, and others, I felt like a total loser, but he said I shouldn't feel that way; I should make a change. I told him about retaking *Konkour* and applying for business school. He knew I was doing well at work, and he encouraged me to move forward with my plan.

He assured me I was capable of doing it. At work when I doubted my capabilities, especially signing freelance contracts all by myself, he encouraged me. "Go ahead and sign it. You can do it."

When I announced my decision to my parents and my friends, no one agreed. They thought I should finish my current degree. My parents especially saw little chance for me to get accepted again. But no one asked whether I could finish physics.

At a time when I had to make a lot of big decisions, Captain's strength and support reminded me I could walk through fear and move forward. His encouragements were genuine and therefore easy to believe. I needed his confidence at that time of my life.

When I dropped out, the dean called me to her office. She was the first woman to become the dean of our school and cared about her female students. She was calm, kind, and wise. She talked to me to make sure I had plans. She told me she wanted me to continue my education no matter what.

I signed up for the 1999 May *Konkour* and started studying one more time in my life. With all the projects at work, including many business trips by then, motherhood, and the social life of a mid-20s woman, it was hard to find time to study. It was much faster to read and study sociology, philosophy, history, and psychology for business school admission, but it was still all new to me. The only easy subject was math, since it was a much softer version of what I had studied before.

Things got harder when I received more responsibility at work because Reza left Iran to continue his education in France. I had limited time to study.

****

Although Captain and I enjoyed every minute together, we never talked about our emotions. Every time I complained about long waits between our dates and said I missed him, he started kissing me passionately, which made it hard for me to remember even my existence. He never talked about his feelings. I knew he cared about me through his actions and encouraging talks, but I was dying to hear about his feelings towards me.

Once, we had a conversation over a cup of tea in a quiet coffee shop. I asked him about expectations. With an anxious voice, he said, "Do you expect me to walk away from my family?" That made me feel badly about my constant complaints of not seeing him enough. I reassured him that was absolutely not my intention. Missing him was painful, but I was the other woman. What did I expect? The relationship was wrong and complicated and I knew it. We should end the relationship sooner rather than later.

That short conversation was perhaps the most we talked about how we felt towards each other.

Accepting this bitter reality, I dreamed instead of having a son with him and sharing my life with this son. Missing Captain and knowing he didn't belong in my life, dreaming of an international job, which was not easily possible in Iran, slowly became a dream of immigrating to another country, settling down with Parnian, and planning to have Captain's child. In Iran, having a baby as a single mother was out of the question. The child would literally not legally exist, and people's judgments would be intolerable. It simply could not happen. My fantasy was soothing and fulfilling, though. I wouldn't have to share his baby with anyone else. His baby—our baby—would belong to my life. Despite my strong desire to have a partner, I was ready to remain a single mother and would pay any price to raise his child. In my dream, I named the child "Arash," after my favorite mythical Iranian hero who sacrificed his life on an arrow to defend Iran against Turan "Arash Kamangir." (Arash the archer) My dream son, Captain's son!

Our encounters were short and infrequent but passionate. Once in his arms, I felt protected, my heart melted. He asked about everything going on in my life. I babbled like a happy little girl. He listened enthusiastically, kissed me, and played with my hair. He asked questions to make me think about better solutions or gave me comments and suggestions right to the point. No matter my doubts in myself, when he said, "Of course you can do it! You ARE an independent woman," it was easy to believe him.

Every moment with him was electro-magnifying and brought me back to life.

In his busy life, filled with work and family responsibilities, in addition to not being not available enough, he was forgetful. Once, I waited on the street for him for half an hour and finally found a public phone to call him. When he answered it was clear he did not even remember our date. I was furious. I said we were through and hung up.

During the next week, with every minute that passed I fought myself about whether I should call him. A week later, my manager said, "Captain wants you to call him as soon as possible for a translation case." I knew it was not urgent to translate the document. I was dying to call him. I jumped on the phone. I called him again and again. He forgot more dates; we broke up for a few weeks and rejoined again.

Every time we broke up, I promised myself to take a different path to build a future for myself and leave him alone. This relationship was heartbreaking. It needed to be over.

Once, he returned from a long business trip on a Thursday, which is the beginning of weekend in Iran. To distract myself from waiting for his call, I decided to paint my room. Parnian got excited about it. We bought everything we needed including some small brushes for her. Together we planned to make each wall a different shade of gray. While I was trying to have fun with Parnian on our project, every cell of my body was waiting for a call from Captain. I wished he hadn't told me when he would return. My brain told me he wouldn't call; he needed to spend his weekend with his family. My heart reminded me how badly I missed him. I was desperate to hear his voice—even for one minute.

We put music on and started painting. I allowed Parnian to paint anything she wanted on one small wall. We could cover it with a couple of extra coats of paint. She was in heaven, I was in hell. She giggled and painted a happy girl with a dark green skirt surrounded with flowers. "Mom, does this look good?" she asked after adding a little more detail to her painting. Before answering her, I checked my phone to make sure it worked. Then I said, "I love it. This is such a fun project."

We finished painting the room in two days, and for the entire time I waited for his call while I knew he would not call. I went up and down the ladder and brushed paint on the wall, hoping to numb my heartache, but nothing could take him out of my heart.

****

Working on that sailor's training and qualification project, I got to know a pleasant gentleman, Afshin. After we had worked together a while, during one of my breakups with Captain in the summer of 1999, he asked me out.

I thought this would be a good opportunity to stop thinking about Captain and eventually forget about him, as Afshin was a nice and gentle person. I accepted his invitation and we went out for dinner.

Society had relaxed a bit because President Mohammad Khatami was a little more open-minded than hard liners before him, and we were less fearful of *Basij*. Men and women were more comfortable showing up in restaurants or walking in the streets.

Walking next to him, I noticed how tall and handsome he was. His kind brown eyes were inviting. He was caring and sweet, with a good sense of humor that made me laugh.

We left the office separately and joined a few blocks away so no one from work would see us together. I wondered how to tell him I was divorced and had a daughter. I wanted to start a serious relationship. Despite my yearning to be independent, I felt invisible cultural pressure to be part of a couple. Even the thought of leaving Iran alone felt so hard. But my status was a deal breaker for most single men looking for marriage. There were virgin girls; why marry a divorcee or widow? Nonvirginal women were fine for sex, but that was it. I hoped he would be open-minded and nonjudgmental.

On the way to the restaurant, walking along Farmanieh Street, I asked why he wanted to date me.

He was generally shy but seemed comfortable with just me. "Because you are yourself." He smiled charmingly. "You don't hide anything."

"You have no idea about my life. Why do you think that?"

"Through your behavior at work. You're not complicated."

"Afshin, what if I told you I was divorced and had a daughter? Would you still say I was an honest person?"

"I'm sorry you're divorced," he said, "but that doesn't affect my feelings for you."

Did he really like me for who I was? He seemed an honest person.

Since Afshin and I both lived with our parents, once we started dating, we met up for dinner at restaurants or walked through parks, usually on weekends. We were caught by *Basij* one night walking in a park in Northern Tehran, but Afshin bribed them and they left us alone. On weekends my parents took Parnian to my aunt's vacation house, an hour and a half outside Tehran. I didn't enjoy joining them there; I preferred to spend time with my friends. My parents didn't complain. Despite the opportunity of an empty house, I never wanted intimacy with Afshin and didn't invite him over.

Since our most recent breakup, I had seen Captain a couple of times at the office and once at a conference. At the office I was polite, talking about business, while shaking inside and dying to kiss him. I left before everyone else so we wouldn't wind up alone together. At the conference, he sat a couple of rows in front of me. I could see his neck. I didn't listen to any of the lectures; instead, I only watched him and worried about when he would leave. I wanted to sit on his lap and hide myself in his arms. I tortured myself all day. At the end he approached my friend and me and said hello. I quickly said hi and hurried my friend out of there.

Afshin invited me to his friend's house while his friend was traveling. That meant sex, and I was not sure how I would react, but I gathered my courage and accepted the invitation. He was handsome, caring, and kind. We had known each other for a few months. It was around my birthday—the same birthday Captain never remembered.

At Afshin's friend's house, I sat on a chair a few feet from the door. He left me for a minute, then returned and covered my eyes from behind. I laughed. He uncovered my eyes and brought a small jewelry box into my line of vision. "Happy birthday!"

I felt so much joy; I felt genuine love. The gift was a beautiful gold anchor on a chain that he gently clasped around my neck. He drew me to his arms and kissed me. I kissed him back. I was surprised how passionate we were towards each other. I didn't expect it from myself. Maybe I was forgetting Captain. Maybe I was finding my way.

We were all over each other for hours, which passed quickly.

At home, that night I fell asleep thinking about Afshin and our sweet few hours. I fell in love with him.

A few days later I attended a training. The instructor was Captain, and I sat in that training watching him without hearing him, without recognizing any words. His voice resonated through my heart for the whole class.

I didn't answer Afshin's next call, or the one after that. Gradually I drifted off and distanced myself from him. He was confused, but I couldn't communicate. I woke up anxious every morning and I felt nauseous as I got ready for work. I couldn't tell him but I couldn't let him go, either. Why couldn't I accept the nice man who cared about me? Why did I fall for the one who kept me at arm's length all the time? The game of chasing him took all my energy, perhaps. Or was that all I knew about love? I had not seen people loving each other. To understand a romantic partnership, all I had seen was my parents and aunts and uncles around me who either fought with or manipulated their spouses. That is what love meant to me, to pursue and push back, and repeat. Unconditional kindness and acceptance weren't part of the game or I never thought I deserved it. But I was searching for it passionately, in the wrong people.

A couple of months later, his mother passed away. It would have been respectful for me to attend the funeral along with the other ladies at work, but fear of meeting his family and getting into a serious relationship made me refuse. Instead I simply called him and apologized. Kindly, he said he understood.

My heart had no emotional availability for another man. It was time to admit this, so I called Afshin and asked if we could be friends. With a kind but sad voice he said, "Yes, I understand." I felt horrible.

I called Captain. "When can I see you?" he asked warmly. "It has been too long." How I loved—no, needed—to hear that voice. It took me to the clouds.

****

A little after Captain and I had started our romance, he had introduced me to his sister. Sima, in her late twenties, was separated from her husband and thinking about divorce, but like millions of other Iranian women, even with no child, she was not independent enough to simply do it. It was not easy to start a new life—even with a basic lifestyle—while one was not financially or emotionally independent. Captain and his family tried to support her during that time, but that was not simple, either.

For a while she lived with his family. With little hope for the future, Sima became sensitive to people's reactions. Her emotional instability made it hard for her family and relatives to support her. I, on the other hand, a divorced young woman, was well suited to help. Captain introduced us, and we became friends. She trusted me as an impartial third party, just a listener. We had long phone conversations and sometimes met to speak in a park. I don't think I helped much but in that time maybe all she needed was a nonjudgmental ear. For me it was precious because Sima reminded me of her brother. I felt a little closer to him.

****

One night Captain stayed with me in my parents' apartment while they were away with Parnian. I wanted that night to be the longest night. It was late when he arrived. When I opened the door he walked in, dropping his small bag and pulling me into his arms. "We are so impatient for each other," he said. I started talking but he just kissed me more. I could never get enough of him. His touch, the warmth of his breath, and his whispers were magic.

While I was in his arms, he said a few words in English. "I learned English the best in college during sex with my girlfriends in Belgium." This irritated me, but I smiled and let it go. I didn't want to ruin our special night together. Anyway, college had been years ago.

That summer night, our closeness felt euphoric. There was no need for a drink or anything. I felt pretty and sexy in the short nightgown he had brought me from Europe. Lying next to me in his underwear after sex, he caressed me and talked with fondness about his childhood and his mother. He told me where she was buried and how much he missed her. "I never talk about these memories. I'm surprised I am telling you about them." I felt special, chosen. Such tiny intimacies felt good, were a small light in the dark shadow of knowing we had to end the relationship eventually. But as soon as I felt the sweetness of the moment, other thoughts attacked and reminded me that he belonged to his family, not me.

Every time I woke up that night, I looked at him sleeping next to me. It seemed like a dream, a short dream.

In the morning, we were nervous. My parents might come home early; his family might discover his absence.

He left before breakfast. My heart wanted to keep him but my brain let him go.

****

I got admitted to a business school outside of Tehran and re-started school in the fall of 1999. The new college accepted some of the credits I had earned at physics school, but there were a lot more to earn. I had two full days per week of classes. I took metro to go to school, and it was a long commute. It was hard with my almost-fulltime job and so many projects outside of Tehran. But there was no way around it, I needed a bachelor's degree.

My work travel was fun but came with challenges. On one trip with the sailing qualification office, under the ports and maritime organization at Chabahar, a small port located in southeast of Iran, I stayed in the guest house owned by the organization. As the only woman in the house I had to watch my behavior. As soon as I saw a ping-pong table, though, I forgot to do that. I asked Mr. Ghodsi, from the organization, to play. We found the paddles and balls and started.

Two days later, I was in our office at Tavana in Tehran when Mr. Mardan came to me with a teasing smile. By then we were comfortable with each other, like friends. He said, "So, I heard you had fun in Chabahar."

I looked at him, surprised.

"Ghodsi has received a warning for not behaving according to Islamic rules." Not believing in those strict rules, he said, "It's hard to be a young woman traveling to those areas. Watch your behavior, lady. Respect Islamic rules." We laughed, but I felt bad for Mr. Ghodsi. As a federal employee he could lose his job for such a warning. The federal office asked Mr. Mardan to have me do the job remotely or to send a male analyst instead.

A couple of my freelance contracts were in northern Iran by the Caspian Sea and a few scattered in several ports in the south along the Persian Gulf and Oman Sea. They were small and manageable. I signed robust contracts but still had cases where, when I finished the work, including gaining quality system validation, I didn't receive final payment. When I complained to Captain about that, he called them and I got my money.

Not all my clients were like that though. I found lifelong friendships through those contracts with warm-hearted people of Bandar Abbas, Bushehr, and Abadan. They invited me to their houses and I learned the idiosyncrasies of Persian culture in those coastal cities. The highlight of it was hospitality and great food. My clients and their families and I discussed culture, their family matters, and even their secrets. I was honored they trusted me and I did my best to keep their trust. I had to be careful since I was working with small family businesses, all competitors with each other.

I realized people in cities all over Iran longed for freedoms as simple as running a business without bribes. One of the owners, who with his family became my close friends, had refused to bribe the person in charge of the permissions, trying instead to go around him. For that, he was severely beaten in a dark alley on his way home one night.

The father of one of my clients made me a calligraphy of a Hafez poem. At the bottom right corner was the most loving part, a little note that said, "To my daughter." It is a great piece of art, which I framed and still own.

Not all client interactions were sweet though. One client picked me up from the airport and put his hand on mine in the car. He invited me to his house for dinner. I took my hand away, looked out the window, and said I was tired and preferred to stay in my hotel that night. The next day I was uncomfortable working with him. I put a serious mask on my face, which always has been the most difficult thing for me to do since I'm naturally playful and friendly. But we got through the day. Then his wife called and invited me for dinner, so I couldn't skip it although I suspected her husband had forced her into it. She was sweet, an obedient housewife with three kids. I could see unease in her eyes. I made a point to speak only with her and compliment her a lot on her cooking and her children. Her husband put his hand on her shoulder and said, "She is wonderful. A great cook and a loving mother." With a shy smile, she turned her eyes down.

When I returned to the hotel, I didn't feel lonely as a divorcee. I knew what I was going through was worth it. With all the romantic, personal, and professional challenges I faced, I was grateful I was not married to an abusive or manipulative man. I could travel and explore and meet different people and even feel funny about being rejected by the government because of playing ping pong with men. That night and others like it taught me many families kept a pretty facade but had no closeness. Empathy and intimacy were rare gems not everyone could have. The dinner had made me feel better about my loneliness and even my extramarital love for Captain. My life had troubles, but I was not trapped with a man I did not love.

My father started hearing from nosy neighbors who wondered whether I lived somewhere else and why I came home late at night. He supported my business trips but asked me to take airport cabs rather than a cheaper, unregistered cabs. "At least they'll know you were on a trip."

"That's nonsense, but okay," I replied.

****

Starting in 1997, when Khatami was elected president and because corruption made many things buyable through bribing, we began to have a little more freedom on how to dress and act in public. However, lack of human rights, women's rights, and other cultural barriers still showed themselves continuously in everyday life.

New problems stemming from illogical Islamic rules arose as Parnian was growing up. After a long wait in line at a face-painting booth in a park one day, the woman in charge told us, "She is too old for face-painting. I cannot accept her." Parnian was six but tall for her age. I was furious and started yelling at the girl, "Tell me who wrote that rule? She is only six." The woman answered the government restricted face-painting to girls five and under. Parnian was heartbroken and started crying. I tried to stop my own tears while wiping Parnian's. Despite my scene-making complaints, we had to leave. Everyone was looking at us as we left. It was outrageous.

Incidents like that strengthened my resolve to take Parnian out of Iran.

I needed to start seriously planning for emigration. I aimed for Canada, Australia, or New Zealand. The United States was out of the question; not many Iranians received U.S. visas.

When Captain agreed there was a better future for Parnian and me in the West; I felt bittersweet. How could I leave him, but how could I make a good life here? I needed to face reality and start working on it. Thinking of having my dream son from him calmed me down. I slept every night fantasizing about raising Parnian and an Arash in a different country, with freedom, but I never shared this dream with him.

1999 was a year full of adventure and change for me. My dreams of freedom had not been wrong—life was bigger than the walls of a house—but when the little black fish left the stream for the ocean, she faced challenges. I read that book to Parnian many, many times.

****

By early summer 2000, the polarity of desperately desiring Captain alongside trying to be understanding about his situation—our reality—had become excruciating. The movie *Shokaran* (Hemlock) was screening, and I went to see it. It depicted the same type of relationship, with a sad ending. A married man falls in love with a nurse, but when he finds out she is pregnant, he simply goes home to take his wife to a dinner. The nurse, driving to his house, feeling furious, crashes her car and dies. The man simply continues life with his family like nothing has happened. As I felt helpless to express my feelings to Captain, as he was hesitant to follow any type of emotional conversations, I decided to let the film do the work. Troubled and uncomfortable, he sat on the edge of his chair throughout nearly the whole movie, and I realized what a mistake I had made. After, we did not talk about the film, but uneasiness filled his eyes, which perhaps made him think twice about us.

On a warm, breezy September night in 2000, Sima needed to talk, so we met at a park. On a bench surrounded by flowers, sipping tea, we spoke about her frustrations with her husband and the impossibility of divorce without enough support. As with all conversations related to Captain's family, I tried to remain neutral. I said nothing that might cause trouble or create drama. It was difficult to make her feel I understood the situation yet consider the impact on his family of any word I might say.

Then Sima said something that made that challenge much worse: "I am losing my only support. My brother and his family leave the country in less than a month."

My hand shook. I spilled tea onto my *mantow*. Of course, she knew nothing about Captain's and my romance. I pretended I was still listening and babbled encouraging words, but everything after that was blah blah blah. The world looked blurry.

I finally thought of an excuse to leave. I walked unsteadily to my car and called Neda, the only person in my life who knew about Captain, and started sobbing. It was so depressing that I didn't even feel angry at him for not having told me himself.

For nights, going home, walking, driving, or being in a cab, I wiped away tears. It didn't matter that, intellectually, I knew we had to end our relationship. This did not lessen my devastation. I experienced enough pain now each time we said goodbye, not knowing when I would see him next, but that was a small scale compared to this. This loss felt damaging.

Despite my grief, I did not let him know I knew about this news. I waited until he shared it with me, a couple of weeks before he left the country. Then I told him I already knew but had not had the heart to discuss it. He tried to explain the situation, but I said he did not have to explain anything. All that mattered was that he knew he was leaving and hadn't told me.

Giving me such short notice did not seem like a big deal to him. Even though I thought I understood the situation, I got painfully hit by the reality of being deeply in love with an unattainable man.

I was trying hard to hold my life together in my hands, but like sand it was slipping through my fingers, smoothly and fast.

I bought him a classic pen with his last name engraved on it. The last time we saw each other, meeting in his friend's office after work hours, we made love and I cried. He whispered in my ear: "Shabnam, I promise to come back for visits as often as I can." I believed him, but I also had to move on. I hid my face in his arms and cried harder. He held me tighter.

Did he know he was taking the pillar I relied on for my growth? Did he know I needed his approval on my decisions in that important phase of my life? Or had he simply enjoyed my presence in his life as his secret lover, becoming independent under his support and encouragement? And no more?

After he left I finally understood completely that I could expect nothing from the relationship, and I was no priority in his life. I was deeply sad, but somehow not angry at him. He had touched my soul, so his leaving did not turn me against him. I still loved him deeply.

CHAPTER EIGHT

2000 – 2003

After Captain left in October 2000, I felt not just emotionally but physically weak. My first reaction to stress was always nausea. I felt sick to the point I shivered at night and gagged in the morning. On top of everything else, instead of getting my period I started spotting and having bad cramps.

My mother was puzzled by all this and took me to my ob-gyn, our family friend doctor. She was worried when my doctor talked about ovarian cysts because my mother had had many difficult surgeries because of cysts. My doctor ordered an ultrasound.

My mother insisted on going to the ultrasound appointment with me and waiting outside while I went into the technical room alone. The technician started the procedure. After a few minutes, he said he could see the fetus: about four weeks old. I looked at him like he was talking in a different language. Words came out of my mouth without my permission: "I am not married, and I have an IUD." I do not know what I expected him to do, offer supportive words? Make the fetus disappear?

"Well, I can see the fetus. You need to talk to your doctor." He handed me tissues to clean the gel and walked away to collect the printed results.

I could not move for a few seconds. I did not know what to do. I wanted to run to my doctor's office and beg him to tell me the technician was wrong. That he had not done his job correctly. That he had made a mistake. Of course I wanted my Arash, Captain's son, but not like this, not when I had no prospect of leaving Iran.

I remembered my IUD was good for only three years. I had lost track of time, and Captain and I had never protected ourselves any other way. We must have conceived that baby in our last lovemaking. I was paralyzed with terror, but I had to get off the exam table. Another patient was waiting her turn. I had to face this. But how?

Worse, my mother stood outside waiting for me. What would I tell her? I could imagine her screaming in the middle of the doctor's office. Out-of-wedlock sex was against her morality, her religion, and her mindset. I got up, put my clothes on, and cautiously went through the door. My mother could always read my face precisely. She knew I had bad news. Words jumped out of my mouth, again beyond my control. "I am pregnant!" But she did not scream. She calmly took my hand and walked me out onto the street. Was she shocked? Was she numb? Was I alive?

She knew nothing about my romance with Captain. She knew only that I had not felt well recently. She had commented after overhearing my phone calls with a new man I had started dating after Captain left. "Are you careful not to fall for men on your business trips? They are going to take advantage of you. You know better. Think wisely and follow morality."

That night I fantasized that when I returned to the doctor I would hear that the result had been wrong. But the next day at the doctor's office, he said he guessed this result when he had examined me few days before.

As soon as he saw my sad face, he snapped, "We don't have time to be emotional." He described the medications I would have to buy on the black market and the procedure he would do in the hospital.

I looked at the floor and fought tears. I couldn't tell my mother this was the dream baby I longed to have. If she discovered my relationship with Captain, things would be far worse than if she believed the baby was a coworker's. My body felt like twice its normal weight, heavy but numb. My brain would not work. I was a robot, mutely agreeing against everything in my soul.

I stepped out of the doctor's office and allowed myself to start crying. There was no choice: I couldn't leave the country. Where would I go? What would I do? Parnian's father would never let me take her out of Iran. Oh, how badly I wanted that baby, Captain's baby, someone who would remind me of him and be part of me as well. I sobbed, and my mother asked nothing. We drove home in silence.

When we got home, with frustration in her voice she asked, "Would he support this?"

"'He'?"

"The new project manager you talk to on the phone a lot. Don't you go on a lot of business trips with him?"

I had started dating someone new to forget about Captain. I had made sure to be on a date with him when Captain was on the plane flying away. I couldn't bear to be alone during those hours. Without Captain's loving presence, I needed to know I was still loveable.

"I will tell him," I said simply. But the project manager used double protection in sex: condom and self-control.

I went straight to my bedroom so my father would not see my teary eyes and ask questions. He was the last one I needed to know about this whole chaos.

Everything looked blurry. I lay down. Thoughts raced around my brain while my body was still heavy and numb. Should I tell Captain? Would he believe me? What if he wasn't supportive? I loved him. I didn't want to see that side of him if he wasn't supportive. Besides, what could he do? I didn't need his financial help for the abortion, and he was far away. It would only worry and upset him. As usual, tears were my best companion that night. Knowing I would go through with the abortion, aborting my dream Arash, was and remains one of the saddest feelings I have ever experienced.

I got the drugs. I took them, and threw up for a couple of days while they were knocking down the fetus. Then I walked to the hospital with my mother, who supported me gently.

Usually husbands had to sign agreement upon entrance the hospital under this circumstance, but my doctor was one of the owners of the hospital and ordered the staff to accept my mother's signature instead. The procedure was straightforward; they removed the baby from my uterus. The doctor and hospital were good; there was no risk to my life. That afternoon, I left my stillborn child—my fantasy son (who knows, but I wanted a boy)—in the same hospital where my daughter and I were born.

Nobody had asked me whether I wanted to keep the baby, nobody helped me process my grief through the horror of losing both my baby and my dream to raise Captain's child. That was gone forever, and I missed Captain even more. I felt overwhelmed by loss after loss, and I pushed everything under the rug just to manage my daily routines. The next day, permitted by my doctor, I flew to another city for a business trip and tried to forget everything.

****

During 1999 and 2000, I worked hard but still tried not to miss any of Parnian's events at school or after school. My parents were humbly raising her with pure love and absolutely no complaints.

My father held his "exemplary grandfather" title at the park, and my mother watched Parnian's diet, health, and homework. I was there to smooth out the level of discipline my mother believed in, which was still much more freedom when compared to my childhood. Society was different, too. A new generation of parents were open to more freedom for their kids and punishment was less common as a parenting style.

From sending her paintings to a kids' exhibition to attending kids' book fairs and plays around the city in different theaters, we tried not to miss many events.

My little six-year-old loved theater. She volunteered to join me for Othello in the central theater of Tehran and patiently sat and listened through the whole performance. I was glad she came with me but disappointed by all the censorship in the play, including a lot of Desdemona's roles. Her love story with Othello did not fit Islamic rules and needed to be trimmed from the story. It felt like a different story. However, it was better than nothing in those days, and Parnian liked it.

She loved acting and was always ready to put on her favorite play, about the mother goat and her three children. She smoothly played all the roles herself, singing all the songs of the story and creating an entertaining musical. This was part of our routine at every party we attended, and for any guests visiting us. Unlike me, she was never shy on stage. I loved it and encouraged her strongly.

For a few years, she had fun at her music class. Then she was required to practice keyboard at age seven. Keyboard was not her cup of tea, so this caused a tantrum.

She went to the class, but if we forced her to practice at home she punched her little fists on the keyboard so hard I was afraid she would break it. I didn't see any point in pushing it. I just took her away and hugged her until she calmed down. My mother thought I was spoiling her, but I firmly held my opinion. If Parnian didn't like it, she shouldn't have to suffer. Soon, the keyboard went back into the box in storage.

Unlike my mother, I didn't encourage Parnian to become the best in every class she attended. I wanted her to be herself. To me there was nothing wrong with average as long as she enjoyed herself. She would find and excel in her true passion one day soon, but not with force.

When she turned seven, I talked to my parents into making her a "room" in their two-bedroom condo. I wanted Parnian to have privacy and independence and to be able to decorate her room in the way she liked. The end of the rectangular shaped dining room had an extension that could be made into a small room by a divider. My parents agreed, and Parnian was thrilled and immediately started decorating her small space. Her first request was for a bookcase for her large collection of books.

Our nightly book date was our favorite time. Although we missed a lot of them because of my business trips, we had fun on nights we were together. Parnian picked a book and I read it until she fell asleep. She listened to me and with her chubby little fingers played with the small feathers coming out of the corner of her pillow. I knew she was asleep when her right wrist was bent under her chin. How I loved to watch her sleep thinking, *Even if my life isn't easy, everything is getting better, she looks calm.*

She was mostly a happy little girl, but she often returned discouraged from visits with her father. "He says I am not polite enough because I didn't say hello to his neighbor. I did say hello, he just didn't hear it. He said you didn't raise me properly and you are a careless mother. He also said my skirt was too short and you should buy pants for me." I put her on my lap, wiping her tears and stroking her hair. I hugged her tight until she calmed down. I assured that she was polite and suggested she say hello to her father's neighbor even louder next time.

"He did buy me another surprise chocolate egg. Want to see my prize?" Thank goodness she rebounded quickly from his harsh words.

To protect her from his criticism I put pants on her when she visited him. I hesitated to say bad words about her father to her, but there were points that I lost it, then felt guilty for my behavior and the damage I caused. He was her father after all.

She was forced to understand events in her life such as divorce much earlier than she should have. She needed less traditional discipline and more love and compassion.

****

My job was project based. Towards the end of the winter 1999, work began to slow down with Tavana, where I was a contractor, and I reached out to similar organizations to join other projects. Reza left for France to continue his education, and Kamran too was looking for more work. He knew people at a well-known consulting organization, Engineering Management System (EMS). We both reached out to Ali, who was one of Kamran's friends from graduate school. I had met Ali and his wife at Kamran's graduation ceremony.

Ali was an account executive for quality management contracts and had good number of projects Kamran and I could join. He was polite, friendly, and good looking. He made jokes, laughed a lot and talked as if we had known each other for a long time. He said he needed analysts on a few projects. He liked our background, and we decided to start working with him immediately. The pay was not as good as Tavana, but I wanted work.

The first couple of projects were in Tehran. Kamran and I made a team with Ali being the project manager. EMS was a big organization with a lot more structure and more policies for their quality management projects, which gave me the opportunity to learn the field more in depth and from a different point of view.

I enjoyed the new environment. We had preparation meetings at the EMS office then went into the field. A project I particularly liked was a for food manufacturer that produced vegetable oil. By then I had been exposed to many other industries such as sailing, car manufacturing, and car parts manufacturing, but food manufacturing was different, and in order to implement quality system standards on their processes, I needed to understand the food industry standards. A lot of learning and a lot of exploration with a good team. I loved it.

At times, when I was alone at the customer site, I wouldn't know the answer to a question, so I called Ali, who was responsive and helpful. Soon he started calling me just to say hi. He was charming, but this made me scratch my head as it felt like something slightly more than friendly. I was lucky I was able to trust my Tavana colleagues fully, that Reza, Shakeeb, and Kamran treated me like a sister. I wanted Ali to be the same.

Once, he said I shouldn't tell everyone at work I was divorced with a daughter. "A lot of men like to take advantage of nonvirgins, and a young divorcée is a good choice." I didn't take it personally; it seemed like protective, brotherly advice. Besides, he was right: Often I received calls from client managers inviting me for a lunch or from other freelance consultants inviting me to their solo offices to talk about "a new opportunity." Mr. Sina invited me to his home office to talk about creating a new training package for quality management. When he started flirting, I politely asked if I could leave. I wasn't a virgin and I did have a high sex drive, but I didn't want sex like this. He aggressively got closer to me, then took off my scarf and tried to lift me from the chair. He was a powerful man but I swirled away, and grabbed my scarf and bag. As I was leaving, I said if he called me again, I would tell everyone about the incident. I was scared, but I was lucky he didn't pursue anything. I always felt, in that culture, it didn't matter what I wanted. My friendly behavior and my type of job, with a lot of traveling, was interpreted for a woman as I am open to casual sex. Once I got out of Mr. Sina's home-office, I walked aimlessly for a while. I was scared and kept looking back to make sure he was not behind me.

****

I usually took a cab to go home but during the hot summer of 2000, one day after work Ali offered me a ride and I accepted. He started asking questions about my personal life. I didn't find them uncomfortable, but, as I was hoping to expand my job horizons, I changed the subject and asked if he had any reference guides needing translation from English to Farsi, and whether EMS would hire me for the project. EMS had a good-size publishing department and gave employees the chance to translate. But Ali said his wife, who had a master's degree in English, was already working on a translation project and he couldn't manage more than one at a time. I was disappointed. Lost opportunity.

Then he quietly added: "Well, actually, that project has not progressed much since my wife left." He said she was staying with her parents in another city. "Please keep this to yourself. No one at work knows." He offered to bring me the book so we could translate it together. I felt bad for them, but I was happy for the work. Also, by sharing his secret, he made me feel special, like my boss trusted me. But why? He had known me for only a few months. I kept the news to myself but wondered whether Kamran knew it.

Over the trips to the clients in Tehran and other cities, we spent many hours together. He asked a lot questions, and I poured out my opinionated answers, which were considered feminist, and not in a positive way. I loved that he was calm and seemed attentive. He never disagreed with me; rather he shared no opinion at all. He just said, "You have interesting opinions." It made me feel special that he wanted to know about me and that I was interesting to him.

Later that summer, with Captain leaving, I started accepting Ali's regular offers to drive me home. After my divorce and complicated relationship with Captain, I felt like a failure romantically. Ali's attention fed my wounded ego and heart. Any little kindness was a relief, not a deep one, but enough to make me feel better for a little while. I did not think about the long-term consequences of those small acts of engagement with Ali. I was lost in my sadness and focusing only on my basic emotional needs, blind to my heart's still-loving-Captain desires.

That September, I started working with Ali on a project with a lot of trips. We flew to Bandar Abbas to kick it off.

The customer organization provided one apartment to each of us in their guest house community. On the first day, after work, we went straight to our separate apartments, right next to each other. A few minutes later, he knocked on my door. When I opened it, he came in, closing the door behind him. "It's too hot outside," he said. It was hot, but asking for permission would have been nice.

I had changed into a T-shirt and pair of shorts. He said, "You look good in shorts," and "I like your hair like that." He stepped closer, touched my hair, put his hands on my face, and started kissing me. I was startled, but I didn't resist. Although I felt no chemistry and certainly no love, his attention fed a desperate need in me. When he pulled out a condom I was surprised but again didn't resist. I could not tolerate the scent of his body, which only highlighted how inferior this was to my time with Captain: There was nothing more lovely than inhaling Captain's scent when I was lost in his arms, but Ali's odor repelled me. Tears ran down my cheeks, but I hid them and pretended I was fully engaged.

Gradually I forced myself to accept physical closeness without emotional intimacy. It left me confused, but the temporary relief soon became a habit.

After all, Ali was successful at work and had a good reputation in the industry. It was appealing to see people count on him and accept his words—he was no Farshad, that was for sure. For example, two days before an audit in one of the projects, he came to the factory and went to the stock room directly. He grabbed a bottle of oil and turned it upside down. It started leaking. He looked at the client's quality manager and said, you are not going to pass your audit until you practice all the procedures my team wrote for you. We were all amazed that he knew to go directly to the failing point. I was so impressed. Systems implemented under his supervision got a lot of compliments from lead industry auditors. I was so proud on the day one of the most difficult auditors said, "Systems implemented by Mr. Ali are so reliable that they make my audit day relaxing and easy." It was true.

I gradually started asking more about his life, but his answers were brief. I asked him where he met his wife and was surprised to learn he had had an arranged marriage and came from a religious family. They lived in a holy city, Mashad, in northeast Iran.

There had been no divorce in his family; it was a shame his mother could not accept. "I have to find a way to bring my wife back," he said.

It was clear we were fillers for each other until we knew what the next step of our lives would be. Ali filled in when Captain left in October and I felt emptier than ever. He filled in when I had my abortion. I was depressed and didn't know what I wanted from life. I put on a mask to look calm and went on dating Ali.

****

My birthday came, November of 2000. Ali and I were on a business trip, and in the evening, he came to my room in the hotel. The light was dim, and as I lay on the bed, he rummaged through his bag. Then he handed me a little jewelry box. "Happy birthday. I hope you like this." I was surprised and happy; the last thing I expected was jewelry. We weren't that close, and he was careful with money. I calmly opened it and saw a simple gold ring. I looked at him with the biggest confusion in my eyes, but I thanked him. He instantly saw he had made a mistake. "I just liked it, it is just a gift." Still I felt totally confused and started crying.

I had always wanted a ring from Captain as a symbol of our connection. I never expected a wedding ring. I just wanted to have something from him touching me all the time. Instead I got one from Ali.

He asked why I was crying, and I said I only that I was touched. Reality was bitter and difficult to accept. Ali accepted my short answer. In the end, his gift made me feel good, and I wore the ring on my right hand.

****

Captain called me a few weeks after his departure, and hearing his voice brought me back to life. I didn't say a word about the abortion and made myself sound happy until he said, "I miss you." Then I started quietly crying. I said I missed him too but understood and accepted his decision. Did I?

I mentioned my telephone call and my past relationship with Captain to Ali. I told him it was now just a normal friendship, but this created our first disagreement. He obviously did not like the fact that I had a relationship that was not completely over. He didn't seem to notice the irony of challenging this while trying to get his wife back; then again, such double standards were the norm in Iran. He had not fallen in love with me, he just liked to spend time with me.

As winter wore on, I grew attached to Ali. I wanted to see him every day. His calm nature appealed to me. He didn't seem emotional - angry or frustrated - all the time like my father. It didn't seem to be part of his personality.

Soon, I asked him to join me at the parties and gatherings Neda, Reza, Kamran, and I had. We had fewer parties after Reza left France, but he came back for visits often.

The first time I asked Ali to join me was at Reza's house. As we climbed the stairs to Reza's condo Ali said it was his first party like this. "What do you usually do?"

"We dance, mingle, sometimes drink, and laugh."

Excitedly, he said, "I have been a good boy until now. You are a bad influence on me."

Parnian was usually a charming part of our parties, but since it was my first time bringing Ali, I left her at home that night. I wanted them to meet on a different occasion with fewer people, or maybe I wanted him to ask to meet Parnian.

That night, although we enjoyed the party I felt a subtle change in myself. I was more careful about my behavior with other men. I rationalized it: I was easing Ali into a new culture. Later, Reza, knowing me well and with his sharp eyes and his straightforward behavior, pointed it out. "With Ali there you seemed uncomfortable talking to other people. You weren't yourself. Next time, bring our sweet Parnian. We miss her." I didn't answer.

For my part, I was surprised by Ali's behavior that night. He seemed comfortable talking to others—especially girls. I felt jealous watching him ask them questions similar to the ones he asked me. I always thought he was interested in knowing me personally. Was he simply this charming with everyone?

Ali never asked to meet Parnian. Instead, when I brought her to a gathering with friends for dinner in a restaurant, he simply said "hi" to her and shook her hand. She was not impressed. Parnian, used to uncle Reza and Kamran's kindness and attention asked why Ali was so cold. I thought he must not know how to deal with young children.

****

In early 2001, a few months after Captain left, he came back to visit Tehran and I went to see him at his friend's house. My heartbeat sped up as I approached the house, where it would be just him and me.

He opened the door, and we hugged each other tightly. There was no feeling better than that. We started kissing each other passionately, but strangely, I did not become aroused. What was it about? Was this loyalty to Ali? Why? How? We were not exclusive. Was my hesitation because of my recent pregnancy? I apologized and said I was in a relationship.

Looking away from me, he said he understood. He sat down, lit a cigarette, and stared into the corner of the room. I sat close to him, holding his hand and thanking him for understanding.

"Tell me about Parnian, your work, and yourself." I talked and talked and he listened to me intently, gave me great suggestions, and asked the right questions, giving me food for thought as usual. He said he wanted the best for me and he would do anything to help, like always. We held each other's hands the whole time.

When it was time to leave, my heart felt heavy. No matter how many times we said goodbye, it always hurt like a fresh wound. The smoothness and depth of our interaction just highlighted how shallow my relationship with Ali was. With Ali, it was a lot of effort to have a conversation or get him to respond to questions. He was evasive. It was partly because he was in a difficult phase of his life, but it was also him being reserved and skeptical about me. My visit with Captain that day confirmed I had no emotional intimacy with Ali. However, Ali was reality. Captain was fantasy.

****

Boarding a plane for a business trip to the south, I had a little cold but thought nothing of it. When we got off the airplane, I felt more congested with a little fever.

Typically, Ali would come secretly to my apartment to spend the night on these trips. That night when he came over and saw how bad I felt, he went out and returned with medicine and orange juice. I was touched.

I felt worse overnight and could not work the next day. He came to check on me after each meeting. It felt so sweet and intimate. He continued taking care of me for the three days of the trip while I lay in bed with the flu. He brought me more juice and medication and cheered me up by telling jokes. I was sick but happy and appreciative. It felt like a wonderful partnership.

A few days later when I asked if he had any news from his wife, he said, "Her mother has been trying to convince her to come back to her marriage. I am trying to maintain the house as clean as I can, hoping she comes back."

This stung considering how tender he had been on our trip. Although intellectually I knew he was filler for me, too, I took it as another rejection. That triggered me to try harder to keep our relationship. So, when he said, "Parties are not a good environment for Parnian," I left her at home. When he said, "What must Neda's husband think when she dances like that in front of other men," I stopped dancing at parties.

Later that summer, Ali and I attended at a party at Neda's sister, Maryam's house. Neda insisted I take Parnian with me to play with her son. Parnian loved Neda's son, who was her age, so I brought her along.

Maryam was a sweetheart, and we had become close friends over time. When we got in, I felt the party calmed down a little bit like the girls became quieter. Neda's friends had mentioned to her before that they didn't like the way Ali looked at their bare legs when they wore miniskirts. Maryam came to welcome us and, looking at me from head to toe she commented, "You look like a real lady with your long skirt and long-sleeve shirt. We look like bad girls here." She laughed. I knew what she meant, but I was the one who was embarrassed.

Parnian usually went to sleep around 10 at parties. By then she was a tall child, heavy to carry. Before, Kamran or Reza would help me take her to the car when she was asleep. That night, though, Kamran kept his distance, knowing Ali didn't like him to talk to me. Ali stood there with Neda, Maryam, and a few other friends as I went to the bedroom to pick up Parnian. The door was open and everyone could see me struggle to lift her in my long skirt and high heels, but I received no help, only silence. I barely found my balance and said a quick goodbye. I could see needles coming from others' eyes looking at me and at him. I felt disrespected and humiliated by him in front of my friends. Going to parties was not as fun anymore.

After that, I felt uncomfortable and self-conscious around my friends. I was silent when later Neda over the phone asked, "But what is his problem with an innocent little girl?" I started avoiding the gatherings and parties. To make Ali feel less suspicious of Neda's influence on me, I interacted with her less and less. I was betraying myself.

We both secretly felt rejected by others and tried to make it up with each other. Neither of us knew a healthy way to cope with the result of our previous relationships. Each one of us took it personally and tried to heal by proving we were loveable and wanted. We fled to each other instead of giving ourselves a chance to self-reflect. This was easier—for the short term, anyway.

Ali was both available and wanted to be with me. I could not see beyond that. Yet, becoming romantically and sexually involved with someone other than Captain broke my heart. I needed just him and nobody else. Perhaps by keeping the relationship with Ali, I hoped I might accept the reality that the man I truly loved was gone. At least I might be loveable by someone else.

What stopped me from leaving Ali wasn't the fear of being alone, it was the terror of not being loved, especially by a successful professional who believed any girl would go out with him. I needed to do my best to avoid losing that game because I was divorced, because that made me not good enough. The desperate need to be loved dominated my heart. With extreme lack of self-belief and fear of rejection, I started giving up some of my most important rights that I strongly believed in being a mother, being a woman, becoming emotionally independent, and enjoying my desires. In my naive mind, I hoped to magically create a trustworthy and emotionally intimate relationship if I could accept his values. Obviously, I had not learned my lesson yet, the same lesson I thought I had mastered when I left Farshad.

Women learned to put up with a lot and keep a man happy, especially if he had some career success. Prestige and accomplishments were so shiny that emotional connection and closeness could be compromised for them. Although I was totally against this in theory, I was acting on what I had learned subconsciously. I judged my mother when she told my father, "You don't even have enough money to be worth my affection." I judged my aunts for putting up with their husbands because of their financial power. I even judged my friends for compromising love for prestige. I refused to admit I was doing the same thing.

Financial independence and holding a professional job—the goal I had striven for so long—were part of my life. But now I saw they weren't everything. What was everything was being accepted by a man accepted in society.

****

It was my first day as a quality management system consultant on a new project. I was sitting in the quality manager's office talking about project execution strategies when her phone rang. Mona excused herself to answer it. When she talked to me she talked fast and confident, with a smile; on the phone, it was with patience and kindness. I watched her. She was in her late 30s, thin but not too tall. An oval face with white skin and green eyes. She constantly fixed her scarf to keep herself covered, but I could still see a few strands were colored blond. She was pretty.

"Ok, great. You'll get Rozhi from daycare. Thank you! I am finishing a meeting. I'll be home soon too."

That intimate voice threw me to a different world. I thought what a blessing to have a supportive husband who took the baby from daycare! It made me lonely, but I dragged myself back to the conversation.

Mona said, "I'm sorry, I have to leave in 15 minutes. I have three daughters. So hard to manage everything."

Ali was at a different client site, and I decided to walk for a while before taking a cab to go home. It was a hot summer day in 2001, but I needed to think, and walking calmed me. Feeling lonely and not having closeness to a partner was a heartache.

The next week, I spent more time in Mona's office to kickstart the project. We spent our lunchtime together and got to know each other at some personal level, still scratching the surface. We learned we lived close to each other, and she offered to drive me home one day.

I had fantasized her home with three beautiful daughters and their dinner table all together with Mommy and Daddy. I was curious to see how close my fantasy was to the reality of her life. So, I said, "Your husband seems to be helpful with kids."

"Kind of," she answered, making a funny face.

"It was so sweet hearing you talking to him on the phone the other day."

"He is not like that all the time. He is busy, and I mainly take care of the kids. I love my little daughters but three is too much."

"But you seem like a cute family. I wish I had that."

"Sometimes I feel so overwhelmed. I try to avoid complaining to my husband."

"That's nice of you."

"Not to be nice to him. He gets aggravated if I complain."

This was disappointing. "All men are like that? It is like as soon as you complain they get angry or they say you are so sensitive."

"How do you know about that, not being married?"

"Well, between me and you, I am divorced. I have a daughter too."

At this point Mona turned toward me with wide eyes. She gaped at me so long I feared we would get into an accident.

"You are so brave. I envy you," she finally said, turning back to the road.

I thought how wrong I was to think she had the perfect life. I was confused, but her comment felt like a boost. I had divorced the man who would otherwise have damaged my life and my daughter's life.

She said, "Do you have time to talk today if I ask my mother to take care of my daughters for a couple of hours? My husband is on a business trip."

We picked a quiet coffee shop and ordered cafe glace, ice cream mixed with iced coffee. She spoke for two hours, with rage and tears, until she was tired. She told me how her university professor husband, educated in France (seen as a great achievement), had blamed her for not delivering boys and forced her to conceive a third time. She told me about his infidelity. And she told me that when she had asked for a divorce, he had said, "You can go anywhere you want but you won't get the kids."

I felt sad and, selfishly, relief I was not married to such a man. (I was obviously in denial about my current relationship.) Listening to her, I also felt rage, hate, and despair. How could she get out of this mess?

We left the coffee shop. She had to come back to reality, go get her children, go home, be a good mummy, and keep her husband happy. Or at least pretend.

****

As a side project, Ali with two of his friends were constructing a building in the northern part of Tehran. He enjoyed the customizing process for his future condo. During the summer of 2001, when it was all done and ready for him to move in, he started asking me about furniture. I thought he still had the furniture from his first marriage, which would belong to his wife per tradition. I was puzzled when he asked what type of sofa or dining table followed the fashion. Then he started to disappear for hours on weekends and be inaccessible.

When he first mentioned some furniture he had bought, I asked what would he do with his wife's furniture. "She took it a few months ago," he snapped like I asked the wrong question. Then he changed the subject. But then I asked about his divorce situation, and he admitted they had divorced a few months before. His short answers enraged me. I did not know who I was in his life. Why hadn't he told me?

Then he said he wanted to let me know that every time he visited with his mother in Mashad, she took him to see unmarried young women for possibilities for an arranged marriage. When he had removed me from the Mashad project, I had accepted his excuse that he didn't have enough budget and needed to go alone. Now it all made sense. I was furious but silent. We were in his car, and when we got to my street, I got out without saying goodbye. He looked down but said goodbye. I didn't answer him.

That night, I took off the ring he had given me. The next day while I was in training at EMS, he came into the room and said good morning with a big smile like nothing had happened. He stared at my finger and noticed the ring was gone.

"What are you up to after class?" he said.

"I'm going home." I wanted him out of my life.

"Let's go out. It's been a while since we've had dinner together." I looked at him in disbelief, but I agreed; we did need to talk. I wondered who I was in his life with everything he was hiding from me keeping me at arm' length.

Usually, I had to call him after work if I wanted to know where he was. That day, he was waiting for me outside the classroom door to walk me to his car. He tried joking around, but I was silent, tired of his attempts to get me to forget about his other life.

At dinner, he put his hand on mine, touching the finger that was bare without the ring. "I want you to come to my new house and see my new furniture. I hope you like my taste. Tomorrow after work?"

I was curious to see his house, and I also wanted to ask him who I was in his life in private, so the next day we went. The unit was nicely built, but his taste of furniture wasn't appealing. He acted kind, romantic even. Why did he want me to like the furniture if I was just a filler for him? Had he become attached to me, as I had to him? I wanted this to be true even as I knew we weren't right for each other.

I did not want to upset him in his brand-new apartment and decided to wait and talk about relationship ambiguity another time. I praised his effort to build such a nice place.

****

On a consulting work trip—a quick overnighter—to Bushehr, on the shore of the Persian Gulf, Ali came along. We flew to Bushehr early and I met with my client during the day.

After work, Ali suggested we catch the sunset from the boardwalk. The weather was nice and the gulf calm and quiet. I had taken a lot of business trips to Bushehr in the past and loved spending time by the water. I loved staring out and feeling the breeze. That night felt nothing like my old trips. I didn't even want to reach out to my old friends there. All I felt having Ali with me was the constant tension of not knowing what type of a relationship I was in. Did he want to stay with me or I was still a temporary filler? I wanted to be either serious or over. Although I knew we were not good for each other, I could not end the relationship myself.

As we walked, I saw Afshin, the man I dated to forget Captain a couple of years ago. Now the first officer of a commercial ship and ready to become a captain on his next trip, he looked handsome in his white uniform, walking towards us. He saw me too, but I ignored him, feeling so nervous. I didn't know how to introduce him to Ali without creating drama. We passed each other, and from the corner of my eyes I saw questions in his. I am sure he did not expect that behavior from me. I did not expect it from myself.

Afshin and I had stayed in touch. Almost twice per year, every time he came back from his sailing trips, he called me and we had warm, friendly conversations. I was eager to hear about his trips and his experience. Now I felt awful for what I did to him. I texted him and said I would explain everything later.

It seemed there was always something Ali wanted to hide from me, which made me nervous and controlling towards him. I felt I should live up to his values to win the competition with other women he was approaching to marry. Why aren't I good enough?

At the same time my anger and frustration created a power struggle. It seemed he had all the power. I wanted to take the power over perhaps for revenge. But this made no sense; I'd have been better off starting over on my own.

The next day at Bushehr's small airport, we were at the gate when I saw Afshin waiting for the same flight back to Tehran. That part of the airport was filled with people waiting for the door to open so they could walk to the airplane. But we could still see each other. I avoided eye contact.

Ali's phone rang and he answered. I could clearly hear a young woman's voice sweetly saying hi. He said hello warmly, stood up, and stepped away. Tears came down without my control. In only one glance I saw a big puzzle in Afshin's eyes. I tried to wipe my tears as quickly as I could. By the time Ali came back, I had stopped crying and was looking down, silent. I did not want to talk.

I called Afshin the next day to apologize for my rude behavior. I was embarrassed. He was as calm and understanding as ever. I said Ali and I knew we were wrong for each other and I did not know why I continued the relationship. Afshin listened to me and with great empathy said, "I care about you, but it seems there is nothing I can do. Please take care of yourself."

I laughed weakly. "I'm not taking care of myself, but I will try."

I hung up wondering why I could not disconnect myself from Ali while I could see Afshin's open and caring heart for me. It seemed he would take me back if I wanted that. Perhaps I was still not ready to share my heart with anyone but Captain. Perhaps I wanted to stay with an emotionally unavailable man and keep my heart to myself because I was not ready to give it to another person. How much did I believe that I deserved honesty, kindness and love?

****

Work was going well and I had many projects, but my loneliness was all-encompassing. I had lost the trust of my best friends: Neda, was uncomfortable around Ali, Reza was out of Iran, and Kamran felt bad that he had introduced me to Ali. I had only one person listening to my frustrations: Shakeeb, my dear colleague and project manager at Tavana. Although he was only a few years older than I was, his wise old soul made me feel he was Grandpa Shakeeb.

We worked together on a project in the northern part of Tehran where public transportation was not available. He often drove me to one of the streets closer to my house, and we talked about everything. Because I was so overwhelmed by my relationship with Ali, every conversation eventually went back to my frustrations. I needed to vent, and he was nice to listen to me. He was nonjudgmental, and I felt comfortable with him. I talked and cried and he patiently gave me supportive comments.

Shakeeb saw I was suffering from lack of self-esteem. He and his wife had taken some self-awareness classes and were happy about the results. He explained the self-awareness classes were based on state of art psychology theories to create a group therapy for people who were going through difficult times. That included majority of people in Iran I thought. He suggested I join a support group that was working on self-awareness, so I did.

The group was women only and had a religious and passionate male leader, Dr. Mo, whose doctorate was in theology. He was conservative enough that we kept our scarves on in the class. We would meet up weekly in one of the members' houses. Dr. Mo gave us assignments so we could practice self-awareness during the week, then come back together to share our experience. I loved my first assignment: Lie down and look at the clouds to see what you see in them. This was supposed to develop our imagination skills.

It was a long way from the visits my friend Mina and I had at her professor's house a couple of years ago discussing Jean-Paul Sartre's ideas, but in its own way, it was good for me. It was eye opening. I started learning about this new and amazing concept of self-awareness.

Although literature and books were still my escape, it was nothing like before. Neda and I had had deep philosophical conversations at one time, but I took that away from myself too. How had Ali, who had no appreciation for literature and had not read one line of a literary book outside of high school, become the main person in my life?

This support group became my little hope. Despite my busy schedule, I made time since I felt the importance. I had read many books about freedom and human rights, but this was a totally new way of learning: listening, practicing, and sharing.

Dr. Mo explained a new subject every week: self-love, the inner child and how to connect with her, forgiveness and letting go, the influence of the past in our present life.

I was receptive to these concepts, but some of them were too advanced for me, considering my limited understanding of psychology. Before I could grow, I needed to heal. I was emotionally broken and could not fully absorb those subjects, but it was a great start.

For one session Dr. Mo planned to teach about letting go. He asked us to bring one item that reminded us of past pain. The item needed to be new or in good condition. I looked through everything I had and picked a beautiful green silk sleep gown Captain had given me. I had never worn it, and he was who I needed to let go of. I gave the gown to another lady, a random person I chose. Her eyes stuck on the softness of the silk, she said, "I love it, thank you." I received a white silk scarf with small pink and blue flowers. Parnian means a silk fabric with floral pattern, so I took the scarf as a sign I would be able to make a sweet history of my love story and pay more attention to Parnian. I had not spent enough time with her recently.

At the end of each class session, Dr. Mo asked us to make a circle, hold hands, and listen to a popular song by Moeen called "Life is Beautiful." It was about hope for the future, the beauty of life and letting go of the painful past. The song had been banned in Iran; the Persian singer lived in California and released the song there, but Dr. Mo had acquired it on the black market and everyone knew it: "Let go of the past, the past is past, think about the future, …".

I did make more effort and pay more attention to Parnian, but my love story did not become history. It remained alive and fresh like the little flower on a cactus leaf that comes alive and colorful with a little water every few months, like Captain's calls or visits.

****

The U.S. State Department had a program called diversity visa, a lottery. To apply, I had to mail the paperwork to the States, but the Iranian government sometimes suspected the purpose of the letter, and many of them never made it. For such popular program globally, there was less than one percent chance to be selected. If the letter got through and won the lottery, the person would be then invited for an interview in one of the U.S embassies outside Iran (there was no U.S embassy in Iran). If they passed the interview they would be granted U.S permanent residency: a green card. The chance of passing the interview and obtaining the green card was 50%.

I wanted to leave Iran, but Ali had not shown much interest in that. I was hoping if we stayed together, I could convince him that life offered more opportunity in the West.

The vastness of America fascinated me. If there was so much information on the Internet, how would it feel to be there at an actual library in a university in the States? How would it feel to see all those art galleries in New York that I had read about in my English books and CDs? How would it feel to watch all the movies I longed to watch? Parnian could take dance classes at school. She could choose a major in college that she wanted rather than being forced to study medicine or engineering. She could become an adventurer journalist and travel the world. If I could continue my education in the States, maybe I could get a job and travel the world to spread the latest technology and information from the States to other places in the world. So many dreams could be realized in America.

My mother was visiting Uncle Mohsen in the States. After three times trying to obtain a tourist visa through different countries, in summer 2001, she had finally obtained one through the U.S. embassy in Turkey. She happily flew to see her beloved brother after many years. She called and asked me to fill out the diversity visa form and send it to my uncle's address in California, pretending it was just a family mail. Then my uncle would send it to the state department.

I wanted to leave Iran but I felt bad not sharing the opportunity with Ali. He had recently been rejected for a tourist visa to the States. Against my mother's wishes, I asked Ali to provide his information and fill out the form too. He hadn't known about such a possibility and was glad to try. I was surprised by his excitement and took it as a positive step towards the thought of immigration. I mailed our forms to my uncle and he sent them to the U.S State Department.

During the spring and in the beginning of June, everyone was talking about the presidential election again. People were encouraging each other to vote and re-elect Mohammad Khatami. We were able to breathe a little easier under his presidency but the country's basic oppressive infrastructure was the same to me. I could see the past four years had allowed people to communicate more, but we were far from accepting each other's opinions like in the democracy discussed in Plato's dialogues. I didn't believe in the election, because no matter who won, it was still an Islamic regime. I didn't vote. Instead, I committed to leave Iran.

My mother's visit was going well for her but not for us because my father was angry at having to handle her responsibilities and looking for any excuse to yell at me.

Because of my busy schedule, full responsibility for Parnian fell on him that summer. She was eight years old, and he did not want to leave her home alone, so during the week, since she was not in school, he either stayed home or took her with him everywhere he went. When one weekend, mid-morning, I told him I wanted to go out without Parnian, he was angry. Later, I was in the kitchen cooking and on the phone talking to Ali, trying to understand his evasive answers about his schedule for the day. Was he going out with other girls? To get out of my detective questions, he finally asked if I could meet for an hour in the park close to my house. My father, perhaps listening to the conversation, came into the kitchen. "You are wasting your time with this man. He has no interest in you. He is playing with you. You are a coward like your mother. Pay attention to your daughter." I did not hang up when he started yelling; I let Ali hear all that. It hurt to hear those words, but he was right. Feeling miserable, I stayed home that day. Then I bought two tickets to Shiraz for the next day, called out of work (which surprised Ali), and left my dad to breathe for three days. Parnian was thrilled. Mommy-daughter trips were her favorites.

****

By mid-2001 I had saved some money. My mother suggested I borrow some more from the bank and buy a small condo. It would be a good investment for my immigration plan. Parnian and I dreamed to live in our own house. I started searching. My cousin Nima joined me at real estate agencies and to see the houses. We found a place that worked but was five thousand dollars more than my budget. However, I knew I would receive the money in a month from one of my contracts. The condo was in a good location; I could rent it easily. Ali did not offer any financial help; I assumed he had used all his money on his construction. My mother asked my wealthy uncle, Hasan, but he said he did not have any money at hand.

I suddenly thought of Captain. I called him, and he sent money to his friend within a couple of days with no hesitation. He said buying that condo would create more financial stability in my life. I bought it and returned the money he lent me within a month.

On the day of the closing, a hot summer day, my father stayed home taking care of Parnian since my mother was still in the States visiting my uncle. I arrived early at the notary office for the closing process. Slowly, four other couples showed up, and the last person was the condo's owner and builder. Earlier in the morning Mr. Mardan and Shakeeb had called to offer their company for the closing. I had thanked both of them and said I was fine. I felt nervous though when I saw other couples all together and I was the only single woman there.

I sat in a corner chair watching. The husbands were going in and out bringing water for their wives and juice for their children. This made me feel lonely but skeptical of the honesty of their behavior. Was it real intimacy or just survival behavior to get the family going and create the picture perfect family?

The closing itself was easy; everything was straightforward and quick. At the end of the process, when we had all signed all the paperwork, the seller, an older, traditional man in his wrinkled old gray suit we called *Haaj Agha* (a respectful term for older religious men) said, "You see all these women? All four of them now own condominiums, but their husbands bought it for them. You are the only one who came here alone and bought it yourself." I was surprised when the traditional-looking owner said, "I'm proud of you." I needed those encouraging words at that moment.

I was a homeowner! I called home and let Parnian and my dad know that everything went fine. Parnian said, "*Maman* maybe one day soon it will be just me and you living there." It melted my heart and brought a big smile to my face. I assured her that it would be soon, and I would try to have fewer business trips to make that happen. At work later, everyone congratulated me, but I heard nothing from Ali.

In buying the condominium, I felt more financial stability. Yet, financial strength did not help me to feel powerful emotionally. I still thought I was not good enough. It did not occur to me that I was capable and strong and could therefore choose my lifestyle. My emotional intelligence needed a lot more growth.

****

Ali and I would usually go to his house on Thursdays, which is the first day of the weekend in Iran. The first time he invited me to his house on a Tuesday, I was puzzled but did not question it. I was walking on eggshells, not asking questions for fear of losing him. There was a thick, invisible wall between us, but one thing was clear: Going to his house meant sex. I thought maybe he missed me. My high sex drive had eventually dominated my heart and I had accepted our mechanical emotionless sex, but I still hoped to create emotional intimacy through sex. I wanted more touching and cuddling, but even cuddling didn't give me reassurance of a closeness I was looking for. I still was not used to his body scent. I still missed the closeness I had with Captain. Tuesday sex with Ali didn't change anything.

When I asked him on Wednesday night whether we are planning to go to his house on Thursday, he said, "I am leaving for a trip to the north early Thursday with my friends, which is why I had you over on Tuesday. I didn't want you to feel the lack of sex. I care about you." I did not like hearing that and was annoyed by yet another surprise from him. I was not shy about wanting sex or expressing my desire during sex. But in his eyes, a good woman should be shy during sex. My being comfortable with myself brought out biting comments. "You really like sex. Is it because of too much experience?" He loved reminding me I was not a virgin and therefore not eligible to be his wife.

That Thursday Ali went to the north, and I went to visit Parnaz, one of my work friends. I shared my frustration about what happened and how Ali treated me. She had her own woes. She had been dating her co-worker and developing emotions towards him when he suddenly disappeared. Next thing she heard was that he had married another girl under the influence of his family. Parnaz was divorced and the other girl a virgin. Parnaz was heartbroken, crying bitterly. A virgin girl had won the man Parnaz loved. All I could think of was who knew if she was a virgin or a fixed virgin. There were ways to fix it for the girls who attempted sexual relationship before they got married. The doctor did a surgery and fixed her like she never had sex. So many stories I had heard.

Sadly, it reminded me of my friend Anahita. During her college years she was in love with a boy secretly. Once, she found their house empty and had the boy over. They had passionate sex, but her parents arrived earlier than expected. They were furious. Her mother took her to doctor to fix her virginity. The next suitor available, she was forced by her parents to get married. A few years later she divorced and could not keep her daughter. Her husband allowed her to see her daughter just once a week because, lawfully, he could.

The following week when Ali was talking about his trip, out of nowhere he said that the age of prostitution was as low as 16. He mentioned they were available everywhere, especially in the northern touristy cities.

****

In the summer of 2002, we hung out at Ali's house most Thursdays. The undefined nature of our relationship was becoming intolerable.

At his house, we usually started the day well, like starting over, until something reminded me of the ambiguous status of our relationship. One thing was me being uncomfortable in his house. Another was him hiding me from all his family and friends.

Tired of talking, one day I sat on the sofa, depressed, crying. I found myself saying, "I want a family. I want to have more kids." I stopped my tears and continued: "If you cannot decide about our relationship, please break up. I cannot do it."

He came and sat next to me and put his arm around my shoulders. Unlike usual, he showed emotion. He said, "I want to have a family and kids too. Give me a little time. I have to change my own beliefs and my family beliefs. It takes time." As unclear as that answer was, it was something. He seemed to know how to calm me down right when I was about to break.

My desire for a family was bigger than my yearning for emotional intimacy. But was this just because I thought my uncertainty would be replaced by the security of cultural approval that would come with marriage and a family? Was it because my ego did not want to lose the game of catching a successful man?

I had had so many other dreams earlier in my life. I was sidetracked. I had forgotten about all my dreams of becoming independent. I had forgotten who I was. My ego was driving full speed and my heart was in starvation mode.

****

Ali and Parnian did not interact much. He did not encourage me to talk to him about her and my concerns for her. If I had to talk to Parnian's teacher, he said, "Did she do something bad at school and you have to apologize? Do you need to be more disciplined?"

In the summer of 2002, Ali, Parnian, and I planned to go to Ramsar, a beautiful city by the Caspian Sea with a few friends of ours.

To get out for sightseeing, every morning I had to wake Parnian earlier than she was used to. She didn't want to wake up, and I had to spend time and play with her until she finally would. The second day, I noticed Ali's face was tense, watching us playing. He said, "You are spoiling her. She needs more discipline. We are late and need to leave."

If it took time to figure out what Parnian wanted to eat in a restaurant, he frowned. "She's a big girl. Why doesn't she read the menu herself to choose what she wants? You pay too much attention to her. It is not good for her independence." Parnian was nine years old, and I enjoyed taking time to discuss what she wanted to eat. I left his comments unanswered.

****

Later in the fall, one Thursday when we arrived at his house he checked the mailbox and saw an unfamiliar letter. He showed it to me and opened it. He had won the diversity visa lottery for the first phase.

Ali was among 100,000 lucky winners!

He was ecstatic. He immediately started learning about the process and finding the forms he needed to fill out to send them for the interview preparation. I had been attending English classes continuously ever since my divorce, so he asked me to help him with the forms. When they were all done, he asked me to go with him to visit a lawyer for a final check. When the lawyer asked about his marital status, he said he was single. He introduced me to the lawyer as a friend who helped him with English. In fact, I was there as second pair of eyes for him to avoid missing the details the lawyer talked about.

"Wow, man," the lawyer said. "You are a good catch with all your education, your professional job, and now a green card on top of it. Girls will be dying to marry you." Ali had a big satisfied smile on his face. I sat there silent.

He grew less and less accessible. I checked his phone and connected the dots of his lies for where he was: out with other women. I was hurt and resentful, but If I said anything, he would deny it.

He decided to attend English classes and asked me about the one I attended, which was one of the first English schools allowed to have adult mixed-gender classes. When I said I liked it, he started the new semester with me. We had classes three times per week with an hour between work and the class during which we did our homework together.

If I tried to discuss our relationship, it was like talking to the wall; after a few minutes he asked an unrelated question, driving me nuts and leaving me helpless. "Give me time. Let's talk later." I understood he needed time accept the idea of marrying a divorcee. How long did he need to change? But he didn't want to break up with me either. We were both confused.

While he knew why I was sad, all he did was redirect our sad conversations. He tried to distract me by being charming. I resisted to some extent, but soon gave up. He used his sweet talk, hugged me, popped a candy in my mouth, or tickled me to make me feel happy, but the root cause of the problem was unresolved.

Love is not expressed only in sweet talks and sweet hugs. Love is expressed in active listening and providing a helpful answer when it is time to resolve a conflict. Without mutual understanding and heart-to-heart connection, sweet talk and sweet hugs are short lived. They are at best Band-Aids and at worst manipulation.

This whole situation made me think more seriously about immigration. Parnian and I needed to get out. I started looking into other immigration possibilities. I had an online friend from India. We had met in a Yahoo online chat room, one of those first online chat rooms on the internet and chatted often. He told me about the possibilities for immigrating to New Zealand and Australia; he was going there with his family. I found a lawyer to assess my current situation against requirements for immigration to New Zealand. In 2002, I still had a year and a half left to graduate from college. The lawyer said because I had good work experience, I should apply for an MBA at a good school in India that was familiar to New Zealand's state department. My parents could take care of Parnian while I could afford living and studying in India for two years, then off to New Zealand with Parnian. I had a gut feeling I could convince her father to let her go; by then they didn't communicate much.

School had been a challenge considering everything else going on in my life. But the conversation gave me hope, and I started taking school more seriously. Ali was evasive as usual when I told him about this plan, so I read whatever I wanted to into his words: Maybe he would come with me if he didn't pass the interview for the diversity visa. But even as I was fooling myself, I was shoring up my plan to get out of the country.

I was relieved he might leave Iran. It was nothing like the devastating feeling I had when Captain was leaving. Ali leaving smelled like freedom, peace, and the end of a long, tiring war. I would not miss him. Intellectually I could see I was not loved and I did not love, but I could not get out on my own.

The stress of everything was getting to me. After a few months of my losing my appetite, feeling fragile, and crying for any silly reason, Aunt Sara and her husband, now close to us, decided to take me to a doctor. The doctor, Monir, was my cousin Marjan's close friend. Marjan had become a pharmacist and moved to Canada with her husband. I had met Monir before; she was a sweet lady with kind manners.

In her office I talked about my loss of appetite and crying. Aunt Sara said she was worried I lacked vitamin B and iron and asked for a blood test.

On our second visit, discussing the blood test result, Dr. Monir *joon* said, "I asked for a blood test to make sure you are fine, but Shabnam *joon*, I think you are just stressed out. You need to be more realistic *azizam*. Life is tough. Nothing wrong with your body."

Of course, Aunt Sara and the doctor didn't know about my relationship with Ali. Even my parents didn't know the details. All they knew was that I was sad. I thanked her and we left. I need to be more realistic. I didn't know how. Anxiety and fear weighed too heavily on my shoulders. Constantly competing with other women and not securing a place in Ali's heart strengthened my sense of not being good enough. Fear had become an undercurrent in my life. I felt powerless, and I desired power badly. Perhaps that was what had happened to Mona, Parnaz, and many more women in unhappy marriages.

I couldn't see that a man who constantly tries other women is confused and incapable of offering love, closeness, or emotional intimacy to anyone, even if he is the most successful man professionally.

****

A few weeks later, in February 2003, as Ali was getting closer to his interview time, he received a letter from the States noting that it was his last chance to make any change in his file, including adding any new family member. Surprisingly, he shared the letter with me. I had learned from Uncle Mohsen before, and told Ali, that according to U.S immigration law, if he didn't add a family member to his file now, applying for a spousal green card later in the U.S, while having a green card oneself, would take four to five years. That was almost as long as it took to become naturalized.

A couple of nights later, he gave me a ride home from English class. When he pulled over to drop me off, with no introduction and in a condescending tone he said, "Do you promise not to cry or miss your parents and Parnian if I take you to the U.S.?" After all his plans to go alone and after meeting all those other girls, I was stunned. Now me?

By then we had been together for almost three years in a fragile, minimally invested standoff. I didn't know why he wanted to marry me. Maybe he didn't either. Maybe he felt powerless, too. Whatever it was, I asked if I could think about it that night. After all my talks, questions, and emotional reactions, now he was surprised, perhaps not to hear yes right away, but he agreed to wait for my answer. Finally, out of nowhere, it seemed I had gained the power I wanted. But did I want to marry Ali for a life in the United States?

CHAPTER NINE

2003 – 2004

What went through my head that night? Nothing bright. I wondered why he chose me, and my ego felt satisfied: I wanted to win this competition. But my heart was concerned with how to put Ali and Parnian in one picture. Was it even possible? Ali made no effort to show her kindness. He ignored her almost all the time. I thought I could fix it. I could create a circle of love between them. How I would do this when I wasn't even in that circle was a mystery, but I didn't think about that.

We didn't love each other, but I said yes, maybe for America. But he might not even get the visa. I still wanted to leave Iran, and he never showed real interest in other opportunities. Then what? Do I leave without him?

The next day I called to hear what he had in mind. He said we should marry as soon as possible so he could add me to his immigration file. I said it would take me awhile to get Parnian's father's permission to take her out of the country. I didn't even know where to start.

But Ali confirmed what I had pretended to myself he didn't mean last night: "It would be better for us to go and get settled and then Parnian and your mother can join us. While we are still in Iran, Parnian should stay with your parents. This will help her get used to you not being around."

And I thought I was selfish! Hearing his selfish suggestions, I felt furious and humiliated. He had no plan to put him and Parnian in one picture.

I shut down my anger. I told myself I could create the circle, but had no confidence in my ability. Still somehow I silenced that furious heart of mine. I accepted his humiliating proposal. Perhaps the ego still wanted to be the winning girl in this beauty contest. Or, what if we could go to America if he got the visa? I would surely find a way to get Parnian there and make a better future for her anyway.

After few moments of silence he said, "I am sure when we have our own child, I will feel differently toward Parnian. Without my own child it's hard for me to understand your feelings as a mother."

"I hope so."

I told him although he had only a 50% chance of getting approved for the lottery green card, I wanted to leave the country no matter what. If not for the U.S, then Canada, Australia, or New Zealand. He said, "Other countries are not as good as the U.S., but we can think about it."

I was worried, feeling sick in my stomach knowing I was making a bad decision. My yes was as loveless as his proposal. We were off to a bad start and I hoped for a magical change.

When I told my parents that Ali proposed to me, my father approved. "He seems to be a responsible man with a good job. You will feel better when you are married. You won't feel as lonely and depressed anymore." He said he and my mother would take care of Parnian since I wasn't legally allowed to take her to my second husband's home. Perhaps he too was tired of me and my crying and aloofness. He thought Ali was the medicine to my depression.

My mother left the house when Ali came to ask for my parents' permission because of Ali's heartless conditions. She said this marriage was a worse mistake than my first. "You are humiliating not only yourself but your daughter." I could not think logically. Her advice, as correct as it was, went in one ear and out the other. I told her I had made my decision.

Ali was surprised by my mother's absence, but my father implied that she was just emotional and not feeling well. I had told Ali how my mother felt about his suggested plan for Parnian. He laughed and said, "I will fix it, and we will get along."

My father and he talked for a while and I sat without interfering. My father said, "Under no circumstances will

I accept Parnian living anywhere but here. This is her house. Shabnam is young and needs to get married, but I am the only man to raise Parnian." Ali looked at me with satisfaction. I could see him saying see, I told you, this is the best way. I remained silent, keeping the mask firmly in place and hiding my inner turmoil.

Then, as if to reassure my father, Ali said he and his brother had carefully analyzed a list of young women, and I had come out on top. Like a product. My father looked down, powerless to clean up the mess I had created. He didn't believe in us either; like me, he hoped for a miracle.

Shaking Ali's hand as he left, my father looked at him intensely and said, "Remember Mr. Ali, life is not all based on logical analysis. We need to consider emotions too. We'll take care of her child but don't forget, Shabnam is a mother." He let his hand go. Ali said nothing, leaving with a satisfied smile.

We were trying to change each other to build that picture-perfect family, but we were painting different pictures. Ali wanted to keep his traditional beliefs, and open up only a little to progressive thoughts. I idealized a fully progressive lifestyle. His painting was an impressionist landscape that looked great from afar, but I would not find any place in my house to hang it. Mine was a sculpture like Auguste Rodin's Thinker, to display in the most important place in my house. My progressive thoughts made Ali curious in the beginning of our relationship, but he was not ready to assimilate them later.

Because he was educated, held a prestigious job, and accepted my career ambitions didn't mean he could abandon the strongly rooted traditional beliefs he had grown up with. Aside from girlfriends, whom he was not marrying, he did not believe in women's desires or their freedom to express those desires. I told myself that by choosing me to marry, he had changed his beliefs. I fantasized opportunities to bring him along for more of what he called "Western behavior."

Selfishly and more selfishly, I planned to tell my nine-year-old Parnian about that decision after I made it rather than bringing her in from the beginning when Ali proposed. With my preoccupied mind and heavy heart, I was not sure how to do that. I took her out to her favorite pizza place and after a few happy discussions about her school and her friends, I told her I wanted to share some news with her. Her eyes were surprised, worried, and impatient to hear the news. When I said I was getting married, her look turned to horror.

"Don't tell me it is uncle Ali." When I said it was, she started screaming and threw her pizza into the air. It landed on the floor right next to the table. I picked it up and tried to calm her down as everyone turned to look. I took her out to the car where we sat together in the back seat. I hugged her while she screamed and cried. I held her tight. I promised her to make things better, but my promises felt empty. She still did not know I would be leaving her with my parents when I moved in with Ali—

and that she would be staying here if and when Ali and I left Iran.

My heart was broken, I hugged her and cried with her.

After that devastating experience, I asked Ali if we could see a counselor. I was surprised and touched he accepted to go. The experienced counselor heard our story, saw my tears, and in less than half an hour said we should not get married. "This is a wrong decision." But we ignored her. Sometimes reality is so bitter that hope for a magical change can keep us going in the wrong direction. Parnian and I had a rough couple of weeks as I gave her the rest of the bad news. I cried with her, but I didn't change my plans. I just bribed her by promising a better future. As unsure as I was, I felt that was the way to go to a better future. I wasn't lying, it was the uncertainty of the future that made me feel I was not honest with her.

My mother's siblings encouraged the marriage. After all, as a divorced mother, I was lucky to have any proposal, let alone from someone financially stable who owned a nice condominium in an upscale neighborhood, was educated, had a promising immigration process going on, was a good-looking guy, and didn't have a child of his own. Of course I should compromise. Of course I should give up my child. He could certainly have chosen to marry a virgin instead.

But regardless of how it may have looked, with my time away on business trips or having romance, I loved Parnian desperately. Mothers simply could not win in Iran in that time. If they had a life of their own they were inattentive mothers or, as in my case, spoiled girls whose parents filled the job. If they stayed in a loveless and abusive marriage, they sacrificed their own needs for emotional connection, most likely taking it out on their children and continuing the damaging cycle.

I had fights in my head and my heart. I never missed any school event and I was always involved with her daily plans. The little time we spent together was fun and intimate. I selected and read books to her that made her think and she liked them. She had a lot of questions, and I tried to answer all of them. All her secrets about school and her friends were safe with me. As much as she loved my parents' care and love, she always asked for private mother-daughter time to tell me her stories. I listened to her carefully.

With all the limitations under the Islamic regime, I still found all the events for children's entertainment and took her to expose her to more variety in life. We enjoyed our mother-daughter dates. Of course I wanted and did my best to provide the best for her, but the culture did not accept my lifestyle—my right to have a mind and interests. Instead I should have sacrificed everything, repressed it all and focused only on spending every minute with her.

I had no answer to my big question: How could I possibly leave her completely to my parents?

Some women stayed in bad marriages to avoid losing custody of their children. Were they right? Was I wrong? My cousin with two children stayed with a husband who didn't allow them to visit her parents often, forced her to wear the scarf inside, did not allow her to wear make-up, and commanded her in all different ways, from raising the children to how she talked to others and who she talked to. She was just waiting for her kids to be 18 years old, and then she would leave. Compared to women like her, I felt selfish, like an irresponsible mother. But what were her children learning about women's rights? Women's roles in the family? How would her son treat his wife? What would her daughter give up to gain her husband's approval? We were both considered wrong, but we were both doing the best we could in a male-dominant, misogynist culture.

****

My father and I flew to Mashad where Ali's family lived so we could formally meet them. His older sister and her family would come to Tehran for the wedding, a small, brief ceremony since we were in rush to add my paperwork to Ali's immigration file. The immigration story was a secret however, and no-one in his family except his brother knew about it. His family was totally against him leaving Iran.

Adding me to Ali's immigration file postponed his interview for a few months and added more paperwork to the process. Although I did not have Parnian's father's permission to take her out of the country, I could have added her information to the file, making it easier to get her immigration visa later, if Ali agreed, but he did not. Adding her to the file could make her father upset, he said. Or the U.S. State Department might reject the whole file if it had too many people.

To soothe Parnian's broken heart, I built time with her into our schedules. Ali and I planned to have her one night each weekend at our place, and I would stay one night each week at my parents'. Ali asked for my mother's presence for those nights Parnian stayed at our place; he didn't want Parnian to get used to being alone with us. I promised Parnian to visit her after work every day. And I explained to her that all this was to prepare us to live in America. I told her America was not an easily achievable goal and we needed to work hard and sacrifice for it. I transferred her to one of the best English schools in the city and got her new books in English, anything to teach her about life in America and get her excited for living there. One thing I didn't tell her was that it would take a few years for her to join me. I just told her I had to go there first to find out how to get her there. She trusted my promise; she would join me.

Persian New Year came two weeks after Ali and I married. The country usually has a two-week holiday, and people travel to visit their relatives, and we were expected to visit Ali's family in Mashad. Ali did not let me take Parnian as he had refused to tell his family about her, so I made sure Ali and I stayed for New Year's Day with Parnian and my parents and then left for Mashad. My parents, trying to help my marriage stability, planned a trip to the Caspian Sea at the same time I was in Mashad, with plenty of entertainment to keep Parnian busy and happy. I was heartbroken and wanted to be involved with the fun time she would have. I missed that whole trip with her.

While staying with his mother in Mashhad, we needed to keep two secrets perfectly hidden: my daughter's existence and Ali's plans to emigrate.

While in Mashhad, I received a Happy New Year call on my cell phone from Negar from Canada, where she had moved in 1999. While I spoke with her, Ali led me to the bedroom, closed the door, and sat next to me. When Negar said she had gotten free from her controlling husband, Ali's face turned red. As soon as I hung up, he said, "We don't have to tell my mother your close friend lives in Canada and got divorced. She will feel concerned about our marriage."

Marrying Ali may have soothed my wounded ego, but it gave my heart deeper cracks. I silently ached.

****

It was about six months before we heard from the U.S. embassy for our interview. During that time, I visited Parnian almost every day and we spent two nights per week together. I wasn't distracted by Ali's relationship-threatening behavior from before the marriage. I was more triggered by Ali's efforts to convince me I was not Parnian's mother and my mother was playing that role perfectly, so I wanted to be a better mother for her. I felt more energy and put it all into Parnian.

I took fewer business trips and was more available. Parnian and I made plans and spoke about so many things. My mother disapproved of many of her friends. She didn't like their bold behavior or the fact that their mothers were divorced. She didn't trust them and their mothers. When I reminded her that Parnian's own mother was divorced, she retorted, "That's different. I am here to watch her." From that moment on, hanging out with those friends of Parnian and their divorced mothers became a mother-daughter secret for Parnian and me.

When Ali was around the atmosphere was different. The nights we stayed at my parents', to get there after work, he drove as slowly as he could in the right lane to arrive as late as possible, close to bedtime. Since he stayed there too, Parnian couldn't join me in my bedroom. We wanted to hold each other's hands and fall sleep those nights, but Ali said, "You should not overdo having her close to you all the time. You'll just make it harder for her when you're gone." I didn't buy into such comments but didn't argue either. Was she supposed to erase her mother from her entire life?

One of those nights Ali and I were staying at my parents, Parnian brought him some new books I had bought a couple of days before. He put the books aside without looking at her. "I am talking now. I will look at them later." But he never did. I decided to stay at my parents' without him.

Night after night I cried and asked what I could do to make his heart open to Parnian and make a warm relationship between them, but he was silent. I asked him to say something. If he said anything without looking into my eyes, it was just, "You're angry now. We'll talk later." In most cases he went to bed while I paced in the living room, spending sleepless nights. The more I tried, the colder he became towards Parnian.

Parnian asked me whether she could call Ali "Dad" because she didn't have much interaction with her father. When he did pick her up for a visit, he either left her with his sister or, while buying chocolate for her, criticized her dress code and behavior. In her little heart Parnian hoped Ali, with his warm behavior toward others (he was trying hard to get along with my mother) would become a warm father figure for her.

I knew Ali's answer would break my heart but asked him anyway. He said, "Of course not. If she gets used to me she'll be sad when we leave." That night I walked around the small living room and cried until morning. I didn't know how to deal with that much dejection.

****

When we received our interview appointment in June 2003 I panicked. It was becoming real. Our appointment was in Abu Dhabi, UAE. We planned to stay in Dubai, a two-hour drive to Abu Dhabi, but more touristic.

The night before our trip we attended my maternal cousin's wedding, which was modern and therefore held it in secret, hidden from police and *Basij*. That was one hell of a fun wedding in a garden outside of Tehran. Everyone was laughing, dancing, and drinking, and having a great time.

People wished me luck for our interview. One said, "This is a great opportunity. I envy you."

"Thank you," I said, "but I am so afraid of living far away from Parnian."

"Don't worry about her. Your parents have accepted her like their own child. You were always traveling and were busy."

Other people kindly reminded me, "Watch your handsome husband with a U.S green-card. Plenty of beautiful young women at this wedding wish they could steal him."

Everyone supported Ali's approach. To their eyes, I was my parent's daughter but not Parnian's mother. Since she was a tall baby even at her age, nine, everyone kept charmingly saying we looked like sisters. Parnian and I both hated it!

Perhaps they meant to calm me down, but what they did not realize was my motherly love and attachment did not disappear just because my parents took great care of my child. I felt judged, not comforted, by their words and wishes. Eventually I stopped talking about my emotions. I simply thanked everyone for their kind words.

Brené Brown skillfully draws a line between sympathy and empathy: When people sympathize with you they don't feel your pain, they only draw your attention to it. Those who empathize feel your pain and reassure you they'd like to help. That's what was missing that night and through my life, and I didn't know how desperately I needed it.

Nobody approved of me as a mother except the only one whose approval I cared about: Parnian herself.

****

When we got to Dubai I felt sick. I was horrified at what we were about to do. I also remembered this was the place Ali came for his type of fun, prostitution. I did not want to be there. It only got worse when Ali took us to the Russian beach and got distracted staring at girls there, and then to an Iranian club with Iranian singers. It was probably one of the lowest-class clubs in all of Dubai, but it was cheap and drunk girls danced sexily.

Worse, he called himself open-minded for taking his wife these places, not that he had asked if I wanted to go. With my overwhelming anxiety, I just tagged along, silently sickened by the disturbing atmosphere.

The interview was quick and easy, and now we just had to wait for a background check, the result of which officials would post online. "When you see your number, come back to see if you get the final approval," the interviewer said. She handed us our paperwork and closed the window.

I went home feeling disgusted with myself.

We waited a few weeks but the result did not come out. Ali emailed the embassy but received no answer. We decided to go back to UAE and talk to them in person.

We returned in the last week of September. This time I was past feeling sick; I felt numb. At the embassy they told us our affidavit form (financial support by an American citizen to guarantee the immigrants wouldn't be without money and a burden on the society), which uncle Mohsen had provided, needed to be notarized and re-sent. In a rush we contacted my uncle and he took care of it and resent it overnight.

Back at the embassy the next day, a half-Persian, half-American girl glanced at our file on her computer and said she could not issue the visa because our background check was not complete. Lottery green card visa requests expire on September 30 of each year if the request is not granted. It was September 29th.

I felt relieved. As much as I wanted to leave Iran, not getting the visa did not bother me at all. I wanted a better future for Parnian and me together and didn't want to leave without her for unknown number of years.

Ali, on the other hand, was sad and silent. I told him now we could start making new goals to build our life. We could consider Canada or Australia. But he was upset. I tried to convince him that even if we didn't get to emigrate, which was my dream of all time, we could still build a good life in Iran. I didn't believe what I was saying, and he was not convinced.

One of his positive personality traits was being persistent. He suggested extending our trip another day and returning to the embassy to plead our case. I said that would be pointless, and besides, I had an audit the next day at a client site that could not be postponed. I asked him to get over it. We had not gotten the visa. But he insisted. He asked me to have my co-worker cover the audit.

So on the last day of September we returned to the embassy. A different officer looked at our file for a few minutes and asked me two simple questions in Farsi. Then he looked at us directly with emotionless eyes and said, "Come back for your visa at 3:00 p.m." We looked at each other with disbelief. We got the visa. We really did. I had given up, but Ali's persistent personality had not.

I was a mess: nauseous with anxiety, excited for the opportunity I had wanted since reading The Little Black Fish as a little girl, and heartbroken at the knowledge I would be leaving my daughter for who knew how long.

The next day in Tehran I hugged Parnian tightly and cried bitterly. She said, "Mom, it is all for good, and we will all live in America one day soon." She was the one reminding me, "You told me it is for our better future. We will build it together." I could not calm down. I hugged her tighter and cried harder. Ali stood back, watching. My parents came closer to us with tears in their eyes.

****

We had six months to enter the States. We decided to take the entire time to wrap up our work and personal projects. I hired people at Tavana, delegated my responsibilities to others on my projects, and helped Ali wrap up his projects.

For the last 50 days of our residency in Iran, Ali's mother came from Mashad to stay with us. She was distressed and blamed my influence for taking her son out of the country. Ali tried to calm her down and spent a lot of time soothing her emotions. I was silent when she complained. Once she said, "My son would never have left his country. You put these thoughts in his head."

I had a lot to finish at work and for school. I had finished my coursework for bachelor's degree in business in fall of 2003, but I had to finalize my graduation and pay off my student loans to receive my degree and transcript. This all took me away from home more than 12 hours a day, leaving me almost no time with Parnian.

My friends at work, Kamran, Shakeeb, Mr. Mardan, and Reza, had expressed their concerns for me and Parnian being apart for an unknown length of time. One February early afternoon, the sun was trying hard to warm up Mr. Mardan's office. We sat at a table connected to his desk discussing projects. I was drained. The sun made parallel lines coming through the half-open vertical blinds, probably trying to get some light to my heart, but it was not strong enough. After we were done talking about work, Mr. Mardan, who had raised concerns about my emotional health before and had asked whether I was sure the marriage decision was right, asked me, "How are you feeling? Would you like to talk about it?"

Staring at the parallel shade lines, I said, "I don't know what to do. I can't believe I am leaving Parnian."

"Think about the future. You always wanted to take her out of Iran. You are going now, and she will join you."

I tried to smile. "But when? It will take years to get her visa."

Then suddenly he asked, "What if Ali doesn't want to stay in the States? What would you do? Would you stay?"

I didn't think twice. "Yes," I said. Feeling so confident in answering his question energized me. It assured me that no matter how terrible it felt now, I was making the right decision—the only decision that could possibly give Parnian and me a tolerable future. It was like the weak February sun put all its force together and sent good warmth directly to my heart.

Mr. Mardan smiled as if to say I trust you. You will take care of your life.

As we got closer to our departure time, everything became more emotionally difficult. Saying goodbye to everyone was hard. Mr. Mardan and his wife arranged a little farewell party for me at the office. All the members of our small team showed up. We had a great time reviewing a lot of memories. They got me a beautiful gold necklace and bracelet set that I still have. I was leaving so many beautiful memories with them, my true friends in that office! My heart ached. Everyone wished me strength and resilience. Grandpa Shakeeb looked concerned but patted my shoulder. "I know you can do it. Parnian will join you soon."

I hugged Mr. Mardan and cried. He echoed Shakeeb. "Iran has no bright future for you or Parnian. Go."

Captain had come back to Iran a few times, but, wrapped up in my misery, I was not in touch with him often. I hadn't even seen him, only spoken on the phone a few times. When I called to let him know I was emigrating, he was visiting Iran. I didn't provide any detail. He tried to get more information out of me. He asked if he could see me and I abruptly answered, "My husband would be upset." I didn't say that I was in an unhappy marriage, that I was leaving my child behind, that I felt emotionally a wreck, that I still loved him deeply.

He was encouraging and happy that I got to emigrate to the U.S, but he said, "Shabnam, you don't sound happy. Are you hiding something from me?" Oh, how well he knew me! "I don't want to make you uncomfortable, but remember I am here for you anytime you need help." His voice and direct words, the way he knew me inside and out, and in general his existence made me fall in love with him over and over, not only every time I talked to him, but every time I thought about him, every day.

During the last few days, every chance I had to be alone, I lay in bed hugging my pillow, crying helplessly. I would fight and would eventually bring Parnian to the States. But how long would it take? Was I breaking her trust in me? Would she understand why I left or would she feel rejected? Would her feelings and developing personality be repressed by that society and my mother's traditional approach, so different from mine? Would my father's drunk behavior (much less than before but still) scar her? Would my parents' fights (also less than before, but still) disturb her peace of mind? Would we have the same connection? Could I still be involved in her everyday life, listen to her worries, and help her through the learning process of dealing with life?

Would she hate me?

I had to move forward. Time was passing and I needed to be realistic and quickly prepare for upcoming changes.

"Mom, when will we live together again? Is it too expensive to call me every day?" Her questions were unbearable. I came up with any possible comforting answer. I taught her how to use email and opened a Yahoo account for her. I got her fast internet so we could connect every day. We made a mantra to make sure our hearts were always connected and close to each other: "We believe we will be back together soon again," and we repeated it three times every night before sleep.

She had been cooperative since she was born. She accepted my lifestyle and danced with me through any song I played, on any stage. We were best friends.

When I started packing, the first thing that came to mind were a few of my beloved books. Although emotional misery, work and school had kept me from reading them for the last couple of years, they were precious to me, so I stacked them next to the suitcase. When Ali saw them he put them aside and said, "Let's put them in the bag later if we have space, our workbooks are more important." I knew it meant you are not bringing those books. I chose a bigger purse and hid my favorite books in it to avoid arguing. I couldn't imagine living without them, but I didn't have energy to negotiate.

March 5th, 2004, that last night before our flight to the United States, was one of the hardest nights in my life with all the tears and promises Parnian and I were exchanging. We were giving each other hope and encouragement to be able to get through the difficult time of being apart.

"Don't worry," my father said. "We will take care of this priceless treasure for you. She is the light of our lives and we love her very much." But this just made me feel worse.

I lost it in my mother's arms when she said, "Remember I always dreamed of living in America. You go ahead, and take us later."

I knew my parents were the best in this world to take care of my Parnian, but Parnian and I needed each other differently.

At the airport, walking towards the security line, I turned to see her one last time. She stood there in her light-gray school uniform, hugging my mom, both of them crying. Her headscarf slid halfway back to show her hair, which I had braided for her early that morning. My tears made everything blurry. I desperately needed Ali's support, but he was wrapped up with his own anxiety and did not have the capacity to give my broken heart any attention. Instead he told me I was overreacting. "This is not good for her. She is in good hands."

I stepped on the escalator going down. He stood behind me. I could not see Parnian anymore.

In the airplane, I turned my head from Ali and tightly hugged my bag with my favorite books in it. Taking off felt I was rising above life and looking at the story of my life from the top.

What future am I planning for Parnian? What future am I planning for myself? What happened to the determined 1998 and 1999 version of Shabnam, or the little Shabnam who wanted to explore the world?

As we rose above the clouds, suddenly, the little black fish came to my mind. She left a small world for a bigger one. She faced danger along the way but she learned a lot. She became wiser and helped others. She inspired other little black and red fishes. I knew the path wouldn't be easy but I promised myself to resurrect the determined Shabnam, renew all her dreams and do anything I could to reunite with my daughter in America, the land of opportunity, as soon as possible.

It was time to use the lessons learned to rebuild myself with more harmony, wisdom, and self-worth.

Quietly, over and over, I said our mantra: "We believe we will be back together very soon again."

The sequel is on its way.

Glossary

Ashura: 10th day of the month Moharam

Azizam: My dear

Baba: Dad

Baghali polo: Made with rice, dill, and fava beans, usually served with chicken or beef shank

Basij: Islamic Guardians

Bebakhshid: I am sorry!

Bekhaz oonvar: move a few steps

Chador: A long loose usually black scarf to cover female body from head to toe

Chelow Kabab: Skewered minced beef with onion grilled on a charcoal or gas grill, served with basmati rice

Cafe Glace: Coffee mixed with ice cream served in a tall glass

Dahe Fajr: The victorious 10 days

Esfand: Last calendar month of Persian calendar. A solar calendar that starts in the beginning of the spring.

Fajr: Victory

Gheime bademjoon: Beef stew mixed with golden sautéed eggplant, cooked tomato and chickpeas, turmeric and cinnamon, and thin fries.

Ghormeh sabzi stew: Sautéed herbs, (parsley, leeks or green onions) seasoned with dried fenugreek leaves and turmeric and mixed with kidney beans, pieces of lamb or beef

Haaj Agha: A respectful term for older religious men

Hijab: Covering for female body and hair

Joon or *Jan*: Dear

Khanoom: Mrs., Madam

Khane doost kojast?: Where is the friend's home?

Kashk e bademjan: Sautéed and mashed eggplant with liquid whey protein and topped with fried onions, chopped walnuts, and mint

Khodahafez: Goodbye

Konkour: Iranian university entrance exam. A standardized test to pass for higher education.

Mantow: A long and loose dress that would be worn on the top women's cloths to cover their body

Maman: Mom

Moharam: Last calendar month of the lunar calendar

Neshani: Address

Nowruz: Persian New Year, March 21st, first day of Spring

Pedar: Father

Riba: unjust gains made in trade or business

Sajadeh: A small prayer rug

Saffron: A Persian spice coming from the flower of Crocus sativus

Salad olivie: A combination of potato and chicken salad

Setar: A traditional Persian string instrument

Sheereen polo: Basmati rice, butter, barberries, orange peel, almonds, pistachios, sugar, saffron, cinnamon, and cumin served with sautéed chicken

Shokaran: Hemlock

Sigheh: A temporary marriage contract

Tar: A traditional Persian string instrument

Tobe Nasooh: Becoming clean of all sins

Touman: Iranian Currency

Velayat Faghih: the Guardianship of the Islamic Jurist

Analytical Questions

➢ What personality type do you assign to each of main characters? (Narcissistic, empath, sensitive, too emotional, too logical, traditional, progressive…)

➢ What was the major common characteristic among different characters?

➢ How did the different personalities interacted? Which ones helped each other? Which ones pushed each other's buttons?

➢ Did you feel any emotional intimacy in this dynamic? Or was everyone absorbed in her or his life dramas?

➢ Do you think there were any chances to create any emotional intimacy?

➢ Do you have examples in your life that you had lack of emotional intimacy? Could you be more empathetic?

➢ Which one of Shabnam's experiences you relate the most?

- ➢ How was the family dynamics and the emotional health of Shabnam's family?
- ➢ Would you consider your family emotional dynamics healthy?
- ➢ How could you improve your emotional health?
- ➢ What sacrifices Shabnam made to move forward? What scarifies have you made or have you had any missed opportunity? How did that affect your life?
- ➢ Do the sacrifices affect the trajectory of your life?

About the Author

Shabnam Curtis, the author of My Persian Paradox, was born and raised in Tehran, experiencing the Iranian Revolution of 1979 firsthand. In 2004 she immigrated to the United States, where she now works as a project analyst by day and a passionate writer all other time. Shabnam teaches memoir writing workshops and has been performing lectures to colleges and universities about her book and the concept of understanding diversity. She is working on her second memoir (sequel). Her articles have been published on The Write Launch, Views & News, The Canadian Business Daily, and Eat, Darling, Eat network. She lives in Virginia with her husband and two dogs.

Her motto is, "We all have a story to tell. Share your story, listen to others' stories. Create more EMPATHY & LOVE!"

www.shabnamcurtis.com

www.mypersianparadox.com